Europe, Globalization and Sustainable Development

Can Europe produce a sustainable future? What difficulties does globalization throw in the way of states that aim to create a sustainable economy?

Europe, Globalization and Sustainable Development explores the many facets of these issues in the light of the most recent developments in Europe. The two focal points of the studies are politics and policy. The contributions to the current European experience made by ecofeminism, the anti-globalization movement and the European environmental movement are examined, as are matters such as education for environmentally-informed citizenship, the possibilities for creating an environmentally-friendly form of industry and the interaction between Europe and the rest of the world in international policy-making forums such as the Johannesburg Earth Summit.

This edited volume considers the ways in which European states and the European Union can and should organize themselves economically and socially in order to address the challenges of sustainable development. It will interest students and researchers of environmental policy and European politics.

John Barry is a Reader in the School of Politics, Queen's University Belfast, UK. He is also co-leader of the Green Party in Northern Ireland. **Brian Baxter** is Lecturer in Politics at the University of Dundee, UK. **Richard Dunphy** is Senior Lecturer in Politics at the University of Dundee, UK.

Environmental Politics/Routledge Research in Environmental Politics

Edited by Matthew Paterson
Keele University
and
Graham Smith
University of Southampton

Over recent years environmental politics has moved from a peripheral interest to a central concern within the discipline of politics. This series aims to reinforce this trend through the publication of books that investigate the nature of contemporary environmental politics and show the centrality of environmental politics to the study of politics per se. The series understands politics in a broad sense and books will focus on mainstream issues such as the policy process and new social movements as well as emerging areas such as cultural politics and political economy. Books in the series will analyse contemporary political practices with regards to the environment and/or explore possible future directions for the 'greening' of contemporary politics. The series will be of interest not only to academics and students working in the environmental field, but will also demand to be read within the broader discipline.

The series consists of two strands:

Environmental Politics addresses the needs of students and teachers, and the titles will be published in paperback and hardback. Titles include:

Global Warming and Global Politics
Matthew Paterson

Politics and the Environment
James Connelly and Graham Smith

International Relations Theory and Ecological Thought Towards Synthesis
Edited by Eric Laffèrière and Peter Stoett

Planning Sustainability
Edited by Michael Kenny and James Meadowcroft

Deliberative Democracy and the Environment
Graham Smith

Routledge Research in Environmental Politics presents innovative new research intended for high-level specialist readership. These titles are published in hardback only and include:

1 **The Emergence of Ecological Modernisation**
   Integrating the environment and the economy?
   Stephen C. Young

2 **Ideas and Actions in the Green Movement**
   Brian Doherty

3 **Russia and the West**
   Environmental cooperation and conflict
   Geir Hønneland

4 **Global Warming and East Asia**
   The domestic and international politics of climate change
   Edited by Paul G. Harris

5 **Europe, Globalization and Sustainable Development**
   Edited by John Barry, Brian Baxter and Richard Dunphy

Europe, Globalization and Sustainable Development

Edited by John Barry, Brian Baxter and Richard Dunphy

LONDON AND NEW YORK

First published 2004
by Routledge
11 New Fetter Lane, London EC4P 4EE

Simultaneously published in the USA and Canada
by Routledge
29 West 35th Street, New York, NY 10001

Routledge is an imprint of the Taylor & Francis Group

© 2004 John Barry, Brian Baxter and Richard Dunphy for selection
and editorial matter; individual contributors their contributions

Typeset in Baskerville by Wearset Ltd, Boldon, Tyne and Wear
Printed and bound in Great Britain by MPG Books Ltd, Bodmin

All rights reserved. No part of this book may be reprinted or
reproduced or utilized in any form or by any electronic, mechanical,
or other means, now known or hereafter invented, including
photocopying and recording, or in any information storage or
retrieval system, without permission in writing from the publishers.

British Library Cataloguing in Publication Data
A catalogue record for this book is available from the British Library

Library of Congress Cataloging in Publication Data
Europe, globalization and sustainable development / edited by John
Barry, Brian Baxter, and Richard Dunphy.
    p. cm.
Includes bibliographical references and index.
 1. Environmental policy–Economic aspects–Europe.
 2. Anti-globalization movement–Europe. 3. Environmental
ethics–Europe. 4. Globalization–Social aspects. 5. Ecofeminism–
Europe. 6. Environmental protection–Europe.
 I. Barry, John, 1966– II. Baxter, Brian, 1949– III. Dunphy, Richard.

  HC79.E5E84 2004
  338.94'07–dc22

                                       2003019160

ISBN 0-415-30276-5

Contents

Contributors	ix
Foreword	xii
Acknowledgements	xxiv

1 **Editors' introduction**   1
JOHN BARRY, BRIAN BAXTER AND RICHARD DUNPHY

PART I
Politics   13

2 **The challenge of ecofeminism for European politics**   15
SUSAN BAKER

3 **Anti-globalism and ecologism in comparative perspective**   31
RAFAL SOBORSKI

4 **Is there a European environmental movement?**   47
CHRISTOPHER ROOTES

5 **Fragmented citizenship in a global environment**   73
MARCEL WISSENBURG

6 **Sustainability through democratization? The Aarhus Convention and the future of environmental decision making in Europe**   94
DEREK R. BELL

PART II
Policy 113

7 Social inclusion, environmental sustainability and citizenship education 115
ANDREW DOBSON

8 The Europeanization of national environmental policy: a comparative analysis 130
ANDREW JORDAN, DUNCAN LIEFFERINK AND JENNY FAIRBRASS

9 Ecological modernization, globalization and Europeanization: a mutually-reinforcing nexus? 152
DEBRA JOHNSON

10 The EU and sustainable development: the long road from Rio to Johannesburg 168
JON BURCHELL AND SIMON LIGHTFOOT

11 The WTO and sustainability after Doha: a time for reassessment of the relationship between political science and law? 186
JAMES TUNNEY

Index 213

Contributors

Susan Baker is Reader in the School of Social Sciences, Cardiff University and in 2003 was awarded a Swedish Royal Appointment as King Carl XVI Gustaf's Professor in Environmental Sciences. Her research interests include environmental governance, participatory democracy and ecofeminism. She has acted as expert advisor to the Swedish Environmental Protection Agency, as well as to UNCED and UNESCO committees. She is on the editorial board of *Environmental Policy and Planning* and has written numerous articles and co-edited several books, such as *Women and Public Policy: the Shifting Boundaries between the Public and Private Spheres* (1999).

John Barry is Reader in the Department of Politics at Queen's University, Belfast. He has research interests in the relationship between moral/political theory and the environment, with particular focus on ecofeminism, the environment and justice, and the political economy of the environment. He is the author of *Rethinking Green Politics* (1999) and *Environment and Social Theory* (1999) and has co-edited several other books.

Brian Baxter is a Lecturer in Politics at the University of Dundee, where he teaches environmental politics and political philosophy. His current research interests are in the area of environmental ethics, especially the topic of ecological justice, and he is the author of *Ecologism: An Introduction* (1999).

Derek Bell is a Research Fellow in Politics at the University of Newcastle. His research interests are in liberal political theory and green political thought. He is currently preparing a book on the relationship between political liberalism and environmentalism.

Jon Burchell is a Lecturer at Brunel University, within BRESE (Brunel Research into Enterprise, Sustainability and Ethics). His research interests include Green parties and movements and corporate social responsibility. He is author of *The Evolution of Green Politics* (2002) and *The Greening of the European Union* (2001) with Simon Lightfoot.

Andrew Dobson is Professor of Politics at the Open University. He is the author of *Green Political Thought* (three editions), *Justice and the Environment* (1998) and edited *Fairness and Futurity* (1999). His latest book is *Citizenship and the Environment* (2003).

Richard Dunphy is Senior Lecturer in Politics at the University of Dundee. His principal research interests are in Irish politics, the European left, and sexual politics. His books include *The Making of Fianna Fáil Power in Ireland, 1923–1948* (1995), *Sexual Politics* (2000) and *Left Parties and European Integration: a Comparative History* (2003)

Jenny Fairbrass is a Senior Research Associate at the Centre for Social and Economic Research on the Global Environment at the University of East Anglia. She is currently researching the impact of devolution on UK sustainable development policy and has previously published on UK and EU environment governance.

Debra Johnson is Senior Lecturer at Hull University Business School. Her latest jointly authored book is *International Business: Themes and Issues in the Global Economy* (2003). She is currently co-editing a book on the EU and Russia and developing previous work on trans-European networks.

Andrew Jordan is a Manager of the ESRC Programme on Environmental Decision Making (PEDM) at the University of East Anglia in Norwich. He edits the journals *Environment and Planning C (Government and Policy)* and *Global Environmental Change*. He has published widely on the politics of British and European Union environmental policy making and implementation. His most recent books include *Environmental Policy in the EU* (2002), *The Europeanization of British Environmental Policy* (2002) and *'New' Instruments of Environmental Governance* (2003).

Duncan Liefferink is a Lecturer in Political Science of the Environment in the School of Management at the University of Nijmegen, the Netherlands. His main research interests are in European and comparative environmental politics, with a particular interest in the dynamic interrelationship between national and European Union environmental policy making. He is the author of *Environment and the Nation State* (1996). He has co-edited several other books.

Simon Lightfoot is Lecturer in European Studies at Liverpool John Moores University. He is the co-author (with Jon Burchell) of *The Greening of the European Union?* (2001). He and Jon Burchell are currently engaged in a research project examining the role of the EU at the recent World Summit on Sustainable Development.

Alastair McIntosh is a Fellow of Edinburgh's Centre for Human Ecology. He is author of *Soil and Soul: People versus Corporate Power* (2001). He lectures at universities and for community groups around the world and is best known through his campaigns for cultural regeneration and land reform.

Christopher Rootes is Reader in Political Sociology and Environmental Politics and Director of the Centre for the Study of Social and Political Movements at the University of Kent at Canterbury. He is working on a major comparative study of environmental movements and green politics at global, national and local levels. Joint editor of the journal *Environmental Politics*, his most recent book is *Environmental Protest in Western Europe* (2003).

Rafal Soborski is a doctoral student and associate lecturer in the Department of Linguistic, Cultural and International Studies at the University of Surrey, Guildford. His research interests focus on the conceptual morphology of discourses resisting capitalist globalization.

James Tunney is a Senior Lecturer in Law at Dundee Business School, University of Abertay, Dundee and qualified as a barrister in the Republic of Ireland. His principal research interests relate to legal issues associated with communications technology, culture, competition, intellectual property, travel and world trade.

Marcel Wissenburg is Lecturer in Political Theory and in the Philosophy of Management Sciences at the University of Nijmegen, the Netherlands. His research interests include environmental political philosophy, liberalism and the changing role of the state in modern society. He is the author of *Green Liberalism* (1998) and *Imperfection and Impartiality* (1999) and the joint editor of other books.

Foreword

Alastair McIntosh

The centrality of place[1]

Consider the paradigmatic value statement that place matters. 'Place' is a soft word, one that, coloured by story, integrates heart with head in humanizing the much more objectified term, 'environment'. Place starts with the ground on which we stand, it spreads out to our local communities and bioregions (perhaps including such social constructs as nation states), and extends into the furthest cosmos. It is geocentric and, often, anthropocentric, capable of placing at the centre of all things the very hearth, or spot, where we happen to be right now.

Whilst such a construct, or rather, empirical experience, is nonsensical in terms of post-Copernican astronomy, it is psychologically valid. Place and places are the context in which we live and die – in which the dust of our bodies comes from and returns to that of the Earth. And place underpins each of the three keywords of this collection's theme. It is paradigmatic to Europe, Globalization and Sustainability.

It is so, first, to Europe, because that word, as used here, developed contemporary meaning in the wake of two major twentieth-century tribal wars which were about territory. These impressed on war's remnant generation an imperative of learning to relate to one another's places with a more dignified respect; something that, it was hoped, and with remarkable success within Western Europe, might negate away the causes that lead to war.

Second, globalization, too, is about relationship to place. It defines how we interrelate both to our standpoint in the 'here', and also to the 'elsewhere'. It does so, not neutrally, but with attitude; with a homogenizing sweep that, for better or worse, subsumes the boundaries and worldviews that would otherwise mark out the identity and distinctiveness of places.

And third, sustainability has bearing on place. It is the acid test of whether or not our interactions with the surrounding ecosystem comprise 'right relationship'. It pushes us to ask: is our relationship proportional, in balance with the web of support structures and feedback systems by which biodiversity, as the fullness of life on Earth, can be sustained? To borrow the accountancy expression, are we running the human race as a 'going concern'? Are we setting up our children's children to live not just any old life, but 'life abundant' into the very fullness of geological time for which an evolved species on this planet ought reasonably to be expected to endure?

In short, we may find ourselves left by modernity somewhat alienated from place, but it still matters, and the veneration with which we develop sense of place through the fullness of time is a touchstone of our humanity. It is what makes us Earth-dwellers rather than any other lifeform.

Geddes' Folk, Work and Place

Given the emphasis on the importance of connection to place and places, it is either necessary to mount a detailed systematic defence of place, or to presume it as an axiomatic value statement. Given the probable readership of this volume as well as my own cultural antecedents, I will presume the latter. This will allow me to devote space to the implications.

Here, then, we are concerned with real people, working out their lives in a Europe that is not just a social construct, but physical reality: a place of stone, soil, elemental forces, plants and animals. Starting from this value-laden concern, let us take our bearings – watching all points of the come-to-pass on the compass grounded in the bedrock of our times. And let us, for argument's sake, start at the place where the papers collected in this collection were initially delivered – at Dundee University.

It was here that Patrick Geddes (1854–1932) once held the chair in botany and was a formative figure in our subject matter. Geddes' biographers variously describe him as a biologist, town planner, re-educator and peace-warrior. Patrick Abercrombie summed him up with the epithet, *A Most Unsettling Person* (Kitchen 1975). Today we see him as a pioneer of human ecology, which is to say, of the study of the interrelationships between the social environment and the natural environment; the study of human communities.

Two aspects of Geddes' thought come quickly to mind. One is his much-quoted axiom, 'By leaves we live', originally part of his farewell address to his students at Dundee. Here, then, was the socio-botanist who saw the building-block connection that exists between the vegetable world's photosynthetic product and human life on Earth. Not for him was the unbelievably naïve notion, readily challenged by simply trying to hold one's breath, that nature is a socially-constructed discourse; that trees are text, rather than text being that which is written on trees. Geddes, then, was a structuralist; an ecological realist. He understood the providential natural processes that buttered his bread and saw humankind in due proportion to these.

The second apposite aspect of Geddes' thought is his so-called 'Notation of Life' (reprinted in Macdonald 1992). He proposed that human affairs could be understood by examining the interactions of three axiomatic categories – Folk, Work and Place.

Consider, then, an international conference such as stimulated the pulling together of this book. And imagine Geddes flying in to attend it from his work in Montpellier, or India. He would have refused to treat Dundee just like any other academic conference location. From the moment his plane broke through the clouds, he would have had an eye to the lay of the land. He would be getting in touch, getting a feel for 'Place'.

He would have noticed that the farms near Dundee are large. And he would surmise from settlement patterns that the countryside has been planned mostly as the preserve of the well-to-do and their servant classes. He would have understood what that implies about patterns of land ownership – indeed, it would have come as no surprise to him to learn that a mere 1,000 owners today control nearly two-thirds of Scotland's private land (which is why in 2003 the new Scottish Parliament passed the Land Reform (Scotland) Act).

Moving from 'Place' to 'Work', he would have observed the harbour facilities on the 'Silvery Tay', leading out into the North Sea. He would have gathered that this was once one of the 'great' cities of Empire. Starting as a market town and port with ease of export to continental Europe, Dundee expanded rapidly as globalization's earlier, more self-confessedly imperial, phase drew in huge volumes of commodities. The city was particularly famous for the Indian jute that came to be milled into sackcloth and rope, colonial decrees having compromised India's own spinning industry in order to maintain jobs back home in Britain.

After having passed through the airport terminal on touch-down, Geddes would probably have picked up not just a national newspaper, but also a local one. He would have wanted to get a feel for the grassroots and, deeper still, the taproot dynamics of the 'Folk' living here. On mounting the airport bus, something of that 'most unsettling person' quality would have been firing up in the Geddesian bones. Passing through the city he would have observed, with an acuity lost to most urbane modern eyes, the 'Folk' of the city. He would have noticed hardship etched into the body language of many a posture; indeed, into the very discoloration of 'poverty teeth'.

Listening to people's accents, observing names and football colours, he would have appreciated that many of those who came to this city during the era of colonial expansion had been pushed off the land, both from nearby and from as far afield as the Highlands, the Borders and Ireland. Their onetime jobs in colonial industries had disappeared back to India or Bangladesh on the homogenized level-playing field of free trade that now better suits the economic imperative. But while capital may be rootless, people are not. So it is that many of Dundee's social problems are the fossilized counterpoint of bygone splendour.

By the time Geddes would have arrived at the conference, he would have been angry. Coming from the tradition of democratic intellectualism that is native to his Scots-Gaelic cultural origins, he would be thinking that there is no point in being an academic, no point professorially professing our vocations and wanking on about sustainability... unless it addresses the malaise of Folk, Work and Place that he saw on his way from the airport. And by the way, I use that masturbatory expression advisedly, as a sadly-necessary scholarly term for the self-gratification that is all our intellectual endeavours can ever amount to unless they serve the needs of either the poor or the broken in nature. Geddes was a Scots internationalist who had internalized the democratic intellectual view that, while knowledge inevitably creates an elite, that privilege is only justified if it serves the community. Knowledge as power is corrupt except when that power is accountably laid at the service of the community.

And so, finally, as Geddes rose to the conference rostrum, he would have arrived as a man of determination; as an academic, unfashionably, with attitude. Not for him academic value neutrality. This would have been a man on a mission, and even before saying anything his wild-eyed elemental countenance would have been troubling the peace of some of our more cloistered colleagues. And as he parted his lips, this would have been the Jeremiad, these are the precise words, that would have thundered forth for due publication in this volume.

> We are indeed the New Troglodytes; hence our restless and ant-like crowding, our comfortable stupor of hibernation, our ugly and evil dreams. Here is a main clue to the sociology and psychology [of our cities by which] we may understand much of the physical degradation of their inhabitants... The sole theory, nay, the whole practice also, of 'economic progress' lies in the steady development of a lower and lower life. Do we not tell the wretched millgirls of our Dundee and Oldham how they must speedily give place to the cheaper drudges of Calcutta and Shanghai, or save themselves and slay these by diving into a yet lower circle of poverty?... And what remedy is there? None that any one knows of... for now is the golden age of Competition, as of Death.

Globalization and the space–time schism

Professor Sir Patrick Geddes wrote those words in his essay, The Sociology of Autumn, first published in 1895 (reprinted in Macdonald 1992). Reading it, we can see that, starting with his Folk, Work and Place 'notation of life', and digging from where we stand at, say, Dundee University, we can quickly find ourselves connected through geographical space with Calcutta and Shanghai, and through time with all the post-Renaissance history of modernity.

Indeed, we find ourselves moved on from Newtonian thinking, where it could safely be said that 'History's about chaps and geography's about maps', and re-connected to a social expression of the Einsteinian space–time continuum, in which place can be seen in true perspective only when considered not just alone in its three spatial dimensions, but also, as being simultaneously situated within the fourth dimension – that of time, of dynamic history.

Not for Geddes would be Fukuyama's pretentious posturing of an 'End of History' (Fukuyama 1993). Neither, for him, would be Fukuyama's fellow globalization exponent and guru to Tony Blair, Charles Leadbetter, who says in *Living on Thin Air*, a book celebrating the 'knowledge economy':

> Strong communities can be pockets of intolerance and prejudice. Settled, stable communities are the enemies of innovation, talent, creativity, diversity and experimentation. They are often hostile to outsiders, dissenters, young upstarts and immigrants. Community can too quickly become a rallying cry for nostalgia; that kind of community is the enemy of knowledge creation, which is the wellspring of economic growth.
>
> (Leadbetter 2000)

Nor would Geddes have been any more impressed by the root of the whole mindset that permits valuing place or knowledge or anything only according to economic performance criteria – a position most formatively expressed in John Locke's 1690 *Second Treatise of Government* where, he supposes, the 'wild common of nature' belonging to all is augmented in its 'natural intrinsic value', only on being 'remove[d] out of the state that nature hath provided', when an individual from among 'the industrious and rational', being obedient to God's supposed expectation that we should 'subdue' the Earth, 'hath mixed his labour with, and joined to it something that is his own, and thereby makes it his property' (Locke 1980: 'Of Property', 18–30).

Here we see exposed the inner wheel of colonization, indeed, of globalization, as the process of commodifying both wild nature and, for that matter, human nature. It might be characterized as a de-spiritualized transcendentalism; an abstraction from this worldly reality that pays no heed to Life and its sources. It sees value only in abstract money terms: the leitmotif being that what can't be counted doesn't count. This is achieved, as Leadbetter unwittingly implies, by denying that which is most human – the living meaning of community, with its roots in settlers, who mixed their labour with lands over which their proconsuls (or more mundanely, shareholders) presumed a divine 'manifest destiny' and, preferably, a Royal Charter, to justify colonization. Now, in the era of globalization, knowledge has subsumed labour as the proprietorial mediator over 'interests'. As Leadbetter puts it, and he is only one of many gurus of such economic liberalism, 'Traditional assets [such as labour and natural resources] still matter, but they are a source of competitive advantage only when they are vehicles for ideas and intelligence which give them value' (Leadbetter 2000).

Deficient from this superficial truism is any sense of real intrinsic value; any essentialist (yes – why not?) recognition that conscious life exists, that life matters, and that cultural diversity and wider biodiversity are more than what can be captured in the mere calculus of, say, contingent valuation methodologies, which seek to value the environment by adding up what people say they would be willing to pay to see it preserved.

I am suggesting, then, that the denial of history, and, with it, that which gives depth and meaning to indigenous cultures, religions and communities of place, are not an accidental by-product of globalization. Rather, deracination is what fuels the engine. The splitting of the socially expressed space–time continuum, so that place can be trampled over in denial of the significance of history, is essential for the casino-economy logic of globalization-as-advanced-capitalism to stack up. As Marcuse (1964) suggested, we have become 'one-dimensional man'. People's cultural history, their relationship in tripartite community – with one another, with the environment, and with their God or gods – must be 'discounted', even destroyed, so that Mammon, the veneration of money, can rise to rule uncontested.

Meanwhile, any attempt to re-integrate the space–time continuum is denigrated. To Leadbetter, as we have seen, it is 'nostalgia'. Others would speak of tribalism or 'dangerous nationalism', and of course, the energy that emerges from politically repressed human aspiration very often does become dangerous. Such, for example, has been the plight of Islam in the face of what it sees as imposed usurious capitalism. Such is the position of any peoples where the implicit meanings of local practices have been steamrollered.

The Marcusian 'system' has to become totalitarian out of its own autopoetic or self-organizing intelligence. It senses that anything short of total control will allow remembrance of alternative ways of being human – allowing for a re-membering of history, a re-visioning of possibilities, and thereby risking a re-claiming of stolen patrimony. The 'spirits of capitalism', as Richard Roberts' critique of managerialism metaphorically describes the forces that we are up against, 'may seem to be haphazard networks, a rhizomic pattern lacking any obvious rational ordering', but, actually, they embody 'a coded, quasi-mythologised vision for a fully managerialised world' (Roberts 2002: 2–3). They fear any analysis suggesting that the root of the global problematique is cultural, even spiritual, because it is precisely these frameworks of comprehension that the latter-day inquisition has marginalized in order to usurp and consolidate power. The result is a progressive dislocation from reality.

Globalization, time and capital budgeting

I would not want to rest my analysis that globalization is characterized by commodification procured by an engineered ahistoricity solely on a critique of exponents like Fukuyama and Leadbetter. Rather, that which makes globalization so particularly interesting is the precise mathematical structuration by which it is constellated. It is, on its own principle that only the countable counts, vulnerable to deconstruction. I refer here to the very calculus by which time is discounted in the formulae routinely applied to achieve advanced capitalism's own yardstick of quantification: I refer to a process known as 'discounting', which is germane to so-called 'capital budgeting'.

Since at least the 1970s, the principles of capital budgeting have become systemic to investment appraisal. Capital budgeting is the discipline that studies, and prescribes, the investment criteria by which corporations (and, increasingly with private finance initiatives, governments) advance their superordinate existential objective – comparative profitability in a competitive market.

Contrary to the ethical teachings of many of the world's religions – medieval Christianity and Islam in particular – capitalism gives money a time value. It presumes that the loan of money is not just a transaction of human conviviality, of mutuality, to be compensated by no more than a zero-real-rate-of-return charge for inflation, administration and bad debts. Rather, it presumes that, in addition to having the primary quality of recording obligations of power between people, money also has a secondary quality; that of self-reproduction – the making of money out of money. This expected rate of return broadly speaking translates as the 'interest rate'.

Interest is defined as compensation for delayed gratification. In orthodox religious discourse it is called usury. On the surface of things, interest recognizes the time, or historic value, of money. Paradoxically, as I shall show, it embodies a logic of abstraction that impeccably undermines real human relationship to time. It thereby engenders, embodies and demonstrates the ahistoricity that, I have suggested, lies at the core of advanced capitalism.

Most people understand how compound interest works, being calculated as interest on both the principal investment and on any accrued interest. Few observers, however, appreciate that the everyday process of charging compound interest has a reciprocal side to it; one that only evolved since the mid-sixties as germane to capital budgeting.

Compound interest is the logic that if I invest £100 at, say, 7 per cent interest (ignoring inflation, administration and any bad debts), I shall end up accumulating £200 in ten years' time. But such logic also carries a reciprocal implication which becomes clear if we consider, say, an investment project where I can expect a return of £200 in ten years' time. Because at our accepted rate of 7 per cent £100 is worth £200 in ten year's time, my future £200 return on investment is said to have a 'Net Present Value' in today's terms of only £100. Put another way, if I require a rate of return of 7 per cent compounded, I will today lend you £100 only if, in ten years' time, you will repay me £200. In economic parlance, I am 'indifferent' between having £100 to spend today, or £200 in 10 years time. Such is money's presumed 'time value'; my compensation for delayed gratification.

Discounted Cash Flow (DCF) methodology is the engine by which such capital budgeting assumptions are nowadays routinely applied in large project decision making. The project just described would be said to yield either an Internal Rate of Return (IRR) of 7 per cent, or to have a Net Present Value (NPV) of £100. The effect of applying a 7 per cent required IRR to the investment outlay is to 'discount' the future cash flow of £200 by 50 per cent.

On the surface of things, interest and its reciprocal in discounting is all very logical and quite innocent. One wonders why, then, such transactions have been so condemned in certain ethical discourses. Why, for example, did Pope Benedict XIV reaffirm medieval Catholic social teaching in his encyclical, *Vix pervenit* of 1745, with such a sweeping statement as: 'The sin called usury is committed when a loan of money is made and on the sole ground of the loan the lender demands back from the borrower more than he has lent' (Kirwan 1991: translator's notes)?

The obvious justification for such condemnation is that interest rates must have been getting out of hand. This was why Protestant reformers, most notably, John Calvin, sought to distinguish between interest and usury, claiming usury to be only the excessive charging of interest. However, Pope Benedict, like contemporary Islamic economists, seems to have rejected this approach. Any rate of interest was seen as corrosive to society. Why?

Apart from the obvious slippery-slope argument leading towards voracious usury, insight into the consequences of any usury whatsoever may be appreciated from reflection on the consequences of DCF, whether this is applied consciously, as with capital budgeting, or implicitly. Any demand for a real positive rate of return on capital implies the logic of DCF. It thereby discounts the children's future. It counts the future as exponentially less meaningful than the present.

The conscious application of DCF, even more than limited liability corporate status, is perhaps the defining characteristic of 'advanced' capitalism. The objection to it rests in the exponential mathematics that discounting employs. The further you plan ahead, the quicker future returns are decayed to a minimal NPV. We have seen, for example, how a 7 per cent IRR degrades future value to half in ten years. Even a mere 3.5 per cent would half it in 20 years. This adds up to why it makes no economic sense to plant forests of slow-growing European hardwoods, or to build constructions that last for more than a couple of generations. The NPV of the stream of future returns (in rentals or other utilities) discounts away to virtually nothing.

Set in this light, the 'sin called usury' emerges as more than just the sin of the loan shark. It is an intergenerational sin against our relationship to time itself; to humankind's situation as a going concern within history. It is an institutional sleight of hand, now axiomatically codified into mainstream Western economics. Neither is it 'inevitable' or 'just the way things have to be'. Pre-Reformation Christian economics, Mosaic economics within early Jewish communities, and contemporary moves towards Islamic banking demonstrate that economic affairs can be handled differently, on a basis of mutuality, if we so choose. This, however, would undermine capitalism, and is perhaps the deepest reason why Islam represents a formidable challenge to Western economics (see for example Choudhury and Malik 1992).

Texts on marketing history such as Vance Packard's classic *The Hidden Persuaders* (1960) and more recent works on consumer behaviour such as Sheth, Mittal and Newman (1999) reveal how corporate marketing sees the name of the game as a battle to command the human psyche. Meaning, originally embedded in a living context of community, place and history, is replaced on the fields of public discourse by extracted, abstracted and invented branded substitutes.

It ought not to pass unnoticed that modern marketing developed out of a post-World War II scenario where mainly-American multinationals feared the peace-time loss of their market positions captured under the exigency of war. These corporations hired the 'depth boys' school of motivational manipulation – a movement so-called after their adaptation to selling branded products of the depth psychology psychotherapeutic insights of Freud, Jung and Adler. Emotional 'triggers' were 'hooked' in ways calculated to stimulate 'needs' that would not otherwise have existed. As such, corporate globalization, seen through the lens of marketing history, is a form of cold war – a covert continuation of wartime overstimulation.

The mechanisms employed in this were, and remain, Pavlovian. Corporate entities are forced to escalate the spiral of competitiveness to avoid predatory takeover. All that counts, and all that is counted, is market expansion and penetration in the gratification of an infantile here-and-now. The battle is for control over the human psyche, and its motor force is the theft of life – violence – under a benign masquerade of 'healthy competition'. This subscript is what causes globalization to leave such a colonial taste on the lips of many, and yet, being hard to see through, makes it difficult to pin down. It is difficult to see the nature of such an all-embracing Moloch. And in small ways, such as when innocently demanding the highest rate of interest from the bank, we are all a part of it.

New and old Europe: globalization versus One World

At the heart of Europe is a paradox. On the one hand it seeks to build a territorially defined peace to which sustainability is integral. But on the other, it seeks to meld this with an advanced capitalist market economy where 'free trade' has become conflated with competitive trade, and where, as we have been examining, this is relentlessly driven by monetarist and marketing mechanisms that privilege ahistorical short-termism and, so, offend against sustainability.

But alternatives to such globalization do exist. The internationalism of a 'One World' perspective, predicated on co-operation rather than competition, can be just as outward looking without reducing the poor and their soil to mere commodities. One World internationalism would not mean an end to competition. Rather, in a reversal of the current ordering of things, it would constrain and permit competition to operate only in the service of co-operation, just as, in democratic intellectualism, knowledge is permitted to express its power only when accountably applied in the service of the community.

Can we imagine, for example, public contracts awarded not to the lowest bidder, but to the one that can demonstrate (within a cost ceiling) the highest level of employee job satisfaction and the most sustainable use of natural resources? Can we imagine, in short, a shift away from corporate survival of the fittest, towards survival of the most fitting within a humane environment?

On the way to full European union, milestones have been passed that perhaps need to be revisited so that values steamrollered by globalizing forces are not lost. During the 1980s, for example, it was commonplace to talk about creating a 'Europe of the regions', with reference to Europe as a 'community' rather than a 'union'. Such thinking honoured place. It should be built upon.

At another level, Jacques Delors had these vitally important words to say about social cohesion in 1992 during his presidency of the European Commission:

> We are in effect at a crossroads in the history of European construction. 1992 is a turning point. Even if on the surface of the sea nothing is yet visible, deep down the currents are beginning to change direction. The Maastricht summit marked the end of the economic phase of European construction ... [and] we are now entering a fascinating time – perhaps especially for the young generation – a time when debate on the meaning of European construction becomes a major political factor.
>
> Believe me, we won't succeed with Europe solely on the basis of legal expertise or economic know-how. It is impossible to put the potential of Maastricht into practice without a breath of air. If in the

next ten years we haven't managed to give a soul to Europe, to give it spirituality and meaning, the game will be up.

This is why I want to revive the intellectual and spiritual debate on Europe. I invite the churches to participate actively in it. The debate must be free and open. We don't want to control it; it is a democratic discussion, not to be monopolised by technocrats. I would like to create a meeting place, a space for free discussion open to men and women of spirituality, to believers and non-believers, scientists and artists.

(Raiser *et al.* 1997: 51)

It is here that we find exposed the deepest name of the game. We could be facing a schizoid splitting of soul if the centre loses its hold – a fissuring into an historically situated 'Old' Europe and a disembedded, ahistorical 'New'.

But it doesn't have to be like that. For it not to be so, we Europeans must insist on values that count for more than dollars can buy. We, like Delors, must insist on nothing less than soul. We must guide our public policies according to that which gives life; that which brings beauty. Achieving a sustainable Europe in the face of globalization will therefore be a question of courage. It means privileging the co-operative ethos of 'One World' internationalism and challenging what Geddes called 'the golden age of Competition, as of Death'.

Note

1 I am deeply grateful to Richard Roberts, Professor of Religious Studies at the University of Stirling and a crucial theorist of globalization and managerialism (Roberts 2002), and to Murdo Macdonald, Professor of Scottish Art History at the University of Dundee and a leading expert on Patrick Geddes (Macdonald 1993) for generously commenting on parts of this chapter. Also to Alastair Hulbert, who previously administered the European Commission's A Soul for Europe project and is now warden of Scottish Churches House, Dunblane.

Bibliography

Choudhury, M.A. and Malik, U.A. (1992) *The Foundations of Islamic Political Economy*, London: Macmillan.
Fukuyama, F. (1993) *The End of History and the Last Man*, London: Penguin.
Kirwan, J. (ed.) (1991 (1891)) *Rerum Novarum: Encyclical Letter of Pope Leo XIII on the Condition of the Working Classes*, London: Catholic Truth Society.
Kitchen, P. (1975) *A Most Unsettling Person*, London: Victor Gollancz Ltd.
Leadbetter, C. (2000) *Living on Thin Air*, London: Penguin.
Locke, J. (1980 (1690)) *Second Treatise of Government*, Cambridge, MA: Hackett Publishing Co Ltd.
Macdonald, M. (ed.) (1992) 'Patrick Geddes: ecologist, educator, visual thinker', special issue of *The Edinburgh Review*, 88 ('The Sociology of Autumn' (1895), 31–9).

—— (1993) 'The democratic intellect in context', *The Edinburgh Review*, 90: 59–60.
McIntosh, A. (2001) *Soil and Soul: People versus Corporate Power*, London: Aurum Press.
Marcuse, H. (1964) *One Dimensional Man: Studies in the Ideology of Advanced Industrial Society*, London: Routledge.
Packard, V. (1960) *The Hidden Persuaders*, Harmondsworth: Penguin.
Raiser, K., Delteil, G., Stewart, J., Santer, J. and Vignon, J. (1997) *Europe under Challenge – Reconciliation and Meaning*, Occasional Paper No. 4, Brussels: Ecumenical Association for Church and Society.
Roberts, R. (2002) *Religion, Theology and the Human Sciences*, Cambridge: Cambridge University Press.
Sheth, J., Mittal, B. and Newman, B. (1999) *Customer Behaviour: Consumer Behaviour and Beyond*, Fort Worth, TX: Dryden Press.

Acknowledgements

This book and the associated conference developed under the aegis of the Centre for European Political Research located in the Department of Politics at the University of Dundee, Scotland. The conference, which attracted an international group of contributors and audience, took place in September 2002. The editors would like to acknowledge a grant from the Department of Politics which enabled the conference to take place and to express their gratitude for the organizational assistance they obtained from our unfailingly helpful secretary, Carol Benoit-Ngassam and from two of the Department's graduate students, Catriona McLellan and Abdullah Yusuf. Heidi Bagtazo has been a very efficent and friendly editor at Routledge. We would also like to thank Alastair McIntosh of the Centre for Human Ecology in Edinburgh for providing the conference with a striking keynote address which he kindly agreed to fashion into a foreword for this book.

1 Editors' introduction

John Barry, Brian Baxter and Richard Dunphy

The central problem which the authors in this book address is that of how to achieve a sustainable form of economic system within Europe in a world in which all states, and the regional groupings which they may create, are subject to the forces of globalization. These three concepts represent the nodal points around which the chapters of the book are organized, and each of the three is in its own right a focus of controversy and debate. This introduction seeks to outline some of these debates in order to enable the reader to grasp the complexity of the central problem. It also situates each contribution within the framework created by the three structuring concepts.

Sustainability

The first concept to examine is that of sustainability. This encapsulates the basic value to which all relevant policies, whether of states or of the European Union, are to be oriented. Some would argue that the particular version of sustainability which has come to predominate in international discussion since its introduction in the UN-sponsored Brundtland Report, namely that of 'sustainable development', is a contradiction in terms (World Commission on Environment and Development 1987). For development as conventionally conceived requires economic growth, and all such growth is sooner or later going to turn out to be unsustainable. Critics of this persuasion argue for a 'steady-state' international economic system, in which growth is stabilized and environmentally-adverse practices are held in check or reduced to nugatory levels (Daly 1993).

Detractors from this position, among whom are to be found equally ardent defenders of the goal of environmental protection, argue that not all growth need be environmentally harmful, and growth may be needed in some areas to reduce adverse environmental impacts of existing practices and technologies. It all depends, therefore, on the exact nature of the growth (Jacobs 1991: 53–61). Some growth is needed in areas necessary for human well-being, unless the human species is to be arbitrarily excluded from the list of species whose interests and needs are to be attended to in the goal of sustainability.

A different issue also needs to be taken notice of at this point, one which also seriously divides ideologues and decision makers thinking about what is required to achieve sustainability. This concerns the distinction between 'strong' and 'weak' forms of the concept of sustainable development. Those who think that sustainable development is not necessarily a contradiction in terms, because not all forms of economic growth are environmentally harmful, often argue that there are nevertheless certain elements of the natural world – dubbed 'critical natural capital' – which should not be harmed or destroyed by economic growth. These are irreplaceable natural resources and services argued to be crucial to the well-being and integrity of the planet's biosphere; such as climate regulation, biodiversity and ecosystem stability. Defenders of such a position thus argue for a Strong version of sustainable development.

Detractors from this position seek to deny that there are any genuinely irreplaceable elements of the biosphere. Provided human beings have accumulated enough capital to employ in new technological ventures, and provided that human ingenuity, an infinite resource, is allowed its full sway, then any inroads we make into natural capital can be compensated for by equivalent amounts of human capital. We may lose species and rainforests, but we will gain roads and airports, and thus we will hand on to our descendants a bundle of resources at least as good as what we have inherited, thereby satisfying the requirement of the Brundtland conception of sustainable development (Munda 1997).

This Weak conception is pretty much a 'business as usual' prescription for economic growth and clearly places no real restriction on amounts or kinds of such growth. In this view, such environmental problems as there are can be handled by conventional forms of technological innovation, stimulated by the demands of the capitalist market place. We are deemed to face no overall crisis of the environment, and any concern we have with genuine threats to human health and well-being stemming from our current economic practices can be dealt with by means of those innovations in production which have been dubbed 'ecological modernization'. The market for less environmentally-harmful products and production techniques may be expected to call forth innovations which provide employment, generate aggregate wealth and lead to effective solutions to those problems (Dryzek 1997: 45–60; 137–52).

An important issue to address in trying to understand the European approach to the issue of sustainability will thus be which of the above conceptions have been adopted by decision makers in the European context. It will come as no real surprise if we discover that the prevailing choice is for the Weak form of sustainable development which puts all its emphasis on the need to foster ecological modernization, or that there will nevertheless be many within Europe who will be inclined to argue for a Strong version of sustainable development and to view ecological modernization as at best a short-term palliative until we find ways of placing the necessary restrictions on economic growth which the concept of 'critical natural capital' implies.

Although these issues appear to be primarily economic, nothing economic is exclusively economic. Alastair McIntosh, in his Foreword to this volume, passionately emphasizes the spiritual dimension to sustainability. He argues that for creatures such as ourselves the natural world is not, and indeed cannot be, simply a bundle of resources for the meeting of our material or physical needs. Some will see in this emphasis on spiritual aspects of sustainability an argument for a new, or revised, form of religion, perhaps for a new pantheon or deity to form the focus of our yearnings. However, it is important to keep certain key distinctions in mind here. Spirituality involves the quest for meaning, and human-beings are clearly seekers after meaning. But religion is only one possible way of finding significant meaning, by locating human life within a transcendental framework. Further, theism is only one, albeit very influential, version of the religious answer. Some religious viewpoints, such as Buddhism, are non-theistic.

Hence, an emphasis on the spiritual dimension of sustainability need not as such commit one to a religious or theistic version of such spirituality. Humanists have always sought meaning within human life, and a version of this approach remains open. However, many environmentally-concerned people find traditional humanism too human-centred (anthropocentric) to the exclusion of those other beings (literally our cousins, if Darwin's theory is accepted), with which we share this planet. Part of such people's conception of the spiritual aspect of sustainability will be the need to find room, within the legitimate search for the betterment of human life, to allow as many of our fellow life-forms as possible to exist and flourish. Clearly, this spiritual element of the sustainability debate engages with long-running and often bitterly controversial issues that lie at the heart of human life. It is vital that, in the course of the extremely important focus on economic issues which also lie at the centre of that debate, this issue of meaning is not lost sight of.

Although issues of spirituality appear primarily to be focused upon individuals, and with how they answer their need for meaning, human beings are social beings. Their lives are characterized by complex social and political relationships, and their implementation of ideas of meaning is conditioned by that fact. We need therefore to ask whether sustainability requires changes in social and political arenas.

Does sustainability require new forms of interpersonal relationships, perhaps less competitive and hierarchical? Susan Baker explores in this connection the contributions of ecofeminist theorizing to our understanding of the ways in which human relationships may require to be restructured in a form which recognizes an essential difference between men and women.

This essentialist claim has met strong resistance over the years from many other kinds of feminism, especially of the socialist feminist school.

The latter views the idea of 'women's nature' as a social construct, the nature of which has to be grasped in terms of the location of women in the structures of an inherently exploitative society, in which large numbers of men as well as women are regularly subject to unacceptable forms of domination.

Baker supports the essentialism of ecofeminism, which she sees as providing a bulwark against forms of oppression of women, and nature, which pure social constructivism seems to licence. She notes that the efforts of ecofeminism involve a challenge to the equality agenda of anti-essentialist forms of feminism, which threatens simply to assimilate women to forms of domination within society and with respect to human-nature relationships. She claims that there is also developing among ecofeminist activists a new conception of what political activity may properly be taken to be, away from the standard concern with participation within political institutions which should rather be strongly challenged for their commitment to harmful forms of domination.

According to Baker, therefore, ecofeminism offers a view of women which, if taken seriously and allowed to influence the public policy of both individual European states and the European Union, would in itself require a radical rethinking of the social, economic and political structures within which we currently live, and do so in a way which moves us towards the goal of sustainability.

Other pertinent issues involved in the socio-political aspect of sustainability concern the nature of citizenship, and the citizenship education, within a sustainable society. Andrew Dobson explores the question of whether Europeans need to develop within their educational systems means of inculcating a sense of citizenship which encompasses environmental responsibility, both towards our fellow human beings, whether fellow-citizens (as conventionally conceived) or not, and towards non-human life-forms. The analysis which he provides emphasizes the importance of environmental citizenship as a matter of accepting responsibilities, particularly as revealed by the idea of the ecological footprint – the concept that human beings have different degrees of adverse impact on the environment, depending upon the nature of the socio-economic system under which they live, and their specific role within it. He concludes that the concept of justice, which lies at the heart of citizenship conceptions, thus has to be recast in terms of justice in the distribution of such footprints.

However, Marcel Wissenburg gives some reason to query whether it is any longer realistic to envisage the possibility of such a mode of citizenship, given that responsibility presupposes power, and increasingly individual citizens are faced with a socio-political reality in which a loss of power, or the increasingly obscurity of its location, seems to be the reality. He argues that the world, under the pressure of globalization, is entering a quasi-medieval period characterized by multiple layers of power and decision making which he dubs 'pluralization', within which it becomes increasingly problematic for citizens to exercise the kinds of active influence and control characteristic of classic republican conceptions of citizenship.

He canvasses two possible responses to this. First the kind of extension of deliberative democracy often championed by the green movement. Pluralization, he argues, makes this a problematic solution for the same kinds of reasons which make representative democracy problematic; that lines of responsibility and accountability are too 'blurred'. Instead he proposes a top-down approach to citizenship, in which the onus falls on citizen-rulers to seek actively to consult all the interested parties among their fellow-citizens, what he calls 'consultative elitism'. He explores some of the reasons why this would be practical – in the form of the correct incentive structure for elites to engage in consultation – as well as not undesirable (a decent society would be possible under it).

The potential for extending democratic forms finds a somewhat more sympathetic reception in the chapter by Derek Bell. He considers the issue of whether sustainability requires new methods of decision making, allowing environmentally-informed and -concerned citizens a direct say in the formulation of the appropriate policies and legislation. He considers the various forms of democratic institutions which might supplement or replace the traditional representative forms of liberal democracies in the light of the Aarhus Convention of 1998. He analyses the conceptions of democracy and sustainability employed by the convention, and examines the way in which the former is supposed to foster the latter. The upshot of his analysis is that the conception of democratic participation used by the convention is insufficiently radical, even given that a fundamentally representative system is arguably unavoidable in modern democratic societies. However, he notes that it is not entirely devoid of radical elements in this sphere – he notes the convention's innovative conception that a right to participate in environmental decisions, given the transboundary nature of environmental problems, has to be extended beyond citizens of the policy-making polity to other affected parties. With respect to the concept of sustainability employed in the convention, he notes its lack of clarity on what was referred to above as the 'Strong' versus 'Weak' issue, and that it is entirely anthropocentric in form. Nevertheless, he argues, the Aarhus Convention provides at least a basis for developments which could give a concerned citizenry greater scope to determine some local environmental matters and to have a more powerful say in the overall direction of environmental policy than is allowed for under prevailing norms of 'participation'.

Europe

The issues so far addressed confront all states and regions of the world. However, this book focuses upon Europe, where an important developing context, represented by the EU, determines how one will try to answer these questions. The EU is both integrating and expanding. The states that choose to join it subject themselves to a new body of laws and institutions which take them away from their traditional focus exclusively on their own narrow self-interest. We need to understand the terms upon which this association is based, and whether it is primarily an economic, or a political and perhaps moral and spiritual enterprise.

Thus, we have to examine the effects of the European dimension upon the nature of politics and policy making within, and even beyond, its boundaries (for, in an era of globalization, boundaries are no longer fixed or impermeable). How far has policy making and sustainability-oriented political activity (as represented, say, by the Green movement) become a European, rather than a state-oriented, phenomenon? How far do states retain both their distinctive national cultural characteristics within the new Europe, and a large measure of control over law and policy within their boundaries? What do we make of what we find when we try to answer these questions, particularly with regard to the issue of sustainability?

Andrew Jordan, Duncan Liefferink and Jenny Fairbrass examine the impact of Europeanization upon the environmental policies of ten EU member states. As ever, the theoretical concept of 'Europeanization' has been subjected to various interpretations by different investigators. Jordan *et al.* use the conception of Europeanization as 'the process through which European integration penetrates and, in certain circumstances, brings about adjustments to domestic institutions, decision-making procedures and public policies'.

What their investigation reveals is that Europeanization thus conceived and applied to environmental policy has been effective to varying degrees within all the member states studied. With respect to the three areas of policy analysis – content, structures and style – the EU's effect has been greatest on the first, and this impact has, over the period since 1970 which has been studied, been 'hugely significant'. However, the details of the interactions between the EU and the member states are indispensable to an understanding of the precise nature of the EU impact on those states and to a fuller understanding of the process of European integration. The authors conclude that the process of Europeanization has been, for many member states, a 'hugely unexpected, unpredictable and, at times, chaotic process' with the states in much less firm control of the integration process than some theorists of that process have claimed.

Chris Rootes examines the extent to which the development of the EU as a legislative and policy-making entity, particularly in the field of environmental policy where, as we have just noted, its activities have become extremely important, has stimulated and fostered the creation of an EU – wide environmental movement. In spite of some elements of EU level institutionalization of Environmental Movement Organisations (EMOs), particularly in the 1970s, Rootes finds that the focus of EMOs within the EU is still largely that of the particular state within which they are located. Different polities and their associated EMOs are actuated by different kinds of environmental concerns. The development of the EU institutions, organizational and financial restrictions upon the activities of EMOs, and the ongoing activities of radical EMOs, those least likely to accept co-option into what they see as fundamentally-flawed EU political institutions and economic practices, all militate against the easy development of something we can properly call a 'European environmental movement'. In the development of such a movement, Rootes argues, the forces of globalization rather than of Europeanization may ultimately have an impact but on present trends it will be a slow and fitful process.

Of course, fundamental divisions within and between Green political parties with regard to the nature and direction of the European integration process are one illustration of the problem Rootes is concerned with. Green parties have long been at the fore in arguing for a fundamental critique of the direction of European construction. They have argued that it is centralized, bureaucratic and technocratic and driven by an endless accumulation of material wealth to the detriment of sustainability. But Green parties have divided on the issue of whether the direction of European integration can be changed from within, using the European Union as a vehicle for the attainment of the goals of sustainability (essentially the position of German, French and Italian Green parties), or whether the EU is a fundamental obstacle to progress and justice and as much power as possible should be returned to the local and national levels (as British and Swedish Greens, for example, argue). These tactical and strategic differences have long stood in the way of progress towards the formation of an effective European Green party, for example. On major issues affecting the future direction and nature of the EU – such as the desirability of a single European currency – the Green political slogan, 'Act local, think global', has too often masked a morass of conflicting positions.

Globalization

Let us now turn specifically to the concept of globalization. The world of states is now, many theorists aver, becoming globalized. This means many things. It refers to economic interconnections, of course – the increase of world trade and the creation of regional economic groupings. But it betokens the interconnectedness across the globe of a whole raft of issues. The environment is a key one, but issues of peace and security are now even more globalized than they have ever been before, and trade and movement of peoples, together with the development of instantaneous electronic communication and information transfer embodied in the burgeoning internet. With these issues come increasing degrees of cultural and therefore of moral interconnectedness. To a certain degree it may be argued that there even exists a globalized political order, centring on the

United Nations, and manifesting itself in a whole plethora of international conferences and reports with their concomitant legal formulations in treaties and conventions. This has been especially noticeable in the field of environmental protection since the Stockholm Conference in 1972.

The concept of globalization seems to imply that between states and cultures there exists some form of equality. After all, interconnection might be thought to imply reciprocity – a mutuality of influence between those interconnected. But many would argue that the reality of the process dubbed 'globalization' is that it is the states that embody liberal capitalism, especially its leading element, the USA, which are developing and strengthening their hegemony over the rest of the world. A further dimension to this claim is that within liberal capitalist states it is the interests of powerful multi-national (or trans-national) corporations which predominate, particularly those which play a major role in the military-industrial complex, and it is seriously open to question how far such corporations can be induced to take the idea of sustainable development at all seriously.

Once again, both Greens and anti-capitalist activists (sometimes referred to, sometimes controversially, as anti-globalization activists) have occupied a broad range of positions. The Green Party of England and Wales, in a 1998 policy statement (Green Party of England and Wales 1998), flatly rejects globalization as a dead-end process, 'driven over the past three decades by the world's leading business and governmental elites', that has resulted in escalating social injustice and environmental degradation and has benefited the TNCs primarily. The party envisaged a fundamentally-transformed EU that essentially 'withdrew' from the globalization game, imposing tariffs on imports in order to promote 'local consumption' and taking control of TNCs, breaking them up into smaller companies.

Other activists have implicitly or explicitly dismissed such calls as totally unrealistic and have argued for *more but different* forms of globalization. This approach clearly informs Naomi Klein's response to the Belgian Prime Minister and (then) EU president Guy Verhofstadt's open letter to the 'anti-globalization movement' in September 2001. In his open letter Verhofstadt had written:

> Your concerns as anti-globalists are extremely valid, but to find the right solutions to these valid questions we need more globalization, not less. This is the paradox of anti-globalization. Globalization can, after all, serve the cause of good just as much as it can serve the cause of evil. What we need is a global ethical approach to the environment, labour relations and monetary policy. In other words, the challenge that we are faced with today is not how to thwart globalization instead but how to give it an ethical foundation.
>
> (Klein 2002: 76)

In her reply, Klein argued that 'I am part of a network of movements that is fighting not against globalization but for deeper and more responsive democracies, locally, nationally and internationally. This network is as global as capitalism itself' (Klein 2002: 77–84). To challenge the hegemony of neo-liberalism was not to reject globalization, but to reject a model that had a tendency to swallow culture, human rights, democracy, and environmental protection inside the parameters of trade. Anti-capitalism, therefore, does not equate with anti-globalization. Rather, Klein argued:

> We have been going through our own globalization process. And it is precisely because of globalization that the system is in crisis. We know too much. There is too much communication and mobility at the grassroots for the system to hold. Not just the gap between rich and poor but also between rhetoric and reality. Between what is said and what is done. Between the promise of globalization and its real effects. It's time to close the gap.
>
> (Klein 2002: 77–84)

The insistence of leading activists such as Klein on the problematic nature of the term 'anti-globalization' is important for a number of reasons. It highlights once again the range of possible approaches to globalization on all sides of the debate, and the degree of confusion that can reign over what exactly it is that we are discussing. It draws our attention to both the temptation – a dangerous temptation, in the eyes of some anti-capitalist activists – that some critics of the current dominant form of globalization may succumb to, namely to retreat within the confines of forms of nationalism, and to the tendency of supporters of neo-liberalism to brand all of their critics as 'narrow-minded' and 'backward-looking'. It questions the inevitability of one hegemonic (neo-liberal) form of globalization.

Rafal Soborski's chapter is concerned with the political relationship between Green activism and anti-capitalist activism (although Soborski, somewhat controversially in the light of Klein's arguments, continues to refer to the movement as 'anti-globalization' rather than anti-capitalist). Specifically, Soborski explores the ideological relationship between the 'anti-globalization' protesters, which are already known to comprise a diverse range of theoretical positions, and the supporters of Green ideology, specifically of ecologism. Both groups share many critical positions, such as a suspicion of modernity, free trade and the neo-liberal capitalist agenda. They also show convergence on their practical nostrums for tackling the perceived problems posed by globalization.

There are also some differences of emphasis between the two groups. Thus 'anti-globalizers', in Soborski's analysis, contain within their ranks supporters of more clearly anthropocentric views. For such thinkers, specifically environmental problems are seen through the lens of their effect on human interests. In spite of these differences of perspective from ecologism, one might, as a result of Soborski's analysis, see the 'anti-globalization' movement as being fundamentally a branch of the more general environmental movement, rather than as representing a new phenomenon entirely. Whatever view one takes on this matter, it is clear that both forms of critique pose serious questions about whether any form of sustainability can be achieved within the context of globalization.

In response to questions such as these, an alternative view of how globalization and sustainability fit together, one which seeks to demonstrate their mutual compatibility, is put forward by Debra Johnson. Here it will be useful to recollect the remarks made at the start of this introduction outlining competing views on economic growth, Strong and Weak versions of 'sustainable development' and the concept of ecological modernisation.

According to Johnson the cement which binds together globalization, Europeanization and sustainable development is, precisely, ecological modernization (EM). She argues that the claims of the environmentally harmful effects of globalization which its detractors often cite, such as the 'race to the bottom' of environmental standards as MNCs relocate to environmentally lax states ('pollution havens') have no strong evidence to support them, and the economic logic of major corporations' activities in any case makes them rather unlikely. Instead, ecological modernization has provided a means whereby businesses can both be environmentally responsible and turn a profit, with the great bonus that EM emerges from within the competitive market environment, rather than being forced upon businesses by discredited command and control systems of regulation.

In her view Europeanization, that is to say the emergence of an increasingly integrated EU, has provided a boost to EM within Europe as the result of deliberate policy innovation, unlike the case of globalization, where the process of EM has been largely left to the workings of the market. This, she contends, bodes well to give the EU a competitive edge within the increasingly environmentally beneficent word of EM. With increased economic growth there is the possible application of the Kuznets Curve, which suggests that although some sorts of environmental damage at first increase with increased economic growth they then start to decrease. Hence, on this analysis, the overall outlook for the environment under the forces of globalization is actually a rather positive one.

That is one, rather positive, view of the ways in which the European Union has been active in the context of globalization within its own boundaries. But it is also important to ask how the EU has tried to put into practice in the global economic and political forums the commitment to sustainability which it proclaims within the European context.

Jon Burchell and Simon Lightfoot analyse the role of the EU in the Johannesburg Summit of September 2002. What they find contains some good, but some, perhaps rather more important, bad in the EU performance, both at the Summit itself and in the preparatory meetings in the years immediately preceding the conference. In some areas, particularly climate change, the EU has been taking a lead, particularly in maintaining some momentum after the Kyoto agreement was rejected by the USA. But in many other areas the EU, while being prepared to sign up for measures to secure environmental and developmental aims, is unable to take any effective action to implement them.

Partly this is due to some deep-rooted policy commitments such as the Common Agricultural Policy, which protects EU farmers from competition from developing countries, and allows them the opportunity to dump their subsidized surpluses upon those very countries, to the considerable disadvantage of the latter's agricultural sector. Also it is due to the fact that the Directorates within the EU responsible for different policy areas have rather different abilities to influence the overall EU policy agenda. Directorate Trade, with its neo-liberal agenda, has much greater influence than do the environmental or development directorates. The concept of sustainable development, to which the EU has publicly committed itself, is viewed as the specific remit of the environmental directorate, rather than as a principle that has to be integrated into all the policy areas of the EU. Overall, then, Burchell and Lightfoot argue, the EU still has a long way to travel to reach its goal of a sustainable union.

We need also to inquire whether a society governed by the rule of law, and committed to sustainability, will find it easy to find legal remedies to combat unsustainability, particularly when globalization (and its sub-elements, such as regionalization) is brought into the picture. In this area, one of the issues that needs to be confronted, argues James Tunney, in the final chapter, is the necessity of developing 'a more robust and indeed sustainable concept of sustainability'. In his discussion of the World Trade Organisation and the whole sustainability debate after Doha, Tunney argues passionately for a triangular dialogue between politics, political science and law. He identifies the 'failure to understand the role of institutions, legal systems and law' as 'one of the greatest failings of the conceptualisation of systems of global governance'. For Tunney, greater understanding of the legal processes of regional bodies such as the EU should allow for more effective strategies of engagement, including legal strategies, that might advance the environmental agenda. He concludes that 'proactive, effective responses, predicated on robust analyses that recognize the reflexive disciplinary relationships that exist' might benefit from a concept of sustainability that has been refined and developed in the 'forge of legal debate'. A failure to proceed in this direction would constitute an Achilles' Heel of the whole 'Europe, Globalization and Sustainability' debate.

Clearly there are points of disagreement between the approaches and views of the authors represented in this book. In some cases disagreement concerns the most useful or necessary approach to adopt towards the resolution of the problems which have been identified – as with Tunney's concern at what he sees as the imprecision of the key concepts employed by those less used than he is to what is required to make a law judiciable. Some disagreements concern what the possibilities are for the creation of sustainability, as in the tension between the accounts of Dobson, Bell and Wissenburg over the role of, and possibilities for, democracy and citizenship within a sustainable Europe. Sometimes it is within the central issues of economic organization that we find differences being aired – over the role of ecological modernization and Europeanization in creating sustainability, for example, with Johnson supportive of a beneficial 'reinforcing nexus', and McIntosh seeing deep spiritual difficulties lurking in the whole materialistic ethos which this approach is often taken to exemplify.

These differences of view and approach are only to be expected where human beings are involved in a problematic and complex endeavour. Our authors have at least demonstrated by the clarity and seriousness of their discussions that the issues are amenable to reasoned debate. Such debate is not a sufficient condition for the resolution of the problems that they have been addressing, but it is surely a necessary one.

References

Daly, H. (1993) 'Sustainable growth: an impossibility theorem', in H.E. Daly and K.E. Townsend (eds) *Valuing the Earth: Economics, Ecology, Ethics*, Cambridge, MA: MIT Press.

Dryzek, J. (1997) *The Politics of the Earth: Environmental Discourses*, New York, NY: Oxford University Press.

Green Party of England and Wales (1998) *Act Local, Act Global: Greening the European Union – A Challenge to Globalisation*, London: Green Party.

Jacobs, M. (1991) *The Green Economy: Environment, Sustainable Development and the Politics of the Future*, London and Boulder, CO: Pluto Press.

Klein, N. (2002) *Fences and Windows: Dispatches from the Front Lines of the Globalization Debate*, London: Flamingo.

Munda, G. (1997) 'Environmental economics, ecological economics and the concept of sustainable development', *Environmental Values* 6: 213–33.

World Commission on Environment and Development (1987) *Our Common Future*, London: Oxford University Press.

Part I
Politics

2 The challenge of ecofeminism for European politics

Susan Baker

Introduction

This chapter explores ecofeminist theory and its critique of mainstream Western ideologies about women and nature. It begins by outlining how ecofeminism can be grouped into two broad categories. It explores each in turn, paying attention, en route, to the divisive issue of essentialism. It then examines ecofeminist political activism, before identifying the ways in which ecofeminism is significant for the development of European politics. The conclusion points to the weaknesses of ecofeminism, but also shows how it presents a very refreshing challenge for feminist analysis and politics.

Ecofeminism as critical analysis and as politics

Ecofeminism is both an analysis of society–nature relationships and a prescription of how these relationships can be transformed (Buckingham-Hatfield 2000: 35). On the one hand, it presents a highly critical analysis of the principal philosophical and cultural attitudes that underlie mainstream Western ideologies about women, the natural world and their interrelationship (Baker 1993). Drawing upon the feminist concept of patriarchy and combining this with insights gained from environmental and peace activism, ecofeminism argues that a common, dualistic belief system, rooted in the principle of domination and subjugation, underlies modern, negative attitudes towards both women and nature (Plumwood 1986: 120).

Western beliefs are characterized by ecofeminism as primarily rationalist ideologies, which hold that the domination and control of nature and of women is morally and politically justifiable as it forms part of the 'natural order'. The 'natural order' is viewed as hierarchical, an understanding that seeks to loosen the links that embed human beings in the natural world. In this worldview, men are seen as set above or apart from the natural world, as inhabiting the spheres of the rational, the discursive, the public and the realms of the mind. Their ties with the natural, emotional, sensual and private spheres of the body, in contrast, debase women. Ecofeminism rejects this Western belief system, because it is seen as having led to the subjugation of women and to the destruction of nature.

To counteract this dominant ideology, ecofeminism aims to reconstruct a new understanding of the place of human beings within the natural world. In particular, it is aimed at situating women, nature and, sometimes, men in a more balanced and equitable relationship with each other. This involves the development of a new set of attitudes to nature and women, one that is based upon acceptance of their inherent, intrinsic value (Diamond and Orenstein 1990: xi).

On the other hand, ecofeminism can also be characterized as a diverse range of women's environmental activities. As such, it can be seen as a practical response to the reality of environmental degradation. Ecofeminism, as political activism, arose from what had hitherto been two different social movements: the environmental movement and the women's movement. From within the latter, it has inherited much from the women's peace and spirituality movements. Its focus is upon counteracting the myriad ways in which the degradation of the natural environment impacts upon the daily lives of women, especially in the Third World.

Moving our analysis of ecofeminism beyond this simple set of statements presents a great deal of difficulty. This is because of the diversity of positions, critiques and arguments that lie behind the single term 'ecofeminism'. At least ten distinct types of ecofeminism can be identified (Buckingham-Hatfield 2000: 37). The resulting uncertainty in attributing the title 'ecofeminist' to individual thinkers, to activists or to groups also makes the task of exploring the political significance of ecofeminism all the more difficult.

Nevertheless, a convention has grown up in the literature that divides ecofeminism into two broad groupings: 'cultural ecofeminism' and 'socialist ecofeminism'. I recognize that such categorization can do harm to the diversity of activities within the movement. Furthermore, it can result in oversimplified characterizations of its underlying ideas and in too sharp a juxtaposition of its principles and arguments. Bearing this danger in mind, I have adopted this two-fold division in my analysis. I believe that it offers a useful heuristic device that will enable us both to explore in broad general terms the contribution of ecofeminist theory and to gain insight into the significance of ecofeminism for the development of European politics.

Cultural ecofeminism

While seeking its inspiration from a wide variety of sources both inside and outside the women's movement and from across a range of feminist theory, cultural ecofeminism draws heavily upon the tradition of radical feminism (Spretnak 1990: 5). Radical feminist analysis has located women's oppression with men, particularly with male sexuality, which is regarded as the site of male power.

Central to the argument of radical feminism is the belief that there exists an innate female nature, which differs from the gendered self of the male. The essence of this difference lies with women's unique power to reproduce. Some radical feminists would argue that, by virtue of this life-giving power, women are inherently superior to men (Eckersley 1992: 66). The life-giving capacities of women are not limited to the birthing act, but extend to women's connections with the rhythms and cycles of time, especially through monthly menstruation. I return later to a fuller discussion of this, when I explore the issue of essentialism.

Cultural ecofeminism has extended this central tenet of radical feminism to argue that women, by virtue of their biological capacity, have a closer relationship with the natural world than do men. Women's reproductive capacity connects them directly with the natural world. Here nature is understood as diffuse, as primarily an active force, rather than as a specific natural environment or location. The argument for a special connection between women and nature owes much to the rejection of the traditional Western approach that sees women, nature and ultimately God as other, alien, outside the self, as estranged. Different ecofeminists place different emphasis on features within that belief system as the root cause of this estrangement, pointing at times to classical philosophy (Platonic dualism), to mechanism in Enlightenment thinking or to anthropocentric Christianity. Plumwood, for example, has developed a sophisticated critique of the dualistic thinking embedded in Western thought, that sets nature against society (Plumwood 1992). She shows how, in the dualistic belief system inherited from Greek philosophy, the public world of commerce, culture and politics became valued over the private world of the particular and the personal (Baker 1999). Ecofeminism here becomes an epistemology, an approach to knowledge that sees a set of ideas or belief systems as responsible for the exploitation of nature and of women. This stands in contrast to the position of materialist ecofeminism, which holds that economic and social arrangements are the root of the problem. This is discussed further below.

As well as being of importance for our conceptualization of the female, the connection between women and nature is of significance for social movement activity. The female connections with nature, natural rhythms and biological reproduction, it is argued, have allowed women to keep sight, throughout history, of the mutually interdependent relationship that exists between humanity and the natural world (Merchant 1980). Thus women are understood to be in a unique and advantageous position to engage politically, culturally and socially on behalf, and in defence, of nature. The maintenance of the connection between women and nature also means that women are ideally placed to begin the task of articulating new sets of relationships that can benefit both women and the environment. This 'standpoint theory', as it is known, is based on the belief that only those that are oppressed can understand and counteract the relationship of oppression. Oppressors have too many vested interests to see or to act in a clear and unambiguous manner.

The cultural ecofeminist project of reconstructing a new relationship with nature is undertaken through what we can call a number of re-affirmations, wherein particular aspects of the human condition are re-appraised and given new value (Baker 1993). The value placed on different aspects or attributes of the female differs among ecofeminists, but they share a primary project of attributing positive value to birth and motherhood and of celebrating women's reproductive and life-giving powers.

It is here that the positive contribution of cultural ecofeminism can be most clearly situated. Through their emphasis on and celebration of the body, a new feminist culture is evolving that is concerned with the material, natural, emotional, subjective and private realms. The development of feminist culture provides women with the opportunity to contribute positively to the current project of reconstructing a new approach to humanity, to nature and indeed to gender itself (Merchant 1980, 1992). It has, for example, led to the development of an ethics of care within ecofeminism (Buckingham-Hatfield 2000). The development stands in contrast to 'male culture', with its focus on the rational, economic and the public. By emphasizing the mind, male culture seeks to transcend natural constraints that, ultimately, lead to the exploitation, rather than care of, nature (Pepper 1996).

Another way in which cultural ecofeminism seeks to go beyond traditional, exploitative understandings of the female and of nature is to override the prevalent influence of patriarchy by drawing upon the myths and beliefs of older, non-patriarchal cultures. Central to this is the recourse to past philosophies and belief systems, so prevalent that some would argue that 'ecofeminism is a new term for an ancient wisdom' (Diamond and Orenstein 1991: xv). In drawing upon older myths and beliefs ecofeminism has also given place to celebration, especially that which honours the embeddedness of all earth's people in the multiple web and cycles of life (Baker 1993). Celebration is aimed at spiritual renewal, healing and at the reaffirmation of the value of women's birth-giving powers. The healing is centred on the Mother Earth, and the rituals are often connected to the celebration of the rhythms and seasons of nature. The return to celebration and the revival of ritual has facilitated the development of new focal points of activity for ecofeminist women. Moreover, as a primary communal event, it allows women to deepen their sense of belonging to a wider community (Starhawk 1988: 155). Here we can see New Age leanings within radical, cultural ecofeminism.

The use of the imagery of the web is common in ecofeminist writings. This contrasts sharply with the imagery associated with the 'animal kingdom', the more traditional term that is used to articulate a hierarchical relationship between human beings and nature. This links well with the concern within cultural ecofeminism to develop a language that expresses and holds the connections between reason and emotion, thought and experience in ways not possible with current language. Daly, for example, has done much to reclaim the value of women through the re-appropriation, re-construction and re-configuration of language (Daly 1978). The breaking of traditional linguistic bounds is seen as essential for women to be able to re-articulate their relatedness to each other and to all living life forms. This is important, as many ecofeminists, especially those influenced by New French Feminism, do not wish women to remain in mystical and inarticulate relationship with nature (Christ 1990: 61), but rather to be able to express and communicate that relationship in new ways.

Distinguishing cultural from socialist ecofeminism

Acceptance or rejection of the claim that women have an innate nature or essentialist characteristics, a position known as 'essentialism', provides a key way of distinguishing the two main tenets of ecofeminism, namely cultural and socialist ecofeminism. The return to essentialism is also the source of considerable disquiet, one could almost say alarm, within the broader, contemporary, feminist movement. Because of its importance, both for our understanding of ecofeminism and for wider debates within feminist theory, I will spend some time looking at the debate on essentialism before discussing socialist ecofeminism.

Essentialism

The rejection of the essentialist argument and the adoption of the position that female nature is socially, as opposed to biologically, constructed have been crucial to the development of liberal second wave feminism. Thus, a central argument in the early development of the women's movement and feminist ideology has been that differences between the sexes are not rooted in female biology, but rather that such differences are the product of social factors and therefore they can be changed. Simone de Beauvoir, one of the key figures in that development, forcefully argued that 'One is not born, but becomes a woman. No biological, psychological, or economic fate determines the figure that the human female presents in society: it is civilization as a whole that produces this creature' (de Beauvoir 1952: 249). Since de Beauvoir, liberal second wave feminism has continued to argue against any emphasis on the link between women and nature. Some, most noticeably Firestone in her *Dialectic of Sex*, went as far as arguing that female liberation requires that reproduction becomes a technological process, removed from women's biology altogether (Firestone 1979). Only then, she has argued, can women become truly free.

In keeping with the tradition laid down by de Beauvoir, many contemporary feminists would strongly distrust the ecofeminist re-connection of femaleness with the sphere of reproduction and thus with nature. Such connections are seen as dangerously conservative. Indeed one could say that for many contemporary feminists they represent the antithesis of the aims of the post-war women's liberation movement. For them it threatens nothing short of the re-imprisonment of woman in her body, from which she has long sought to gain her freedom and to assert herself, both politically and economically.

However, despite the assertions of de Beauvoir and her status as one of the founding theorists of second wave feminism, the essentialism versus social construction debate was not put to rest, but rather has continued to simmer, albeit it at the margins of feminist theory. Through its emphasis on the connection between women and nature, cultural ecofeminism has once more moved the debate to a more central stage in feminist theorizing. Rather than seeing woman as freed by her disentanglement from the body, cultural ecofeminists argue that true liberation requires the positive affirmation and celebration of women as embedded within nature as birth-givers. Women gain their freedom through recognition of their essential, biologically grounded, female nature.

Many contemporary feminists will accept that cultural ecofeminists are right to point out that it is not woman's reproductive capacity that is the source of her oppression, but rather the 'hierarchies that many men have built upon them' (Biehl 1991: 10). However, general feminist acceptance of the cultural ecofeminist position on biology stops there. There are two interrelated reasons for this. First, cultural ecofeminism is seen as smacking of biological determinism and, second, in the light of the struggle of second wave feminism for women's equality, the emphasis on female biology and 'women's nature' is regarded as politically and socially regressive.

Dealing with the first of the arguments, many contemporary feminists feel increasingly uncomfortable with what they see as the cultural ecofeminist assertion that certain *personality* aspects of women are innate, such as their relationship with nature. As such, they cannot be changed through political and social engagement. As Biehl, who is very vocal in her anti-ecofeminism, has argued:

> ecofeminism's healthy impulse to reclaim women's biology has in many cases become an acceptance of some of the same constricting stereotypes of 'women's nature' that have long been used to oppress them. When ecofeminists root women's personality traits in reproduction and sexual biology, they tend to give acceptance to those male-centred images that define women as primarily biological beings.
> (Biehl 1991: 11)

Others, like Randall, would caution against their stress upon biology because of its politically conservative consequences. She argues that:

> One longstanding feminist criticism of such an approach has been that it is precisely these differences that have been cited to justify male dominance. This certainly is a dangerous possibility with arguments for an 'essential' biologically rooted feminine nature. The claim 'different but equal' has always been difficult to mount in the face of one group's entrenched power.
>
> (Randall 1991: 28)

In short, the cornerstone of cultural ecofeminism is rejected because the stress on women's biological capacities is seen as oppressive, one that denies women access to the rational world and portrays them instead as over-determined by their biology (Eckersley 1992).

In response to these concerns, many of the key theorists of cultural ecofeminism, including King (1983), Plumwood (1993) and Warren (1994) have declared that they reject essentialism and the idea of an innate, female, gendered self. Yet, at the same time, they, especially Plumwood, are reluctant to ignore the women–nature link. This is because the claim that women have 'an elemental affinity with nature' (Daly 1978; Collard 1988) is crucial to cultural ecofeminism.

The rejection of essentialism by key cultural ecofeminists has, however, proved to be far from an easy or indeed completed task. First, it is difficult to see how the link between women and nature can be made without invoking biological reproduction as a key element in that link (Evans 1993: 184). Second, theorists like Plumwood have, as yet, failed to develop alternative models of the self, or of the female character, that can replace their earlier essentialist characterization. In constructing that model, they still have to find a way out of the potential trap of accepting the view of women that patriarchy provides. Third, they are also blocked by the epistemologically challenging task of having to avoid making the assumption that we know which traits of the female character to choose as authentic and enduring (Evans 1993: 183).

While respected ecofeminists such as Plumwood and others have struggled to loosen the grip of essentialism on their arguments, I would make a stand against their hasty, albeit not entirely successful, retreat from essentialism. I believe that there is need to confront head-on the fears that essentialism hold for feminism and for feminist theory. In defence of the essentialism of cultural ecofeminism, one could argue that the fact that male culture has drawn upon female reproductive capacity as a source of oppression is not sufficient grounds for arguing that reproduction is *in itself* oppressive. Cultural ecofeminism rightly makes a distinction between reproduction as a tool of oppression and reproduction itself as oppressive. It acknowledges that women's biological capacity has been used as a tool of oppression, but denies that it is oppressive in itself. On the contrary, women's biological capacity can also become the source of women's liberation because, through re-establishing and re-articulating the connectedness with biology, women can realize their own nature. Herein lies the hallmark of women's freedom. Essentialism liberates thought from the trap of using male-identified consciousness to devalue women's biological capacity. Male-identified values can promise nothing more than a false consciousness of 'equality', achievable only through the internalization of male values, norms and actions. Without essentialism, the danger is that we will take flight in the face of the resultant negative evaluation of women's biology. Facing essentialism, we are provided with one of the key tools for the construction of a theory of female-identified consciousness.

Essentialism is also liberating in its social and political consequences. It allows women to know and reaffirm their relationship with the living world and to understand themselves through identification with the wider mystery of life, birth and the rhythms of nature. This facilitates movement beyond the atomizing individualism of current society, which serves to alienate women from the self, from each other as well as from the wider world.

Nevertheless, while accepting essentialism in its positive aspects, I urge caution in our identification of the female with her biology and in the assertion of the female-nature link. Male culture, society and political structures have used this linkage to their advantage. Science and technology have also been misused. This does not mean that we must abandon either, rather that we must work to develop a new framework within which scientific investigation can unfold and its fruits can be applied ethically. Similarly, biology is not the problem, but rather the problem is the interpretation, use of, and power over, that biology. In confronting the ideological underpinning of that power, cultural ecofeminism is a deeply radical and highly political challenge to mainstream Western thought and its political practices.

Socialist ecofeminism

It is in its efforts to bypass what is seen as the morass of essentialism that the second main type of ecofeminism, what is known as materialist, socialist ecofeminism (at times also referred to as socialist-anarchist ecofeminism) comes to the fore. While some socialist ecofeminist writers recognize that we should not ignore the reality of the biological, and that this cannot be entirely subsumed within the social, by and large socialist ecofeminists reject both essentialism and what is seen as the related biological determinism of cultural ecofeminism.

Crucial to the socialist ecofeminist position is the claim that the exploitation of nature is related to exploitation in society. This argument places emphasis on social and political, as opposed to personal, aspects of domination (Pepper 1996). The reason why women have different experiences of nature from men is not due to their 'essential nature' but, rather, to the fact that we live in a gendered society. Socialist ecofeminists hold that it is the social role of women, such as the provision of food and childcare, which identifies them more closely with nature. As Mellors has argued, women and nature are in a historically contingent relationship, that is, they have a socially constructed connection (Mellors 1997: 195). In addition, socialist ecofeminism would argue that men and women, as well as nature, are political and ideological categories, where women's oppression is interwoven with class, race and species oppression (Warren 1990).

Socialist ecofeminists have explored how the interrelationship between women and the environment arises. They point to the fact that men and women have different social positions and therefore they have different environmental needs and experience environmental problems differently. In rural and poor communities, for example, women's disproportionate responsibility for family health and family subsistence differentiates their experience from that of men (Mellors 1997: 198). This strongly materialist analysis contrasts with the idealism of radical ecofeminism.

However, like cultural ecofeminism, socialist ecofeminism suffers from some fundamental weaknesses. One of the problems with the socialist ecofeminist theory is that, if female values are seen as socialized, they can be changed. This leaves us with an unsatisfactory idea of the female, wherein it becomes little more than the product of patriarchy. Lacking an ontological escape route, this condemns the female to remain a by-product of a dominant male culture and politics. In addition, if the relationship between women and nature is simply false consciousness, why continue that relationship, however modified, in a socialist future? Where then lies the future of ecofeminism and, for that matter, of the environment?

The future for some lies with the construction of a socialist society. Much of socialist ecofeminism, as exemplified by Mellors, has been an attempt to modify Marxism with an ecofeminist analysis. Here, the material world of motherhood, like the material world of industrial production, becomes an important agent in shaping a future socialist society. There is also much emphasis on the need for that future to build upon and reflect the daily lives of women. This awareness of the daily reality of women's lives is, it is claimed, not sufficiently acknowledged in the analysis of cultural ecofeminism. As Mellors has argued:

> The difficulty in laying stress on the 'naturalness' of motherhood is that it is overlaid with problems of fertility, poverty and socially constructed images of mothering. It is hard to posit a universally common 'mother-identity' when women have children in a wide range of circumstances, rarely entirely of their own choosing.
> (Mellors 1992: 237)

Thus, in keeping with the position of many contemporary feminists, socialist ecofeminism, far from seeing motherhood as natural, regards it as a social experience. A good experience of motherhood then becomes conditional upon the presence of a support network for a woman (Dally 1982). It is also here that we begin to see ecofeminism emerging as primarily social-political action, and it is to this we now turn.

Ecofeminism as socio-political action

Focus of action

Cultural ecofeminists argue that because of women's unique role in biological reproduction their bodies act as important 'markers for ecological stress' (Diamond and Orenstein 1990: x). The claim that women are more responsive than men to environmental problems provides the motivation behind women's aspirations for a better environmental future. Given the emphasis on the reproductive capacity of women, it is not surprising to find that cultural ecofeminists direct most of their political actions at areas where environmental degradation impacts upon women's capacity to bear and rear children.

The impact of environmental degradation upon the reproductive capacity of women has long been an area of concern for women's groups, not just for ecofeminists. The increased production and utilization of carcinogenic products, to take just one example of economic activity, is adding a new urgency to this problem. Such toxic production processes can pose a very direct threat to women's reproduction capacity. Some ecofeminists target their attention on reproductive technology. Here links are made between the contemporary commodification of human reproduction and the development of a mechanistic approach to the natural world (Rich 1976).

It is well known, especially by advertisers, that the woman, in her capacity as homemaker, is largely responsible for deciding what the family consumes and eats. It is largely women who buy the food for the family diet as well as other weekly products that are purchased within the household. Women have, therefore, a major role to play in re-shaping family consumption away from environmentally unfriendly towards environmentally friendly goods (Baker 1993). This, for example, is one of the main concerns of the London-based ecofeminist group, the Women's Environmental Network (WEN).

Although many of the early works in ecofeminism concentrated on the experience of women in the developed world, towards the end of the twentieth century the question of gender and the environment in the context of globalization become central (see Mellors 1997 for further details). This links well with the concerns of socialist ecofeminism. As mothers and carers, ecofeminists have not only expressed concern about the impact of industrial pollution on their families but have also widened their focus to include their Third World sisters. For some time, environmental groups in the developed world have been working with overseas development agencies to highlight the dangers involved in the exportation of both toxic products and production processes to the Third World. Many of these products and practices affect both men and women. However, as the environmental movement draws upon the insights of the women's movement, it has become clear that the social and economic position of women in the Third World makes them more vulnerable than their male counterparts. They are more marginalized, usually work harder, especially if engaged in agricultural labour, have a less adequate diet and are often denied a voice in the political, economic and social spheres (Fiéloux and Bisilliat 1987; Mies and Shiva 1993). As a consequence, they are more likely to suffer the ill effects of environmental degradation and environmentally unsafe practices.

The significance of ecofeminism for European politics

Ecofeminism, by challenging existing mainstream conceptualizations of gender and the relationship between gender and nature, makes several contributions to the development of European politics.

First, it propels us to take a new look at an old debate in feminist scholarship, that of essentialism. In this sense its on-going contribution to feminist theory is important, especially given that the debate remains, as yet, unresolved. In that debate, the essentialism of Daly and other cultural ecofeminists has been counterposed with the idea of the 'socialized' gendered self, whose values are to be cherished. Both positions, however, while they retain the concept of gender, remain theoretically weak. Essentialism can be conservative and play into patriarchy's hands; socialized attributes can dissolve, and with it the concept of the 'female'. Yet, as cultural ecofeminism has shown, the concept of gender must be based on some defining characteristics or features. What ecofeminism asks us to explore in feminist theorizing once more is the thorny issue of whether these characteristics are essential (Evans 1993: 186). If we answer in the affirmative, then feminist theory is challenged to find new ways in which essentialism can be grasped without falling into the trap of biological determinism. If the answer is negative, then ecofeminism theory rightly calls upon feminist analysis to identify what in the socially gendered, female self is authentic and enduring.

Ecofeminism is also significant for feminist political engagement. It has added a new, and increasingly important, addition to the remit of feminist activity, that of activism in relation to the environment. Ecofeminism also offers women a new way in which to integrate into a more coherent framework the various concerns that they are expressing. These include concerns about environmental pollution, world hunger and debt, reproductive technologies and violence against women. In addition, by engaging in new forms of direct action, it offers a new arena for *independent* political and social activism. This independent re-engagement can help to revitalize a movement that is currently suffering, especially in mainland Europe, from an over-dependence upon state feminism. This over-dependence has dissipated the autonomous women's movement in many countries (Baker 1999). As a political practice, it is also helping the women's movement develop its own style of political protest, encouraging the development of non-hierarchical organizational forms and the practice of non-violence. One well-known example of such activity is the women's Peace Camp at Greenham Common. Ecofeminism, especially cultural ecofeminism, is also contributing to the widening of the notion of the political, expanding it to include the practice of ritual and celebration. These activities are political precisely because they are not only aimed at personal change but also at societal transformation. In this sense both the development of an ethics of care within ecofeminism and the exploration of new forms of female culture become political acts. Through these acts, ecofeminism is altering our understanding of what constitutes political change: for ecofeminists it is nothing less than the creation of new beliefs about and practices of living with the earth.

I would also argue that, despite the difficulties that many feminists have in accepting the emphasis of cultural ecofeminists on women's biological capacity, ecofeminism is not as out of step with the mainstream of current feminist thinking as it initially seems. Since the 1970s much of the activity of the women's movement has been directed at consolidating women's difference and the creation of alternative spaces for women. In many ways the ecofeminist emphasis upon women's reproductive capacity is part of this wider trend. This has added the *politics of difference* to the agenda of feminist theorizing and activism. The emphasis on difference is particularly significant because it challenges the hegemonic position that equal opportunities policies have held both within the aims of the feminist movement and within state level policy responses to second wave feminism.

Challenges to the hegemony of equal opportunities policies

Perhaps one of the most challenging aspects of ecofeminism is that it questions the dominant policy response of the state and, increasingly in a European context, of the European Union, to the demands of the second wave women's movement. State-level responses have, by and large, tended to reduce the demands of the contemporary feminist movement to that of equality, understood primarily as the achievement of equal opportunities in the workplace. The new emphasis upon women's difference, arising from cultural ecofeminism in particular, has important consequences for equal opportunities policy. As Hoskyns has argued, the demand for equality seems irrelevant, if not actually damaging, to the concern about recognizing difference (Hoskyns 1988: 45). The achievement of female emancipation becomes far more challenging when the recognition and valuing of difference, as opposed to the search for equality, becomes the primary focus of action.

This focus on difference also challenges the dominance of the discourse of liberal feminists, relative to the discourses of other branches of feminism. Since the 1970s, when equal opportunities legislation came to be developed within European states, the equal rights agenda has become the acceptable face of feminism within mainstream political discourse. While liberal feminists seek equal rights for women, rights as are accorded to men, cultural ecofeminists reject this focus of attention on equality politics. The attainment of equality, argues cultural ecofeminism, would allow more women to have access to 'male' lifestyles. This is a regressive step, as it has the potential to increase the damage done to nature (Buckingham-Hatfield 2000: 36). Faced with this prospect, ecofeminists reject equality politics. They also reject it on ideological grounds. For Andrée Collard, the quest for equality politics locks women into male, false, consciousness. To counteract this ideological false consciousness, women have to keep alive the knowledge and memory of their history. In that history the individualistic, hierarchical, and power-based gods and societies of men replaced the worship of the earth and the Goddess. This memory is vital to women, who will otherwise adopt male values and seek 'equality' rather than 'kinship, egalitarianism and nurturance-based values' (Collard 1988, quoted in Evans 1993: 180).

Importance for the development of the environmental movement

Ecofeminism is also important in that it has the potential to shape the development of the environmental movement, especially the policy preferences adopted by environmental groups. By seeing all life forms as woven into a web, it comes as no surprise that ecofeminists reject the managerial approach towards the natural world, so beloved by conservationists and, increasingly, by the state and by ecological modernized businesses. 'Soft' ecology, such as waste management, is rejected, because it fails to challenge and change the ways of thinking that produce an overabundance of waste and destruction (Conley 1996: 25–6).

Ecofeminism has also implications for the strategy of the environmental movement. Its origins in the peace movement mean that ecofeminism rejects violence as a tactic in their political engagement. In its place, ecofeminists have begun to develop strategies to deal with the ecological crisis that are heterogeneous, life affirming, consensual and non-violent. This is also making a contribution to the development of a new environmental consciousness. At present, the environmental movement is learning to be less anthropocentric in its approach and to build an understanding of nature that accepts the ecological interconnectedness that forms the basis of life. Like deep ecology, ecofeminism makes a contribution to this by accepting the intrinsic value of all life forms. Ecofeminism's unique and additional contribution is to value life-giving as an integral part of that connectedness.

Conclusion

While ecofeminists owe a good deal to traditional feminist critiques of patriarchy they place a somewhat different emphasis upon the elements of that critique. They make a new connection between women and nature. Cultural ecofeminists in particular, argue that our conceptions of God, human kind as well as nature must not only be critically re-evaluated but that all three elements must be re-examined together. This arises from their view that all life is interconnected. Acknowledging this compels us towards the reconstruction of a non-anthropocentric basis to our philosophy of, as well as our practice towards, nature. Part of this project has involved cultural ecofeminism in reclaiming those values associated with ancient pre-patriarchy and contemporary tribal cultures.

Ecofeminism is not, as we have seen, without its problems. It has romantic overtones, especially in terms of its understanding of nature, which may bear little resemblance to the harsh reality of the natural world. In drawing upon the past, ecofeminism, especially cultural ecofeminism, can also be criticized for the tendency to idealize non-Western cultures as well as ancient societies. This tendency may stem from a failure on behalf of ecofeminists to engage in rigorous archaeological as well as historical research. This may arise as a result of the urge to legitimize the modern day project of ecofeminist by reference to historical antecedents. The irony is that this type of legitimization may not be necessary. The depths of the current ecological crisis are without precedent and, as such, may well call forth responses that are themselves outside the range of traditional, that is, historically grounded, patterns of perception and behaviour.

Ecofeminism is correct to point to the role that the Judeo-Christian tradition has played in shaping patriarchal values. However, in drawing from pagan and pre-Christian traditions, ecofeminism has been rightly criticized for trying to ignore the widespread acceptance of the Judeo-Christian tradition within the Western world. It also ignores the diverse features of this tradition, such as the minority traditions of Franciscan and Clarrisen spirituality.

There is also criticism of ecofeminism on the grounds that the postulation of a 'special relationship' between women and nature is weak, not least because it fails to explain racism or class oppression. Further, they seem to ignore the awkward fact that many traditional societies live in harmony with nature, yet their organization form is patriarchal (Young 1990). Similarly, the fact that emancipation of women need not necessarily lead to the emancipation of nature needs to be given more careful consideration. In addition, while it has developed a good critique of the domination of nature, the link between this and the subordinate position of women is weakly developed in ecofeminist theory. It is one thing to note similarities in domination, it is another to argue that they arise from the same source. Patriarchy and the domination of nature can be the product of quite different conceptual and historical developments and this needs to be more fully explored. Patriarchy may not be the root of the ecological crisis, but rather may be a subset of a more general problem of philosophical dualism that has pervaded Western thought from the time of classical Greek philosophy (Eckersley 1992; Plumwood 1992). But, despite their criticism of this dualism, ecofeminists have not managed to escape the dualistic trap, for they too are guilty of positing too sharp a distinction between the private, sensual and biological world of the women and the rational, public and discursive world of man.

On the positive side, while the scholarly basis of ecofeminism has been severely criticized, this may not be as important as the political effects of this movement. As a new social movement, the philosophical rigour of ecofeminism is of less relevance than the ability of ecofeminism to mobilize women around a feminist critique of society's attitude towards and treatment of women and the environment. Thus, in a crucial sense, ecofeminism may be more valid as an ideological critique of societal values and thus a political practice, than as a scholarly endeavour.

References

Baker, S. (1993) 'The principles and practice of ecofeminism', *Journal of Gender Studies* 2: 1, 4–26.
—— (1999) 'Risking difference: reconceptualizing the boundaries between the public and private spheres', in S. Baker and A. Van Doorne-Huiskes (eds) *Women and Public Policy: The Shifting Boundaries Between the Public and Private Spheres*, London: Ashgate, pp. 3–34.
de Beauvoir, S. (1952) *The Second Sex*, New York, NY: Bantham.
Biehl, J. (1991) *Rethinking Ecofeminist Politics*, Boston, MA: South End Press.
Buckingham-Hatfield, B. (2000) *Gender and Environment*, London: Routledge.
Christ, C.P. (1990) 'Rethinking theology and nature', in I. Diamond and G.F. Orenstein (eds) *Reweaving the World: The Emergence of Ecofeminism*, San Francisco, CA: Sierra Club.
Collard, A. (with J. Contrucci) (1988) *Rape of the Wild*, London: The Women's Press.
Conley, V.A. (1996) *Ecopolitics: The Environment in Poststructuralist Thought*, London: Routledge.
Dally, A. (1982) *Inventing Motherhood*, London: Burnette Books.
Daly, M. (1978) *Gyn/Ecology: The Metaethics of Radical Feminism*, London: The Women's Press.
Diamond, I. and Orenstein, G.F. (1990) 'Introduction', in I. Diamond and G.F. Orenstein (eds) (1990) *Reweaving the World: The Emergence of Ecofeminism*, San Francisco, CA: Sierra Club.
Eckersley, R. (1992) *Environmentalism and Political Theory: Towards an Ecocentric Approach*, London: University College London Press.

Evans, J. (1993) 'Ecofeminism and the politics of the gendered-self', in A. Dobson and P. Lucardie (eds) *Politics of Nature: Explorations in Green Political Theory*, London: Routledge.

Fieloux, M. and Bisilliat, J. (1987) *Women of the Third World: Work and Daily Life*, NJ: Fairleigh Dickinson University Press.

Firestone, S. (1979) *The Dialectic of Sex*, London: The Women's Press.

Hoskyns, C. (1988) 'Give us equal pay and we will open our doors – a study of the impact in the Federal Republic of Germany and the Republic of Ireland of the European Community's Policy on women's rights', in M. Buckley and M. Anderson (eds) *Women, Equality and Europe*, Basingstoke: Macmillan.

King, Y. (1983) 'Towards an ecological feminism and a feminist ecology', in J. Rothchild (ed.) *Machina ex Dea: Feminist Perspectives in Technology*, New York, NY: Pergamon Press.

Mellors, M. (1992) 'Green politics: ecofeminist, ecofeminine or ecomasculine?', *Environmental Politics* 1, 2, Summer.

—— (1997) 'Gender and the environment', in M. Redclift and G. Woodgate (eds) *The International Handbook of Environmental Sociology*, Cheltenham: Edward Elgar.

Merchant, C. (1980) *The Death of Nature: Women, Ecology and the Scientific Revolution*, New York, NY: Harper and Row.

—— (1992) *Radical Ecology: The Search for a Liveable World*, London: Routledge.

Mies, M. and Shiva, V. (1993) *Ecofeminism*, London: Zed Books.

Pepper, D. (1996) *Modern Environmentalism: An Introduction*, London: Routledge.

Plumwood, V. (1986) 'Ecofeminism: an overview and discussion of positions and arguments', *Australasian Journal of Philosophy*, Supplement, 64: 120–38.

—— (1992) 'Beyond the dualistic assumptions of women, men and nature', *The Ecologist* 22: 1, January/February.

—— (1993) *Feminism and the Mastery of Nature*, London: Routledge.

Randall, V. (1991) *Women and Politics: An International Perspective*, Basingstoke: Macmillan.

Rich, A. (1976) *Of Woman Born: Motherhood as Experience and Institution*, London: Virago.

Spretnak, C. (1990) 'Ecofeminism: our roots and flowering', in I. Diamond and G.F. Orenstein (eds) *Reweaving the World: The Emergence of Ecofeminism*, San Francisco, CA: Sierra Club.

Starhawk (1988) *Dreaming the Dark: Magic, Sex and Politics*, 2nd edn, Boston, MA: Beacon Press.

Warren, K. (1990) 'The power and promise of ecological feminism', *Environmental Ethics* 12: 2, 121–46.

—— (1994) 'Introduction', in K.J. Warren (ed.) *Ecological Feminism*, London: Routledge.

Young, I. (1990) *Justice and the Politics of Difference*, Princeton, NJ: Princeton University Press.

3 Anti-globalism and ecologism in comparative perspective

Rafal Soborski

Introduction

The aim of this chapter is to compare principles of Green ideology with the standpoint represented by what is usually known as anti-globalization or anti-globalism. Whereas Green ideology has been present in the political arena since at least the 1960s, with its roots dating back to the nineteenth century (Dobson 1995: 33–4), and intensification of its global consciousness in the 1980s (Sachs 1993: 12), anti-globalism is a new trend and has not developed enough to be treated as a mature political ideology. Ideology should offer a vision of a desirable society based on core beliefs about the human condition (Dobson 1995: 2), whereas the message of anti-globalism is issue-oriented and predominantly negative, constructed vis-à-vis processes it rejects. Anti-globalism, not being a complete political ideology, is susceptible to other ideological trends, which colour it with their own features. It seems to be sufficiently non-specific to be merged with ecologism, and the latter is also particularly prone to alliances with anti-globalism. The relationship between them is reciprocal: Green ideology uses arguments taken from anti-globalist discourse, while anti-globalism borrows from the ideological matrix of ecologism. As a result, in both systems of beliefs common arguments and threads are to be found. These two currents form a peculiar ideological 'field', whose semantic content consists of both well known 'classical' themes of political ideologies, and of relatively new concepts deriving from ecologism on the one hand, and from the critique of globalization on the other.

The analysis of interdependent influences between ecologism and anti-globalism is not easy as both currents contain numerous subtypes that express themselves in various ways. A widely understood Green outlook on life contains trends of different degrees of maturity, sophistication and radicalism. Within the Green spectrum, there are both ideologically mature, complete trends, as well as approaches which do not form any broad worldview but merely aim at responding to particular environmental issues. Andrew Dobson, in his book on Green political thought, distinguishes between environmentalism and ecologism, and only considers the latter as a political ideology (Dobson 1995: 2–3). Similarly, when Michael Freeden includes Green thought in his morphological analysis of political ideologies (Freeden 1996), he seems to mean ecologism, not environmentalism, which in the words of radical Green intellectual, Wolfgang Sachs, has been reduced to technocratic 'managerialism' (Sachs 1993: 11). In the same way, anti-globalist positions could be ranked on the continuum representing the extent of radicalism, with 'reformist' standpoints on the one hand and 'extremist' on the other, depending on their views in relation to the required profundity of transformation and the role of existing institutions in achieving postulated aims.

This chapter does not limit itself to discussing any particular version of anti-globalism or ecologism. Instead, I have decided to obtain sources from the whole variety of positions situated under the Green and anti-globalist umbrellas. Obviously, limitations of space have eliminated consideration of some trends, such as the environmental policies of mainstream parties, which are accused by radical Greens of giving (hidden) support to ecologically destructive globalization (Shiva 1993; Lohmann 1993). This chapter confines itself to examining countercultural, anti-systemic positions.

This chapter uses a twofold analysis to approach the interdependent aspects of the two ideological currents. First, it examines fundamental components that are common to both ecologism and anti-globalism. By fundamental components I mean the principal beliefs and main concepts within which the two systems operate. This part focuses on the ideological heritage and intellectual background to which these sets of ideas refer. Second, the analysis will concentrate on parallels relating to operative components of the two currents, which are understood here as prescriptions for action, strategies employed in the ideological persuasion and measures suggested in order to achieve political goals.

Analysing fundamental components common to both currents requires the identification of elements of anti-globalism within the Green ideology and of ecological arguments in the narratives, which should be classified as predominantly anti-globalist. This chapter assumes that the current phase of globalization refers principally to the proliferation of global capitalism and thus to the extension of various phenomena that were always rejected by the Greens. Therefore, the base of capitalism, modernity, with its faith in progress is first discussed in order to compare its roles in ecological and anti-globalist argumentation respectively. The analysis then focuses on the current transformation of time and space, the most fundamental dimensions of human reality. The changes of human spatial and temporal conditioning are presented as stimulating current global processes. The latter are shown in the context of their implications for the issues of community and identity, and as significant as far as social justice is concerned. Green and anti-globalist perspectives and concerns relating to these subjects are presented.

Modernity

One of the key words to which neither ecologism nor theories of globalization, and thus anti-globalism, can stay indifferent is 'modernity'. Modernity forms the matrix from which most of the phenomena contested in the Green discourse originated. It means rationalism and control over both natural and social processes. At its inception, modernity revived the ideas of progress and strengthened the Christian anthropocentrism and instrumental attitude towards nature. It also gave shape to the capitalist system initiated with the Calvinist doctrine of salvation. These foundations of Western civilization are currently questioned by the Greens, and, to a certain extent, by anti-globalists.

With anti-globalism the problem of modernity is more complex than in the case of Green ideology. On the most general level of reflection globalization is inevitably, though differently, conceptualized in relation to modernity, even if this means a refusal to analyse the two concepts as correlated. First, globalization can be claimed to precede the processes of modernization. Robertson argues that the germinal phase of globalization began in the fifteenth century. Yet he also admits that the process of modernization added an impetus to the progress of globalization, and he emphasizes that the two processes have a common European origin and that for most of history they shared the same European 'arena' (Robertson 1992). Second, globalization can be perceived as a distinct phenomenon that cannot be explained using the modernity discourse (Albrow 1996). Finally, globalization can be seen as the extension and strengthening of modernity either simply as its continuation or as its more self-reflexive variant. The best-known example of theories linking the process of globalization with the development of modern society was developed by Giddens. He distinguishes four institutional clusters of modernity:

- capitalism
- industrialism
- the nation-state
- militarism.

(Giddens 1990: 55–63)

Although Giddens's views are far from, if not contradictory to, the anti-globalist position, the rudiments of his scheme can be applied to the analysis of anti-globalist perspectives on the main aspects of modernity. Even though anti-globalism remains very complex and equivocal in its relation to the concept of modernity, it is nevertheless possible to discuss individual expressions of anti-globalism according to their stance on Giddens's constituents of modernity. Particularly contrasting views are expressed in the anti-globalist polemics in relation to capitalism and the institution of the state. As far as the capitalist system is concerned, the 'radicals' who remain uncompromising towards the capitalist system see it as the ultimate reason for injustice and the arena of exploitation. On the other hand, more moderate anti-globalist discourse expresses sympathy for the Keynesian form of capitalism. Radicals argue that globalism is essentially the newest form of the capitalist system following its earlier incarnations, such as colonialism or imperialism, and that an abolition of globalism means no less than elimination of the capitalist mode of production. The more moderate standpoint, while accepting the principal market relations, argues for their regulation and subordination to the control of society and state and postulates responsible welfare capitalism as a counter-project to undermine neoliberalism. When Richard Falk, the author of *Predatory Globalization*, expresses his nostalgia for the welfare state, like Sweden in the 1970s, which nowadays is unable to look after public good and 'can no longer be Sweden' (Falk 1999: 41), he seems to think that such compassionate capitalism is still possible. However, in Falk's argument it is not capitalism that regulates and reforms itself, but the institutions of the state that should hold the market in leash.

The issue of the state is another controversy within anti-globalism. Radical positions portray the state as the agent of capitalism and thus the promoter of globalization. According to this interpretation the state is closely connected with global business. By its nature, the state apparatus reinforces global capitalist exploitation. Matthew Patterson, in his article 'Globalization, Ecology and Resistance', is highly critical about the state and any social project within the capitalist system:

> Social-democratic politics, as simply a different means of organizing capitalist economies and a different variant of the liberal-democratic state, is itself just as subject to the ecological pathologies of capitalism as is neoliberalism. Such states are still fundamentally capitalist states and, as such, structurally required to promote capital accumulation.
> (Patterson 1999)

The more temperate views agree with the radical position as far as the estimation of the actual condition of the state is concerned and are highly critical of the minimal position the state takes in relation to capital. The example of such polemics is Peter Evans's reflection on 'stateness' in the era of globalization where he is concerned that nowadays the idea of what he calls 'leaner, meaner stateness' is dominant. Instead, he postulates strong state organisms as necessary for the functioning of civil society and even beneficial for business (Evans 1997). According to the advocates of the moderate position, the current lamentable situation is not inherent in the state. It is the doctrine of neoliberalism that should be blamed for the current powerlessness of the state institution and its incapacity to mitigate the social effects of globalization. The state should reform itself, which means it should return to its welfare form. Such opinions contain a significant dose of optimism. Their supporters seem to believe that just as the welfare state originated from the unbearable oppression of industrialism, the pernicious effects of global capitalism will lead to the introduction of certain regulations for the sake of social good.

Michael Hardt in his article describing the World Social Forum in Porto Alegre, notices in practice these two different perspectives on the role of state:

> there are indeed two primary positions in the response to today's dominant forces of globalization: either one can work to reinforce the sovereignty of nation-states as a defensive barrier against the control of foreign and global capital, or one can strive towards a non-national alternative to the present form of globalization that is equally global. The first poses neoliberalism as the primary analytical category, viewing the enemy as unrestricted global capitalist activity with weak state controls; the second is more clearly posed against capital itself, whether state regulated or not.
>
> (Hardt 2002: 114)

The first position, advocating stronger national sovereignty, is represented for example by the French movement 'ATTAC' and intellectuals grouped around *Le Monde Diplomatique*. In fact, some leaders of 'ATTAC' declare that their movement is not anti-capitalist, 'but merely wants to stop short term financial flows disrupting national economies' (Harman 2000). Under the non-sovereign position Hardt primarily groups the movements that protested in recent years against global capitalism in the streets of numerous Western cities (Hardt 2002: 115). Hardt sees the differences between the two outlooks as corresponding to yet another criterion of classification that could be used in analysing forms of organization of anti-globalist movements. According to this:

> the traditional parties and centralized campaigns generally occupy the national sovereignty pole, whereas the new movements organized in horizontal networks tend to cluster at the non-sovereign pole. And furthermore, within traditional, centralized organizations, the top tends towards sovereignty and the base away.
>
> (Hardt 2002: 115–16)

Anti-globalism on the Left is itself an expression of modernity, emanating from the socialist wing of the modern ideological tradition. An anti-modern attitude is unquestionably more explicit in the case of conservative anti-globalist positions which also merge with ecologism. Green ideology seems to be at variance with modern ideas for the reason that the main elements of modernity, as enumerated in Giddens' model, are directly responsible for the emergence and persistence of environmental threats.

Green literature emphasizes in particular the direct connection between globalization and ecological destruction via industrialism and the global division of labour embodied in triumphant world capitalism. Philosophical and ideological principles underlying the modern capitalist system are thus the targets of ecological critique. Greens question the Western version of human history based on the concept of progress, which in turn invokes such terms as growth and development. In the Green discourse development is accused of being the cause of 'the dissolution of cultures which were not built around a frenzy of accumulation' (Sachs 1993: 5). According to ecologists, development, increasingly subordinating social life to the economy, should be replaced by the rule of the 'laws governing all nature', which 'lay down limits to growth; economic, population and technological' (Pepper 1996: 15). Environmentalists call for sustainable development, defined in the *Brundtland Report* as that which 'meets the needs of the present without compromising the ability of future generations to meet their own needs' (quoted in: Ekins 1993: 91) but this is not accepted by deep ecology as a sufficient solution. Wolfgang Sachs, attacking 'shallow' environmentalism as 'the highest state of developmentalism' (Sachs 1993: 3), perceives the concept of sustainable development as a slogan which 'emasculates the environmental challenge by absorbing it into the empty shell of "development" and insinuates the continuing validity of developmentalist assumptions' (Sachs 1993: 9). He disapproves of such 'sustainability' as a call 'for the conservation of development, not for the conservation of nature' (Sachs 1993: 10).

There is no place here for further investigation into controversies concerning the idea of progress and the concept of sustainability within Green ideology. Progress and development are also intensely discussed in many currents of anti-globalism. Globalization itself means, among other things, progress in terms of the increase in global production and global consumption. Left-wing anti-globalism, with its strong concern for social justice, does not accept 'progress' which is accessible for only the rich minority, 'a global middle-class of individuals with cars, bank accounts, and career aspirations' (Sachs 1993: 5). Sachs's argument sounds anti-globalist when he states that 'at the end of development, the question of justice looms larger than ever' (Sachs 1993: 6). He is however much more 'Green' when warning only a few lines further:

> Although only a small part of the world's regions has experienced large-scale economic expansion, the world economy already weighs down nature to an extent that she has in part to give in. If all countries followed the industrial example, five or six planets would be needed to serve as 'sources' for the inputs and 'sinks' for the waste of economic progress.
>
> (Sachs 1993: 6)

Sachs's twofold argumentation demonstrates the difference between anti-globalism and ecologism as far as progress is concerned. This difference consists primarily of the emphasis that the former puts on social justice and the latter on the planet's limited capacity.

Time and space

Progress, in the evaluation of its apologists, is conventionally associated with modernization of the whole world after the West's example. Such reasoning often has an evolutionist slant: Western civilization is claimed to be the ultimate model which all other cultures will finally choose to emulate. This process implies cultural homogenization, conceptualized as the 'Global Village' (McLuhan and Powers 1989), or Ritzer's and Barber's 'McWorld' (Ritzer 1993; Barber 1995). Whereas the former book is a eulogy on contemporary global consciousness generated by the new media environment, the latter is an example of anti-globalist polemics pointing at social and civilizational threats posed by globalization. Barber portrays conflicting forces of globalization: its strong inclination towards a homogenous 'McWorld', is paradoxically complemented by identity-based, particularistic tendencies of 'Jihad'. 'Jihad' designates the reverse of globalizing processes within the dialectics of simultaneous 'universalization' and 'particularization' (Robertson 1992). Such anti-western fundamentalism is a form of anti-globalism and, at the same time, provides the grounds for an anti-globalist argument, identifying fundamentalism as an inevitable consequence of globalization. One of the reasons for the current strengthening of fundamentalist tendencies is the economic and socio-cultural inability of non-Western cultures, as well as significant segments of Western societies, to catch up with technological changes. New technology frames the dominant economic system and imposes novel structures on such essential dimensions of human perception as time and space.

Modernity, with its tendency to unification, substituted objective, universal measures in place of traditionally grounded understandings of time and space that were built on communities' direct experience. Within the modern Cartesian-Newtonian paradigm, linear time and three-dimensional space have become the only valid basis for organizing social life. Nowadays, the Cartesian time-space relations are being invalidated. Although they still organize ordinary human perception, they are not decisive as far as the dominant globalization logic is concerned. In the twentieth century the computer replaced the clock as a symbolic definition of the prevalent technological paradigm. David Bolter introduces the concept of the defining technology in his book *Turing's Man* (1984). A defining technology is one that has such an influential meaning that it provides conceptual frames for human thinking. The device embodying a defining technology has a metaphoric sense and is a point of reference to which biological and social phenomena are compared. Descartes, for example, thought of animals as clock mechanisms, and in the 'classical' modern era the clock was such an important mechanism that even God was compared to a watchmaker. Nowadays, computer technology develops its connections with the art and philosophy of the globalizing world and provides various domains of human activity with metaphors, models and symbols.

Popularization of personal computers is a condition for the pervasive spread of capitalist globalization, which is based on processing and disseminating information. However, it has been the invention of networks providing interconnectivity between computers that has led to global processes in the gigantic web of billions of bits of information. The outcome of the new technological paradigm that functions thanks to an immediate flow of information in the electronic networks is a revolutionary transformation of spatial and temporal organization of social life, which laid the ground for other processes shaping the contemporary world (Castells 1996).

The benefits of technological change in its present shape are often questioned. Manuel Castells, an expert on 'network society', states that as technological evolution progresses much faster than social change, there exists a dramatic gulf between hyper-development of technology and backwardness in the social sphere. While appreciating the great potential of the new technology Castells is disillusioned with its implementation in social *praxis* (Barney 1997). Although modern technology may have its place within the Green canon, ecologists tend to be suspicious towards technology as a 'surrogate world' opposed to the 'real one' (Dobson 1995: 96–7). This may be especially evident in the case of the dominant informational technology which, in the words of Baudrillard, no longer encompasses the world but 'replaces it with a "more than real" simulation' (Nunes 1995). Furthermore, information technology is not absolutely safe in environmental terms. It is, as some Greens would argue, merely more effective in hiding its own ecological cost (Dobson 1995: 99).

Whereas Greens analyse technology under their 'critical microscope' (Dobson 1995: 96), anti-globalism (usually its more conservatist variant) may stress negative cultural consequences of the new technology (Birkerts 1994), or if it appreciates technological innovation, as in the case of most leftist movements, it resists limitations of people's access to technological achievements. The latter attitude is the case of, for example, the cyberpunk subculture, which praises the democratic potential of information technology, while resisting the corporate dominance over its usage and generally the influence of transnational business on global processes (Rucker *et al.* 1992: 54–93). Yet, cyberpunk fails to realize the wider problem of social exclusion in the globalized world. Castells maintains that with the triumph of the new technology all the discourses that have no access to the electronic network of media are reduced to personal communication, which is currently increasingly marginalized (Castells 1996: 405). Economically based exclusion from global communication leaves vast areas of the world unable to influence the dominant logic of the world system. It also prevents poorer nations from adjusting to new forms of temporal and spatial arrangements of social and economic life. Global injustice, one of the main concerns of anti-globalists and Greens, is underpinned by the new technological paradigm.

The impact of new technologies on the relationship between time and space is central to globalization. Technology dramatically intensifies global interdependencies, leading to the 'shrinking' of the world. This process has been conceptualized in different terms: as the world becoming 'a single place' (Giddens), 'compression' (Harvey), or 'the annihilation of space' (Marx) (Patterson 1999). More recently, Castells elaborated on the ontology of space and time in the global 'network society'. Castells distinguishes between the electronic 'space of flows' and the physical 'space of places'. While business and organizations depend upon electronic flows and networks (that is cyberspace, the 'space of flows'), people are still situated in the social context associated with real places. This constitutes a growing dissonance between the organizational logic and everyday experience (Castells 1989: 169–70). Real places and people living in them are either irrelevant to the system and excluded from benefits of being in the network, or, when they stay integrated in the global electronic web, they are vulnerable to global processes initiated outside their control. According to Castells, the split between virtual and physical spaces composes a 'condition of structural schizophrenia'. As Felix Stadler puts it, the fact that 'while the dominant social logic is shaped by the ... space of flows, people live in the physical world, the space of places ... introduces massive perturbation in cultures around the globe' (Stadler 1998).

While losing its significance for the functioning of the system, physical space has become a subject of interest for anti-globalist movements for another two reasons. First, as Zygmunt Bauman argues in his bitter book on globalization, space, or rather mobility within it, has become the decisive factor of the social stratification. Those who are free to move, the 'globals', dictate the rules of the economic and political game, and those, who are imprisoned in their 'places', the 'locals', are deprived of any influence on the world system, as the latter have been removed beyond their local life (Bauman 1998). Second, 'real' space, especially its most important centres, is itself colonized by the capitalist market. The street, once the realm of community, has become a shopping mall, a faceless space where the 'system' finds its physical representation to fulfil the 'wants' of consumers; 'a place to move through not to be in'. The 'Reclaim the Streets' movement combines environmental and anti-globalist features under its concern about the community's good. Its resistance towards 'car culture' is only part of a wider struggle against:

> the privatisation of public space ... [which] ... continues the erosion of neighbourhood and community ... Road schemes, business 'parks', shopping developments – all add to the disintegration of community and the flattening of a locality. Everywhere becomes the same as

everywhere else. Community becomes commodity – a shopping village sedated and under constant surveillance.

(Reclaim The Streets 2002).

Space in anti-globalist discourse is thus an important issue as both a factor of stratification and organizer of global inequality, as well as a dimension of reality to be defended against the capitalist lust of conquest. To prevent space from becoming a commodity it is essential to secure spatial local identities and to protect natural and cultural 'pluralism' of space. Anti-globalism on the Left bases its objection to unification on the approval of cultural heterogeneity. For its part, most of Green ideology opposes homogeneity in the name of biological and social diversity, again advocating the need to follow the laws of nature. These laws 'tell us that both social and ecological systems derive strength from diversity; sameness... leads to lack of robustness and a destructive instability' (Pepper 1996: 15). Conversely, the conservative wings of both ecologism and anti-globalism argue for radical homogeneous communitarianism. Radical Greens as well as conservative anti-globalists stand against loosening the ties between people living in the physical places and, at the same time, they do not approve of social mobility, intercultural contact, and cosmopolitism, all of which are stimulated by the global processes. Instead, they argue for something opposite: decentralized communities where mobility is reduced and relationships between members are 'supportive' and 'satisfying' (Dobson 1995: 104). Such communitarianism based on living 'in place' (Dobson 1995: 104) is said to be most ecologically beneficial; at the same time the idea of place-based communes negates travelling and abandons trade.

The issue of trade is a subject of concern (even if differently understood) of both right- and left-oriented ecological and anti-globalist policies. Trade, especially so-called 'free trade', is a foundation of neo-liberalism and a key word in debates on globalization. This ideology of the market is challenged unanimously by both anti-globalism and ecologism. Green politics argues for self-reliance if not self-sufficiency (Dobson 1995: 101). According to this, societies should produce using their own resources. Trade should be limited to an absolute minimum since it leads to dependency. Environmentalists and anti-globalists are normally less extreme in their views on international trade. However, they agree that free global trade as it is functioning today has dangerous social and environmental consequences. Some of the comments on the nature of the global trade echo Marx's diagnosis:

> increasingly we produce what we do not consume, and we consume what we do not produce. The separation of material production and consumption also involves the removal and abstraction of knowledge about that self-same relationship. Thus neither knowledge of the tech-

nical procedures of production nor the environmental circumstances and costs of production are visible to distanced consumer.

(Saurin 1993: 48, quoted in Patterson 1999)

The latter remains unable to understand both his/her participation, as well as the role of 'contemporary power structures', in generating environmental damage (Patterson, 1999).

The deepening 'separation of producers from consumers' increases the dynamism of capital accumulation and thus deepens capitalism's inevitable consequence: inequality. Social injustice is a principal concern for both Greens and anti-globalists. Greens perceive environmental degradation and social inequality as 'inextricably linked', arguing that ecological problems stem from social ones (Pepper 1996: 16). Apart from their advocacy of a less hierarchical and more participatory society, Greens say that present 'aid' and debt relations between the rich and poor countries encourage environmental destruction. Anti-globalism, especially in its leftwing incarnation, is equally troubled about world poverty. In both ecological and anti-globalist discourse global injustice is conceptualized in terms of the North–South divide. Falk argues that capitalist globalization means the uncontrolled rule of the market, favouring the rich over the poor. This kind of globalization is supported by the neoliberal doctrine. According to Falk, where neoliberalism faces no opposition, it will consolidate current conditions of extreme inequality. Falk describes the social structure of today's world as 'global apartheid', where one-fifth of the population is rich ('North') and four-fifths poor ('South') (Falk 1999).

Whereas neoliberalism is an ideological foundation of capitalist globalization, the agents of global capitalism, transnational corporations, are the favourite targets of anti-globalist and ecological attacks. The characteristic feature of the contemporary division of capital is its concentration in the hands of a few gigantic corporations whose economic power surpasses that of many states. Ecologists abhor the transnational corporations as strengthening the most dangerous aspects of the world market. Corporations fight against any environmental or national regulation which could limit their economic supremacy. In the environmental polemics the latter is vividly depicted:

> trans-national corporations... can stimulate or undermine local industry, can generate revenue but avoid taxes, can monopolise technology, can catalyse modernisation throughout the world – simultaneously reinforcing inequalities and promoting Western cultural hegemony, can create low standards for employees (child labour, temporary low-paid work, alienating workplaces) and can critically alter the natural environment.
>
> (Pepper 1996: 82)

Ecological discourse expresses criticism of the selfishness and irresponsibility of corporations enforcing their immediate profit-driven policies and ignoring not only the planet's future, but also the well-being of the majority of present societies. 'Greens' blame international corporations for the contemporary hierarchy and inequality of conditions and for imprisonment of 'the majority of people in impoverished enclaves [in order to] move production there' (Graeber 2002: 65). Anti-globalists would fully subscribe to this diagnosis and, especially those more conservative, would also focus on the fact that whilst consolidating injustice and exploitation, the ubiquitous corporate 'agents' of globalization introduce uniform patterns of consumption among those who are financially privileged to consume. This 'mcdonaldization of society' (Ritzer 1993) is resisted within both anti-globalism and ecologism as contradicting tradition and local or national identity. Examples of this attitude are to be found throughout Europe. In my own country, Poland, a populist party 'Self-defence' (*Samoobrona*), with a predominantly peasant electorate, proclaims slogans with strong anti-business undertones. It focuses on the issue of food and supports Polish products, which are said to be of very high quality, while discouraging people from buying food produced by huge transnational companies. The latter is said to contain plenty of chemicals and to be produced with the use of GM methods. It is however not only an issue of food quality: while big companies, states Samoobrona, destroy Polish farming, the distributors of foreign products, internationally based hypermarkets, lead to the bankruptcy of native small business.

Similar ideology is employed in France by *Confederation Paysanne*, whose leader, José Bové, has become a well-known figure of anti-globalism after dismantling one of French McDonald's restaurants in August 1999 to protest against tariffs placed on French cheese by the US government after France refused to import hormone-treated beef from the States. Bové's action was grounded on national sentiments. At the same time, McDonald's 'junk food' was again pointed out as a symbol of 'gastronomic imperialism' (Jeffress and Mayanobe 2001).

Operative components of ecologism and anti-globalism

Ecologism and anti-globalism go beyond written polemics and ideological debate. Even within an academic format, the two trends offer concrete schemes of resistance in order to effectively limit harmful consequences of capitalist globalization. The last part of this chapter describes patterns of action prescribed by the two currents in order to achieve their political aims.

Both anti-globalists and Greens choose the actors behind unfavourable practices of the capitalist globalization as their direct adversaries. The two trends are opposed to liberal economists and politicians but primarily they point the shaft of their critique towards transnational business and 'unelected treaty organizations', such as the IMF, WTO and NAFTA (Graeber 2002: 62). Peter Newell enumerates the tactics employed by environmental non-governmental organizations in targeting transnational companies (Newell 2000). The most spectacular way of attacking the transnational corporations consists of a kind of 'propaganda war'. This tactic is pointed at companies' public relations – a key component of corporate success. This 'counter information' discourse:

> centres on attacking a company on the basis of the claims it makes about itself and encouraging customers to sever their loyalties with the company through boycotts. Such campaigns are intended to expose perceived corporate misconduct, force the company to defend its reputation in public, and dent its political and economic power.
>
> (Newell 2000: 128)

Actions against corporate businesses usually include a boycott of their products, as in the case of campaigns against the most abhorred corporations like Nike or Shell. The 'McLibel' case between the McDonald's corporation and members of London Greenpeace is a famous example of boycott and propaganda war (Vidal 1996). It is also an instance of the concurrence of goals between ecologists and anti-globalists. In this case one of the main Green organizations came out with environmental and anti-corporational arguments to which the anti-globalization position would certainly subscribe.

Transnational corporations are concrete and tangible embodiments of globalization. Their products are ubiquitous and their physical representations: offices, shops, restaurants, are located in every city. The most visible expressions of anti-globalism are thus incidents happening on the streets. Thus, McDonalds restaurants, for instance, become the subject of the anger of the crowd gathered to express objections to the actions of more distant and inaccessible agents of global order, such as the WTO. The slogans employed by the demonstrators have both ecological and anti-globalist grounds.

Demonstrations against globalization are sensational events. Western societies have not seen publicly expressed opposition to capitalism on such a large scale since the late 1960s. The organizers of these events seem to be fully aware of the enormous role of the media in shaping current politics. Anti-globalist actions are well-selling media products, and are widely publicized. The outcome is impressive. Within a mere few years, globalization has become a concept well-known to the masses. Anti-globalists are visible and usually perceived as supporters of the poor and vulnerable against the powerful and wealthy. Equally spectacular means of action are used by the 'Greens'. The groups tying themselves to trees or obstructing roads are just examples of these.

The methods used by radical ecologists and anti-globalists in order to enforce their postulates onto the political agenda are thus rarely mediated by official institutions or procedures. Even in the case of the anti-globalist parties who have gained access to official politics, such as the above discussed 'Self-defence', in the centre of their activities are street 'performances' consisting of blockading roads, burning corn, pouring out milk etc. This proves that both ecologism and anti-globalism are characterized by anti-establishment attitudes and mistrust of traditional forms of political activity. It often stems from the conviction that business and political elites have common interests and act in collusion with each other. Instead, in order to popularize their ideas, both ecologists and anti-globalists attract the attention of the television and the press and set up their own web pages on the Internet. The media have their own perspectives and operate with a symbolic simplification. However they show conflict and thus raise public consciousness (Domoslawski 2002). Both ideological trends know the rules of functioning in a society that statistically devotes the largest part of its active life to media consumption.

Ecologism and anti-globalism are thus convergent in terms of actions taken to achieve their goals. Recent events grouping both ecologists and anti-globalists seem to prove the affinity of their interests. The World Social Forum in Porto Alegre was an example of what Falk calls the 'globalization-from-below' opposed to 'globalization-from-above', enforced by neo-liberalism and global financial interests (Falk 1999). In this case it was promoted by the global civil society and a new politics of resistance of both anti-globalist and ecological provenance (Domoslawski 2002).

Conclusion

This chapter has demonstrated that for the most part 'Greens' and anti-globalists are strongly associated through shared views and common concerns, even if they stress different aspects of the problems that preoccupy them. The chapter emphasized the similarities in the discussed trends. From the wide spectrum of the Green ideology, mostly ecological concerns directly relating to the social (and not biological) realm were discussed. The reason for this is that the ecological ideology has the whole of nature as its subject, whereas anti-globalist attention relates primarily to social matters. Anti-globalism does treat ecological issues as extremely important, but this significance follows from their meaning for people.

Ecologism and anti-globalism were compared in respect to their attitudes towards the 'big theme' of modernity with its implications for spatial and temporal organization of social reality, for community, social justice, and culture of the globalizing world. The similarities between the two currents of thought were demonstrated, but the differences in their views were also underlined. It was shown that significant affinities between the two currents frequently depend on their wider, Right or Left, progressive or conservative, derivations. Thus, anti-globalism with a right-wing tinge is closer to conservative ecologism than to leftist anti-globalism. This chapter did not focus on merely the narrative, fundamental layers of ecologism and anti-globalism. Having shown their ideological, conceptual resemblance, it exposed the correspondence between the measures the two ideological streams choose to undertake in order to enforce their arguments on the political agenda. The examples used to illustrate both the ideological narration and activities of ecologism and anti-globalism were taken primarily from the European political scene. They are, however, not specific to this part of the world. By their nature, the two currents have global concerns and often transgress the borders of countries and continents.

In trying to give answers and solve problems, this chapter has probably provoked even more questions. To what extent does the Green ideology contribute to anti-globalism? How does anti-globalism support ecologism? What distinguishes anti-globalism from ecologism? The answers to these questions are hard to discover, as anti-globalism is a new and constantly evolving phenomenon. For ecologists, globalization means usually the extension of capitalism, with all its ecologically destructive consequences. Therefore, anti-globalism is the Green ideology's natural ally. Anti-globalism, on the other hand, uses concepts worked out by the Green movements, and employs the ecological critique of social injustice. The difference between them is, as stressed previously, a difference in the strength of emphasis put on different matters. Ecologism is inevitably anti-globalist, and anti-globalism displays concerns about ecological consequences of globalization. The exact estimation of ecologism's and anti-globalism's share in shaping each other must be limited to the analysis of ideological profiles represented by concrete movements and of specific policies adopted by them in dealing with different aspects of contested reality.[1]

Note

1 I should like to thank Chris Flood for his helpful comments on earlier drafts of this chapter.

References

Albrow, M. (1996) *The Global Age: State and Society Beyond Modernity*, Cambridge: Polity Press.
Barber, B. (1995) *Jihad vs. McWorld*, New York, NY: Times Books.
Barney, C. (1997) *Q&A with Manuel Castells*. Available online: http://www.netfront.to/full_transcript.html (accessed 13 December 2002).
Bauman, Z. (1998) *Globalization. The Human Consequences*, Cambridge: Polity Press.
Birkerts, S. (1994) *The Gutenberg Elegies. The Fate of Reading in an Electronic Age*, Winchester, MA: Faber and Faber, pp. 389–98. Available online: http://archives.obs-us.com/obs/english/books/nn/bdbirk.htm (accessed 13 December 2002).
Bolter, D.J. (1984) *Turing's Man. Western Culture in the Computer Age*, Chapel Hill, NC: The University of North Carolina Press.
Castells, M. (1989) *The Informational City: Information Technology, Economic Restructuring, and the Urban Regional Process*, Oxford and Cambridge, MA: Blackwell.
—— (1996) *The Information Age: Economy, Society and Culture*, vol. 1: *The Rise of the Network Society*. Oxford: Blackwell.
Dobson, A. (1995) *Green Political Thought*, London: Routledge.

Domoslawski, T. (2002) *Swiat nie na sprzedaz. Rozmowy o kontestacji i globalizacji*, Warszawa: Sic.
Ekins, P. (1993) 'Making development sustainable', in W. Sachs (ed.) *Global Ecology. A New Arena of Political Conflict*, London: Fernwood, 91–103.
Evans, P. (1997) 'The eclipse of state? Reflections on stateness in an era of globalization', *World Politics* 50: 1, 62–87.
Falk, R. (1999) *Predatory Globalization. A Critique*, Cambridge: Polity Press.
Freeden, M. (1996) *Ideologies and Political Theory*, Oxford: Clarendon Press.
Giddens, A. (1990) *The Consequences of Modernity*, Cambridge: Polity Press.
Graeber, D. (2002) 'The new anarchists', *New Left Review* 13: 61–73.
Hardt, M. (2002) 'Porto Alegre: today's Bandung', *New Left Review* 14: 112–18.
Harman, C. (2000) 'Anti-capitalism: theory and practice', *International Socialism Journal*, 88. Available online: http://www.swp.org.uk/ISJ/HARM 88. HTM (accessed 13 December 2002).
Harvey, D. (1989) *The Condition of Postmodernity. An Enquiry into the Origin of Cultural Change*. Oxford: Blackwell.
Jeffress, L. and Mayanobe, J.P. (2001) 'A world struggle is underway. An interview with Jose Bove', *Z magazine*, Available online: http://www.thirdworldtraveler.com/Reforming_System/World_Struggle_Underway.html (accessed 13 December 2002).
Lohmann, L. (1993) 'Resisting Green globalism', in W. Sachs (ed.) *Global Ecology: A New Arena of Political Conflict*. London: Fernwood, pp. 157–69.
McLuhan, M. and Powers, B. (1989) *The Global Village: Transformation in World Life and Media in the 21st Century*, New York, NY: Oxford University Press.
Newell, P. (2000) 'Environmental NGOS and globalization. The governance of TNCS', in R. Cohen and S.M. Rai (eds) *Global Social Movements*. London: Athlone, pp. 117–33.
Nunes, M. (1995) 'Baudrillard in cyberspace: Internet, virtuality, and postmodernity', *Style* 29: 314–27. Available online: http://www.dc.peachnet.edu/~mnunes/jbnet.html (accessed 13 December 2002).
Patterson, M. (1999) 'Globalisation, ecology and resistance', *New Political Economy* 4: 1, 129–45. Available online: http://www.ap.nhu.edu.tw/cybersun/course/globalisation.htm (accessed 13 December 2002).
Pepper, D. (1996) *Modern Environmentalism. An Introduction*, London: Routledge.
Reclaim The Streets (2002). Available online: http://rts.gn.apc.org/ prop05.htm (accessed 13 December 2002).
Ritzer, G. (1993) *The McDonaldization of Society*, London: Pine Forge Press.
Robertson, R. (1992) *Globalisation: Social Theory and Global Culture*, London: Sage.
Rucker, R., Sirius, R.U. and Queen Mu (1992) *Mondo 2000. A User's Guide to the New Edge*, New York, NY: Harper Perennial.
Sachs, W. (1993) 'Global ecology and the shadow of development', in W. Sachs (ed.) *Global Ecology. A New Arena of Political Conflict*, London: Fernwood.
Saurin, J. (1993) 'Global environment degradation, modernity and environmental knowledge', *Environmental Politics* 2: 4, 46–64.
Shiva, V. (1993) 'The greening of the global reach' in W. Sachs (ed.) *Global Ecology: A New Arena of Political Conflict*, London: Fernwood.
Stadler, F. (1998) *The Logic of Networks. Social Landscapes vis-à-vis the Space of Flows*, Available online: http://www.ctheory.net/text_file.asp?pick5263 (accessed 13 December 2002).
Vidal, J. (1996) *McLibel: Burger Culture on Trial*, Basingstoke: Macmillan.

4 Is there a European environmental movement?[1]

Christopher Rootes

Is there a European environmental movement? This might seem a curious question to be asking at this stage of the histories of both Europe and environmentalism. There are, after all, many reasons to suppose that environmentalism has now produced a mature social movement. Indeed, one of the arguments advanced in recent years is that it is now so mature, has been so successfully institutionalized, and is now so embedded in 'constructive' relationships with governments and corporations that it is no longer a social movement at all. I do not intend here to discuss such arguments at length. Suffice it to say that I disagree with them, principally because to focus upon their institutionalization is to overlook the extent to which even relatively institutionalized environmental organizations are still in conflict with and present a quite fundamental challenge to the power structures of increasingly globalized capitalism, and because it is also to overlook the new radical environmentalist groups that have arisen during the last decade or two (Rootes 2003b).

But what is the relationship between environmentalism and that other set of increasingly mature institutions, the European Union (EU)? In a world made smaller by the processes of economic, cultural and political integration that we have come to call 'globalization', environmentalism is represented as a global phenomenon, a global response to a global challenge. Sidney Tarrow (2001: 246–7) has rightly observed that 'the main fulcrum around which transnational groups organize are international *institutions*, which serve as sources of group claims, as targets for their protests, and as sites that can bring parallel groups together internationally'. The limited development of such institutions at the global level is an impediment to the development of a global environmental movement (Rootes 2002b), but the EU is by any measure the most developed transnational political system in existence.

If some observers are so impressed by the progress of globalization and the responses it has evoked that they now purport to identify the contours of a global environmental movement, surely we can speak with confidence about 'the European environmental movement'? It is my contention that we cannot. When we begin systematically to examine the evidence, we find not a coherent transnational movement but a series of national movements whose interaction at the European level is surprisingly limited and that are, for the most part, focused upon targets within the several national states. The development of the EU and its competences in environmental matters has attracted environmental groups and, in their early dealings with the EU, those groups enjoyed both access to and the support of the European Commission (EC). However, recent changes in EU policies and structures, as well as the revival of environmental radicalism, have produced a distinct cooling in that relationship and have diminished the incentives to the formation of a publicly active European environmental movement.

Early days

The nature of environmental issues encourages a transnational perspective, and environmentalists are, for the most part, modernizers and internationalists who instinctively aspire to transnational action and seek transnational agreements. It is therefore not surprising that environmentalists were quicker than many other organized collective interest groups to address the recently established institutions of the EU. From the 1970s onwards, the concatenation of a general heightening of environmental awareness, the rise of more activist environmental movement organizations (EMOs), and the assumption of interests in the environment by the EC produced favourable conditions for the development of environmentalism at the European level, and for the development of a mutually beneficial working relationship between environmentalists and the EC.

As relatively new collective actors, EMOs were only loosely institutionalized at the national level and so, by comparison with business and organized labour, both of which were relatively well-embedded in national arrangements, environmentalists were quick to see and to seek opportunities in European co-operation. The EC, as a new institution relatively ill-resourced by comparison with the bureaucracies of national governments, had strong incentives to network with groups interested in EU policy (Peterson 1997: 8). Seeking allies, the EC offered encouragement to those elements of the environmental movement that promised to feed its need of expertise in a rapidly developing policy domain in which scientific understanding of the issues was rapidly changing. The great advantage that EMOs enjoyed in lobbying the EC – and much of the value to the EC of cultivating a relationship with them – lay in EMOs' ability to draw upon an enormous range of scientific expertise, most of it of the highest quality and freely given by scientists because they believed in the goal of environmental protection.

In 1974 the first specifically European EMO, the European Environmental Bureau (EEB) was established, with 25 member EMOs drawn from all the then EU states. Its objective was to enhance the networking and exchange of information among its members and to make recommendations concerning environmental policy to the appropriate authorities, including the EC (Long 1998: 105–6). Although the formation of the EEB may appear, by its timing, to have been a direct response to the EC's first Environmental Action Programme (1973), it was as much a product of the desire of people active in the environmental movement (including those outside Europe) to advance the cause of environmental protection and sustainability by the development of organizational networks whose scope was more appropriate to the transnational nature of environmental issues.

In the succeeding years, the relationship between the EEB and the EC was often close. The EEB derived much of its core funding from the Directorate General Environment (DGE) and for more than twelve years it remained the only EMO dedicated to the European arena. However, in recent years other EMOs have opened offices in Brussels, and relations between the EEB and DGE have become less cosy.

This suggests both the extent and the limits of the Europeanization of environmentalism. The EEB was not, after all, conceived as a campaigning organization in its own right, but as a broadly representative coordination of environmental groups drawn from the widest possible spectrum of European nations. Yet it appears to have disappointed the expectations both of the EC and of many national EMOs, particularly the more activist groups among them. This experience suggests several questions. Have European environmentalists indeed developed such close links or engaged in such transnationally collective action that it is sensible to talk about '*the*' European environmental movement? What have been the effects of recent changes in the structure of the EU and its institutions? What are the prospects for the further development of a European environmental movement? These are the questions that this chapter will address, but first let us clarify what we mean by an 'environmental movement'.

An environmental movement may be defined as a loose, non-institutionalized network that includes organizations of varying degrees of formality as well as individuals who have no organizational affiliation, is engaged in collective action, and is motivated by a shared identity or environmental concern (Rootes 1997b, following Diani 1992).[2] In respect of each of these three elements – network, engagement in collective action, and shared concern – the existence of a European environmental movement is problematic.

Networks

New pan-European environmental organizations were born not out of internationalist idealism so much as out of recognition of the limitations of what could be achieved without them. So long as it was *ad hoc*, cross-national cooperation between environmental campaigners was 'sporadic, limited and informal' (Rucht 1993: 80). However, in order to form more effective cross-national networks, among the differences that had to be overcome were those of organizational forms, preferred tactics, legal systems and cultures.

Most European-level EMOs take the form of more or less stable transnational alliances or loose networks of *national* organizations. The EEB itself is deliberately a network of national organizations, and its executive committee consists, like the committees of the EU, of one representative from each state. By 1992 the EEB represented some 120 organizations (Rucht 1993: 83), and at the end of 2002 it claimed 134 members in 25 countries, including all the EU member states and most of the 'accession' states accepted for early entry to the EU, as well as Turkey and Algeria.[3] Most of the other EU-level EMO networks are the European branches of more extensive international networks whose presence in Brussels is dictated by their recognition of the efficiency of concentrating their European lobbying activities in one place, and by the recognition that, in matters of environmental policy, the EU is now considerably more important than any of the member states.[4] Thus CEAT, the European coordination of Friends of the Earth (FoE), established a Brussels office in 1986, followed by the Climate Action Network (now Climate Network Europe – CNE) in 1989, not least to prepare policy advice for the European Parliament (EP) (Rucht 1993: 81). The European Federation for Transport and the Environment (EFTE) followed in 1992 and Birdlife International in 1993. In addition, the two leading centrally directed transnational EMOs – Greenpeace and the World Wide Fund for Nature (WWF) – opened Brussels offices in 1988 and 1989 respectively. Increasing numbers of more specialized networks are also at least intermittently represented in Brussels or Strasbourg.

These networks are not entirely mutually exclusive. Some national member organizations of WWF and FoE retain membership of the EEB. Nevertheless, the picture is one of increasing specialization. Fragmentation was mitigated during the 1990s by the development of a 'super umbrella' network. At first, this 'Gang of Four' co-ordinated the activities of EEB, FoE, Greenpeace and WWF and developed a close working relationship with DGE, all except Greenpeace receiving EC subsidies to defray the costs of their Brussels operations (Long 1998: 114; Webster 1998). Later this expanded to become the 'Group of Seven' (G-7) and, more recently, the 'Group of Eight' (G-8) (EEB, CNE, EFTE, FoE, Greenpeace, WWF, The World Conservation Union, International Union for the Conservation of Nature (IUCN) and Birdlife International). All are involved in lobbying, but in line with the EC's declared preference for dealing only with pan-European groups that are both representative and expert (Mazey and Richardson 1992: 115), only the EEB is recognized by DGE as a representative organization (Biliouri 1999: 175).

EMOs at European level do not generally compete one with another. Compared with industry groups that represent market competitors, EMOs are 'essentially on the same side fighting the same cause and have a common interest in better environmental regulations' (Mazey and Richardson 1992: 119–20). Thus although there is some competition for funding among the members of G-8, there is 'an unwritten and unspoken agreement to specialize in different areas of activity' (Tony Long, Director of the European Policy Office of WWF, quoted in Biliouri 1999: 175).

Environmentalists were, at least up to the early 1990s, relatively successful at setting the EC's environmental agenda, especially by comparison with industry groups (Mazey and Richardson 1992: 112, 120–1). Indeed, agenda-setting appears to have been their strong suit and to have been an activity that some groups saw as their main role. Where EMOs were weaker, however, was in their ability to stay with an issue all the way through to the detailed drafting of policy (Mazey and Richardson 1992: 123). Perhaps this reflected their initial naïvete about the policy process and their taste for other, more public forms of action, but it was principally a result of their limited resources. There were and are simply too few EMO representatives in Brussels for them to be very effective (Ruzza 1996: 217); the total staff available to them in recent years has not exceeded 30 (Long 1998: 115). Their lack of resources not only limits EMOs' effectiveness in lobbying at the European level, it also limits their activities *to* lobbying, and it limits their capacity for collaboration among themselves.

Resources apart, the most general obstacle to the success of European-level EMOs is the persistence of national differences that impact upon the relationship between EMOs and the EC as well as upon EMOs themselves. Because most of their activities at the European level consist of lobbying and negotiations conducted behind closed doors, EMOs are not, at EU level, competing for public support and visibility (Rucht 1993: 91). Nevertheless, co-operation among them is impeded by the very diversity of the groups and their national backgrounds. They differ in their organizational forms and styles, in their policy styles, in their perceptions of the relative importance of various environmental issues, and in the magnitude of their expectations.

Because the political debate about environmental issues occurs mainly within nation states and has only limited direct impact upon EC policy making, whether it sets the environmental agenda or responds to the agenda-setting efforts of EMOs, the EC is insulated from public opinion. EMOs, by contrast, depend for their legitimacy and their resources upon their ability to command public support, and, in the absence of a genuinely European public opinion, it is public opinion at national level to which EMOs must be responsive. Because their resource bases and the people to whom EMOs are, in one way or another, accountable are mostly within the nation states, EMOs tend to invest in strengthening their national organizations rather than providing the substantial resources required for collective action at European level. Action at the European level is, in any case, made disproportionately expensive by the costs of travel, communication and translation. It is also more difficult to evaluate its effectiveness than is the case where action is taken within a nation state. Unlike many other interest groups, the environmental groups are not formally represented in the preparatory stages of policy formulation, whether they are consulted or their advice sought being entirely at the discretion of the EC or the relevant Directorate General (Rucht 2001: 133).

If we consider the activities of national EMOs, the extent of transnational networking among them is more limited than the existence of transnational network organizations might suggest. Many of the 30 British environmental organizations that responded in 1998 to a survey designed to explore their European connections reported that they were heavily reliant on one another when dealing with EU matters, the smaller organizations especially so (Ward and Lowe 1998a, b). But if this encouraged networking among environmental organizations *within* Britain, it does not appear to have produced dense or overlapping networks nor to have extended to very extensive collaboration with European organizations. Although 24 of the 30 groups surveyed claimed membership of a European network, 20 different networks were mentioned. Although ten claimed membership of the most frequently named network, the EEB, most saw the EEB's function as limited to the exchange of information.

A more extensive survey of national environmental groups in Britain, undertaken as part of the Transformation of Environmental Activism (TEA) project, produced similar results.[5] Of 86 UK environmental groups surveyed in early 1999, only 21 claimed to have exchanged information with the EEB, and only six claimed ever to have collaborated in a campaign with the EEB. Figures for the Climate Action Network were similar. These modest numbers are scarcely the result of any lack of enthusiasm for European collaboration among British EMOs since more of the EEB's member organizations are from Britain than from any other country. In response to an open-ended question asking them to name their most important collaborators, out of a total of 232 nominations the EC/EU was mentioned only twice and not a single European EMO or network was named. The results of similar surveys in the six other EU states covered by the TEA project do not suggest that EMOs elsewhere in the EU were any more likely to be actively involved in EU level networks.

It appears, then, that environmental movement networks within the EU are neither very dense nor very active. Most are highly specialized and most EMOs remain primarily oriented towards the national rather than the European stage. Only a small elite of British EMOs is well and consistently integrated into European networks, and cross-nationally collaborative *action* tends to be confined to the larger multi-national organizations such as FoE (Ward and Lowe 1998a: 158, 162). Otherwise, British EMOs appear to prefer to deal with the familiar milieu of British politics and have not focused their energies upon EU institutions that they perceive to be 'greener' but to which they feel outsiders. It is not simply that national EMOs have made the rational calculation that the costs of action at the

European level outweigh the probable benefits; rather it appears to be simply that habits of action at the national level are more deeply ingrained.[6] There is nothing to suggest that in this respect British EMOs differ from those of other EU states (Long 1998: 117).

Collective action

Environmentalists have staged a few, mostly small and symbolic, transnational demonstrations in Brussels or Strasbourg and at recent EC summits.[7] For the most part, and certainly until very recently, however, these demonstrations have been mounted mainly in order to attract the attention of national media.[8] Lobbying may be undertaken in Brussels and Strasbourg, but the public collective action of environmental movements in Europe occurs overwhelmingly *within* nation states in the form of mobilizations confined to the local or national level. It is, moreover, mainly focused upon local or national issues and aimed at local or national targets.[9] Examination of environmental protests reported in one leading national newspaper in each of Britain, France, Germany, Greece, Italy, Spain and Sweden[10] over the years 1988–97, undertaken as part of the TEA project, discloses only very small numbers of environmental protests that were European in their level of mobilization, the scope of the underlying issues, or their targets.[11]

Protests mobilized at the EU level ranged from 0.4 per cent of all protests in Britain to 4 per cent in France. Only in three states (Britain 6.4 per cent, France 5.7 per cent, Germany 7.5 per cent) was the EU identifiable as the scope of the underlying issue behind the protest in even a modest number of cases. Even the small number of cases in which the EU was the level of the target (ranging from 0.8 per cent in Italy to 4.6 per cent in Germany) included protests whose targets were companies, associations and governments of other EU states.[12] Of the 52 British protests whose target was at the level of the EU, only 12 (less than 1 per cent of the protests for which a target could be identified) were targeted at the EU itself.[13] Moreover, there is no evidence from any of the EU countries whose environmental protests we have examined of any trend towards increasing Europeanism over the decade on any of these dimensions. The picture is instead one of trendless fluctuation (Rootes 2003a).[14]

If this finding is surprising, it is only so because we have been led by years of rhetoric about globalization and by talk of the construction and extension of the European Union (no longer a mere 'Community', nor yet a 'Common Market'!), to neglect the fact that, except at the most elite levels, politics is still very much *national* politics. Mass environmental movement activity, in particular, occurs almost exclusively at local, regional or national level *within* nation states.

Clearly the existence of the EU and the increased breadth of its environmental remit have created new opportunities and these opportunities have encouraged actors prepared to use them (Marks and McAdam 1999). One way in which Europeanization of environmental movements may occur is when national groups invoke the aid of European institutions in their battles with unresponsive national authorities. There is considerable cross-national and temporal variation in the frequency with which this has occurred but, by opening up such opportunities, the balance of environmentalists' actions may be changed in the direction of a common European repertoire. Political opportunities do not merely offer incentives to act; they also shape the ways groups make claims, and the structure of EC institutions encourages a bias towards conventional forms of activity such as discreet lobbying and against unconventional ones such as mass protest.

Thus the character of EU institutions does not encourage all the same kinds of strategies and tactics that EMOs are accustomed to employing in their efforts to influence national governments. The EC itself is less susceptible to mass protest than are the civil services of member states. The European Council (formerly the Council of Ministers) consists of delegates of national governments whose positions have been prepared in advance and at home. The European Parliament has until very recently been a mostly toothless forum largely invisible to the European public. It may now, as a result of recent reforms, have increased powers, but Members of the European Parliament (MEPs), elected either by national or large regional constituencies, still often appear as lost souls in search of a mission, remote from their constituents and insulated from them by mass indifference and their own invisibility.[15] Sometimes this may be turned to the advantage of the environmental movement as MEPs attempt to forge meaningful roles for themselves.[16] Thus the British Greens MEP, Caroline Lucas, has used the resources and immunities of her office to raise the profile of the campaigns to which she has long been committed. Nevertheless, without in any way diminishing the useful work that MEPs may do, the institution itself is not one that encourages the mobilization of collective action.

Moreover, even if environmental policy is now largely European, there is an important residuum that remains the province of national and local governments. More significantly, at whatever level policy is made, policy *implementation* is still national and local. A great deal of environmental movement action is not addressed to the grand scheme of policy making but to battling over the particular ways in which, and the sites at which, policy is implemented. Even semi-institutionalized national EMOs are well aware of the extent to which their vitality depends upon their ability to keep faith with those engaged in local campaigns (Rootes 1999a). As a result, the objects of contention that are most important to national environmental movements remain largely local and national.

Even to the extent that real power lies in Brussels and national governments appear increasingly to be mere agents of the EC, environmental activists will tend to mobilize against those local tokens of European power rather than against the EC itself. The institutions of the EU are, by comparison with those of nation states, both remote and inaccessible. Members of national parliaments, regional assemblies and local councils are much more directly accountable than are MEPs, and much more susceptible to mobilized opinion. For relatively poorly resourced EMOs, they present much more attractive targets for collective action than do any of the institutions of the EU. It is not so much that there are, as Rucht (1997) observes, formidable obstacles to transnational mobilization, as that the rewards for any such mobilization against the EU are so uncertain as to defeat any attempted calculation of the ratio of benefit to cost. Nor is it necessarily the case that the environmental movement's influence at EC level is limited by the obstacles to transnational mass mobilization. Mobilizations restricted to the national – or even the local – level still have the power to disrupt EC-favoured projects, thereby alerting the EC to the issues in contention, and, by putting pressure on national governments, to tip the balance within the European Council.

If there is little evidence of increasing levels of environmental collective action on the European stage, perhaps there has been a convergence in the forms of collective action taken in the national arena. It might at least be expected that by now, as a consequence of the embedding of common institutions and policies at the EU level and the increasing frequency of cross-national communication within the EU, there should be some evidence of convergence upon a shared repertoire of political action from institutionalized consultation through lobbying to protest, or at least of some diffusion of tactics.

It does appear that there has been some diffusion of repertoires of collective action, and that the number of instances of cross-border emulation of protest tactics has increased in recent years. In 1999, Welsh farmers, drawing inspiration from their French counterparts, blocked the passage of trucks carrying Irish lamb, and British truckers blockaded motorways around London. In 2000, a wave of protests against the high prices of road fuel saw truckers blockading fuel depots first in France and then in Britain, Germany and Spain.[17]

However, even when the citizens of European states have mobilized around the same issue, they have usually done so in different ways. Thus in 1995, the German, French, British and Italian publics reacted quite differently to Shell's attempts to dump the Brent Spar oil storage buoy at sea and Greenpeace's campaign against it (Jordan 2001), and to the French nuclear tests in the South Pacific. Indeed, in Britain the salience of both these issues was dwarfed by protests against the export of live animals, an issue that was met with incomprehension in many other EU countries.

In reported environmental protests in the years 1988–97 in the countries covered by the TEA project, moderate action predominated everywhere; only in Germany and Britain were as many as one third of reported protests more disruptive than demonstrations (Rootes 2003a). Large demonstrations became less common everywhere, but otherwise there was little evidence of convergence of repertoire. In Britain, confrontational action became markedly more common during the 1990s as the number of protests increased, whereas in Greece, where confrontational tactics were also relatively common, they declined. Confrontation was relatively uncommon – and declined – in Sweden and Italy. Germany was the only other country where the relative incidence of confrontation increased but this was principally associated with protests against the transport and processing of nuclear waste, an issue that rarely arose elsewhere.

The national peculiarities of environmental movements clearly testify to the persistent impact of national cultures and political structures, and the activities of EMOs at the EU level are not independent of their more frequent activities at the national level. However, national political opportunities are not fixed; they change in the course of dynamic relationships whose structure and timing is nationally idiosyncratic. We have found no evidence that the trajectories of environmental protest within EU member states are converging; rather, the evidence is that they respond chiefly to national political timetables, events and opportunities (Rootes 2003a).[18]

Shared concern?

Even if effective organizations and mass mobilization at the European level prove elusive, a more subtle form of Europeanization may yet occur in the development of common conceptions of environmental politics and of common issues among the various national movements. Certainly this is something that the EC itself has been concerned to encourage, not only for its own administrative convenience but as part of the process of building a common European political culture.

Previous research has shown that there are considerable differences in the conceptions of environmental problems and consequent claims-making among European populations, and that these are reflected in the policies and actions of national EMOs (Dalton 1994). Surveys conducted during the 1980s concluded that, whereas large majorities of people professed concern about the environment everywhere in the EU, in northern Europe environmentalist sentiment more often took the form of 'global concern' than in southern Europe where environmental concern more often expressed 'personal complaint' (Hofrichter and Reif 1990).

The pattern of the issues raised in environmental protests from 1988 through 1997 in the seven EU states covered by the TEA project is broadly consistent with that portrayed by earlier survey data. Issues of pollution and the effects of environmental degradation upon human health were more frequently raised in the southern European countries (Italy, Spain and Greece) than in northern Europe.[19] More surprising was the diversity of the kinds of issues raised in the four northern European countries

(Germany, Britain, France and Sweden). In Britain and Sweden there was a relatively even spread among nature conservation, pollution and urban/industrial issues, transport and animal rights, but in France, protests concerning nature protection and, especially, animal welfare were relatively rarely reported. Most strikingly, in Germany over half of all protests involved nuclear energy, an issue that was only relatively infrequently raised elsewhere, particularly in the more recent years. Not only was there no common pattern, but, apart from a modest decline in the distinctiveness of the issues raised by environmental protests in southern Europe, there was no apparent trend towards convergence (Rootes 2003a). If there is shared environmental concern among the citizens and environmental activists of EU states, it is concern shared only at the most general and abstract level. It is the particular concerns of the citizens of particular nation states that predominate.

Even where the issues are the same, the patterns of knowledge and concern often vary considerably from one country to another. In 1993 about one third of southern Europeans had not even heard of global warming and their levels of knowledge of the phenomenon were generally low, yet their levels of concern were all above the EU average. In Denmark and the Netherlands the pattern was reversed: levels of knowledge were high but concern was relatively low (Rüdig 1995). There is evidence of increased global environmental consciousness among the better educated in the more affluent countries, but that consciousness is largely limited to those better educated citizens, and there remain considerable differences from one country to another in the predominant forms of environmental consciousness of the general public. It is not, however, simply that people are more concerned about environmental issues in the north and west than in the south and east. Environmental concern is nearly universal and at very high levels. Where Europeans differ is in the *kinds* of concern they voice, the *priority* they attach to environmental issues, and the *forms of action* they are prepared to take in the expression of their environmental concerns.

More than thirty years of broadening and deepening the EU have not produced a common European environmental consciousness. It may not matter too much that mass publics do not share global environmental consciousness if the educated elites who are mobilized by EMOs do, but there is evidence that, despite their best intentions, the thinking and values of even EMO elites are heavily imprinted with the peculiarities of the national cultures from which they come.

The persistence of national differences and effects of European integration

Although there has everywhere been a trend towards the institutionalization of EMOs, the extent to which it has occurred and the forms it has taken have varied significantly from one European country to another.

Comparing Germany, the Netherlands, Switzerland and France, van der Heijden (1997) found the first three to be highly institutionalized but the last scarcely institutionalized at all. There are important differences in the specific features of institutionalization in each of these countries, as there are in the other European countries which have recently been studied systematically (see, on Germany, Brand (1999), Rucht and Roose (1999); on Spain, Jiménez (1999)). The imprint of nationally specific institutional structures, prevailing constellations of political power and competition, and of political culture is evident everywhere (cf. Tarrow 1995). It also appears that there are significant, albeit temporally variable, differences among the patterns of action employed by EMOs in the several EU states (cf. Koopmans 1996, Kriesi *et al.* 1995). Whether and how EMOs lobby or mobilize in Brussels will be influenced by the way they are used to behaving at national level.

Thus it is said that the EU level is especially congenial to the British because the structure of power in the EU (weak legislature, strong executive, preference for informal policy networks) is similar to that in Britain (Hey and Brendle 1992, cited in Long 1998: 109). It may seem paradoxical, then, that the unresponsiveness of British governments has been seen as a spur to British EMOs' embrace of Europe (Ward and Lowe 1998a: 156) and to their playing a leading role in the formation of European EMO networks (Lowe and Ward 1998c: 88). However, the paradox dissolves when it is recognized that the unresponsiveness of British governments to EMOs was not structural but conjunctural: it was especially during the years 1983–92 that British EMOs sought to increase their leverage upon the British government by appeals to Brussels, Strasbourg or Luxembourg (Lowe and Ward, 1998b; Dalton 1994); sometimes to good effect.[20]

For the most part, European integration has entailed the generalization across the EU of the best practice developed in pioneer states. Those states that were first movers in environmental protection (Denmark, the Netherlands and Germany) have largely dictated the agenda and the regulatory regime for the rest, particularly for those smaller states (Ireland, Portugal, Greece and Spain) that did not have well-developed environmental protection regimes and that had at best limited capacity for independent policy formation on environmental issues about which they had little scientific expertise.

These differences have been mirrored in the environmental movements of the several states. States that pioneered environmental protection are generally those in which EMOs have become most developed, while laggard states tend to have smaller, less well supported and, usually, less well institutionalized environmental movements. Laggard states are also more likely to be 'colonized' by EMOs originating in the pioneering states and to sustain EMOs that are relatively dependent for ideas and resources upon those developed or raised elsewhere.

In the leading states, the relationship between the environmental movement and the national government is generally one of well-developed interaction with established channels of communication. Although it is far from being a relationship of equals, because in these states EMOs have demonstrated their capacity for independent fund-raising and popular mobilization they tend to be treated with respect by their interlocutors in government and, increasingly, in industry. As a result, they are increasingly drawn into partnership and away from confrontation (Jamison 2001).

In the laggard states, the relationship is more complicated. Because EMOs in these states have not, for the most part, been able to mobilize large numbers of people and substantial independent resources, they are more dependent on access conceded to them by national governments rather than created by national EMOs' own actions. Laggard states may thus be inclined to see EMOs as actual or potential partners in meeting the state's obligations to the EU rather than as rivals. Indeed, in Spain, EMOs have difficulty finding the personnel and the resources necessary to take advantage of the opportunities created by the decentralization of the state and the incorporation of EU environmental legislation as well as by their own past actions (Jiménez 1999). The relationship is, however, complicated by the fact that, especially in these states, ill-resourced EMOs are more likely to resort to the tactic of taking national governments to the European Court or otherwise seeking to embarrass them in the European arena as a means of drawing attention to governments' performance failures. Thus a relationship of mutual dependence is also a tense one in which the potential for conflict is embedded.

The attitude and relationship of national EMOs to the EU varies, not least as a reflection of EMOs' relationships with national governments and in response to national governments' responses to EU environmental initiatives. Although the advantages of a common European environmental policy are widely recognized among EMOs and the benefits of EU-wide co-ordination of EMOs' activities only slightly less so, the extent to which national EMOs look to the EU for action varies according to their expectations of the responsiveness and competence of their own national government.

In this respect, Britain is a particularly interesting case. Neither consistently a laggard nor a leader in the formation of EU environmental policy, Britain, as the first industrial nation, experienced some of the earliest and worst effects of pollution and made pioneering efforts to mitigate it. A distinctive and, by continental European standards, idiosyncratic style of environmental policy was developed, and an extremely well-developed conservation movement was, decades before the most recent wave of environmental concern, relatively well embedded in a highly developed policy community. Challenged from the 1970s by new, more radical EMOs such as FoE and Greenpeace, the traditional bureaucratic accommodation of the environmental movement in Britain came under particular strain during the decade from 1983 when Conservative governments committed to the revitalization of the capitalist economy were increasingly combative in their relations with the EC at the very time when EU environmental protection measures were proliferating most rapidly. It was this exceptional concatenation of factors that provoked British EMOs into so vigorously playing the EU card (Lowe and Ward 1998b: 19–22). The slowing of environmental policy innovation in the EU after 1992 and a progressive shift in the policies of the Major government produced a return to a more normal balance in British EMOs' relations with the national government and the EU; a relationship that the election 1997 of a surprisingly environment-friendly Labour government has consolidated.

Neither in leading nor in laggard states is the environmental movement undifferentiated. In most states, some EMOs are more institutionalized than are others. Some are, as a matter of policy, more conciliatory and easily incorporated than others. In general, it would appear that the relationship between the state of development of national environmental regimes and the degree of radicalism of EMOs is curvilinear. In the leading states, the internal development of EMOs and their relationships with government and industry both conduce to a relatively high degree of institutionalization, to the moderation of conflict potential, and to the absence or marginalization of environmental radicalism. In the laggard states, the weakness of the internal development of EMOs and their relative dependence on government encourage the moderation of conflict potential and the (more precarious) marginalization of environmental radicalism. It is in those states that are neither consistently leaders nor laggards but where, for political conjunctural reasons, the normal relationship between EMOs and national government is disturbed, as it was in Britain during the 1980s and early 1990s, that the potential is greatest for deliberately provocative appeals to EU institutions and radical environmental mobilizations.

Effects of recent changes in the EU

At first sight, a number of recent institutional changes in the EU should work to the advantage of environmentalists and make the EU level more attractive to EMOs. Increased qualified majority voting and the increasing desire of national governments to avoid responsibility for EU policies have combined with increasing 'pillarization' within the EC to empower policy networks in the shaping of policies arising from frequently vague intergovernmental bargains (Peterson 1997: 17). Furthermore, with the advent, post-Maastricht, of 'co-decision' among the EC, European Parliament (EP) and European Council, increasing power has flowed to the EP. This is important to environmentalists because the EP has shown itself to be more hospitable to a range of broad social interests, including environmentalism (as is evident in recent legislation on biotechnology and food safety), than the EC whose most powerful Directorates often appear to have become more tightly locked into the promotion of the interests of the producers within their associated policy networks rather than those of consumers. The recent strengthening of the Green group in the EP is another development that may be expected to increase EMOs' interest in and access to the EP.

Even so, as recently as 1998 British EMOs rated the EP only fifth, below even national government departments, as an important channel for influencing EU policy (Ward and Lowe 1998a: 159). Moreover, if recent institutional developments appear to favour environmentalism, other, less formally structured processes do not.

For some years the EC has attempted a 'shake-out' of interest groups accorded the status of interlocutors in favour of a sharper focus upon a stronger 'inner core' (Mazey and Richardson 1993). This was inevitable as an understaffed Commission sought more effectively to ration the resources it devoted to listening to the ever-increasing number of lobbyists active in Brussels, but its effects have been to privilege a small number of better established groups at the expense of a larger number of smaller, newer and/or less institutionalized groups. Few groups not already established in the EU arena have entered since 1992. 'The integration of the environmental lobby seems to have become increasingly frozen' (Ward and Lowe 1998b: 29). The rise of 'secondary lobbying' – whereby the latter groups lobby others that they believe to have the ear of the EC – is seen by some observers as widening the array of voices that are heard in EU policy networks (Peterson 1997: 18), but its more obvious effect is to enhance the privilege of the already entrenched and to extend to them not merely an aggregative function but also a gatekeeper role; if other voices are heard it is indirectly, their messages not merely translated but interpreted.

The increased centrality of more tightly defined policy networks privileges the powerful and the efficient. The problem for the environmental movement is that few of its constituents are either. By comparison with industry lobbyists environmentalists are neither well-resourced nor do they enjoy guaranteed access in alternative forums. Largely because of their dependence upon a small number of highly committed but overworked professional staff and a larger number of erratically part-time volunteers, most EMOs are not well-placed to take full advantage of the opportunities that the EU appears to offer, or to reliably deliver the policy advice and expertise officials seek.

The environment as a policy area and EMOs themselves prospered in the EU at a time when the EC was relatively young and uninstitutionalized. EMOs found a ready audience in Brussels both because the EC lacked resources and expertise in a policy area in which it had only newly acquired competence[21] and because the new internationalist EMOs, as groups relatively unattached to the nation-state-based political order, flattered the EC by taking it seriously, by appearing genuinely rather than merely tactically European in their perspectives (Mazey and Richardson 1992: 120), and by being prepared to play the EU card against recalcitrant national governments. Despite the fact that environmental movement networks were loose and alliances fluid, they were disproportionately influential, not least because, at the time, many industry groups, more thoroughly embedded in the institutionalized relationships of the several member states, took the EC less seriously than did environmentalists.

All this has now changed. Although the EC may remain small and informal by comparison with the bureaucracies of most of the member states, it has become more expert in matters environmental and, especially, more institutionalized.[22] Environmentalists' rivals and adversaries have, especially since the completion of the Single European Market, taken the EU increasingly seriously, and they have used their tight and comparatively well-resourced policy networks increasingly effectively, not least to take advantage of the second chance opportunities to shape EU legislation that have been opened up by the advent of co-decision. Thus the Internal Market Directorate and its associated policy networks were able to water down environmental proposals in the interests of producers (Peterson 1997: 15). The Directorate General Environment has been encouraged to take industry interests more centrally into account, and in recent years it has shown less inclination to consult environmental groups before making proposals that concern them (Long 1998: 116).

By contrast with industry lobbies, environmental policy networks remain loosely structured and have fluid memberships. Although this fluidity might appear to offer opportunities, the more general effect is to produce compromise environmental policies easily steamrollered by competitors for 'policy space' and especially susceptible to intergovernmental bargains and the reservation of power to national governments (Peterson 1997: 9). Although the better established EMOs are now no less impressed than in the past with the importance of the EU as a policy arena and although they have sought to establish more effective (and more specialized) networks at EU level, their resources have not continued to increase. Indeed, since the early 1990s, the resources of the most radical globalist EMOs – Greenpeace and FoE – have at best stagnated at the very time when the competition over policies, and for access to EU institutions, has intensified.[23]

One consequence is that EMOs appear to be making an increasingly hard-nosed evaluation of the implications of their limited resources. Efficacy increasingly requires the judicious deployment of resources and strategic choices must be made about which activities to engage in. Even the larger and wealthier organizations, such as WWF and Greenpeace, are deliberately specialized. This has effects upon transnational environmental networks. Misgivings about the structural weaknesses and consequent efficacy of the EEB were among the factors prompting the larger transnational EMOs to set up their own European units. Other EMOs have followed suit, establishing more specialized networks in order to husband resources that might otherwise have been expended in discussions with smaller groups within the EEB. Thus the EEB which began as an effort to produce a broad and fully representative co-ordination of EMOs throughout the EU has gradually been reduced to a network of mainly smaller or strictly national EMOs (cf. Lowe and Ward 1998c: 103). Not surprisingly, in view of its increasingly questionable ability to represent the broad environmental movement, the EEB's value to the EC has been eroded and its EC subsidy has been reduced.

At the national level, except for a small elite of EMOs that have the resources themselves to participate directly in EU forums and to bypass the national agencies that were hitherto often their means of access to government (Lowe and Ward 1998c: 104), Europeanization appears to have led to increased interdependency among EMOs (especially within national domestic networks), increased centrality of national governments as lobbying targets, and a shift in the forms of EMO activity towards the politics of policy implementation as EMOs have found it increasingly difficult to set environmental agenda in the European arena (Ward and Lowe 1998b: 32–3).

One effect, then, of the increased 'maturity' of the EU system is that as the EU becomes more important, so, for all but a small elite of EMOs, it becomes less directly accessible. This encourages EMOs to refocus their lobbying efforts upon national governments as an indirect means of influencing the EU. In the national arena, the effect of Europeanization has been to strengthen the position of groups that were already among the elite in domestic environmental politics (Lowe and Ward 1998c: 102) by encouraging their institutionalization and professionalization. This further privileges the few groups sufficiently large and well-resourced to be highly active in both national and EU arenas and capable of playing multiple roles in the policy process (Ward and Lowe 1998b: 32–3). The consequent tendency to produce elite 'winners' and non-elite 'losers' is mitigated among the more formally organized EMOs by the sense of shared purpose and the acceptance of division of labour and specialization of roles. Some groups – in Britain, FoE stands out – have proven especially sensitive to the need to maintain co-operative contacts with other EMOs as well as being attentive to the concerns of the grassroots activists who are widely considered to be the 'conscience' of the environmental movement (Rootes 1999b).[24]

The stagnation of the flow of resources to EMOs has coincided with an increased maturity of the environmental policy community that dictates an increasing focus upon backroom policy work and responses to increasing demands for professionalism and 'practical solutions' rather than critique. In this climate, protest mobilizations are increasingly regarded, especially by EMOs' ever more expert interlocutors, as amateurish and ill-informed. In order to avoid stigmatization by those EC officials who saw environmentalists as 'obstructionist, anti-growth and heavily dependent upon the media to attack both decision-makers and companies', at least one EMO deliberately changed its style in order to appear to play a more 'constructive' role and appeared as a result to have been more favourably viewed by the EC (Mazey and Richardson 1992: 125–6). As is often the case in the national arena, access appears to have been maintained at the price of domestication.

Thus it appears that in the relations between the environmental movement and the EU, both because of structural changes in the EU and because of the limited (and possibly declining) mobilizational capacities of established EMOs, a window of opportunity is closing.[25]

To EMOs this presents a severe practical dilemma: do they commit an ever greater share of scarce resources in order to undertake the necessary backroom policy work and in the process hope to gain influence over policy even while losing public visibility? Or do they invest their resources so as to maximize their public profile even at the expense of becoming more marginal to the policy-making process and influencing policy mainly by mounting spectacular 'agenda-setting' campaigns? Since few EMOs have the resources to successfully do both, it is not surprising that most have become more or less specialized in one form of activity rather than the other and that most have taken the more predictable path of lobbying. One result is that networking among EMOs becomes increasingly important and a division of labour becomes more respected. There is evidence that this is happening both within national environmental movements[26] and among EMOs and EMO networks operating at the EU level (Ward and Lowe 1998a: 164).

Not the least limitation of this increasing maturity is that it has developed and works best within and among EMOs and generations that have grown up and matured together. Particular tensions arise in respect of relations with newer groups and younger generations who cannot see the backroom policy work and who have neither the capacity nor the inclination to engage in it, and who are exasperated by both the lack of progress towards environmental sustainability and the infrequency of effective, publicly visible action (Rootes 1999b; Wall 1999).

Environmental radicalism and the limits of Europeanization

Whether or not environmentalists respond to the opportunities the EU presents will depend not merely upon their experience of national politics but also upon their preferred styles of political action. Action at the European level is most attractive to those whose styles of action are participatory only at elite level and for whom consultation, negotiation and lobbying are congenial. Generally these are actors whose dispositions are reformist or pragmatic.

By contrast, engagement with the EC is not at all attractive to those whose objectives are more radical, whose preferred styles of action are direct or confrontational, and whose principles are those of democratic mass participation. One consequence of the increasing institutionalization of more established EMOs is the proliferation of new, radical groups with just such principles. It is not that their horizons are limited to the local or the national level – on the contrary, they take very seriously the injunction to 'think globally, act locally' – and they are sharply critical not only of the institutionalized EMOs who sup at the EC table, but also of the institutions and purposes of the EC itself. The environmental radicals reject not merely the bad environmental practice in the EU, but the dominant conceptions of *good* practice within the developed world – the modernist, utilitarian, anthropocentric discourses of 'ecological modernization' and 'sustainable development' (van der Heijden, 1999) and the very kinds of solutions to environmental problems that are proposed within the EU. Thus Earth First! (UK), for example, has not entered established European networks not merely because of the limitations of its resources or the more difficult political climate since 1992, but because it is committed to a different model of political change (Wall 1999). Such groups are likely to continue to be the irritant in the oyster of European environmentalism and they will limit any prospects of easy institutionalization and convergence.

Although the inspiration and networks of the new environmental radicals are more truly global than European, some do organize at the European level, but when they do so their organization takes the form of loose networks designed to share information rather than to lobby the EC. It is perhaps emblematic of this that A SEED, the network established to facilitate the co-ordination of local and national actions of resistance to the EC's trans-European transport network initiative, was based not in Brussels but in Amsterdam.

If the political processes of European unification have limited appeal within the environmental movements of Europe, there are nevertheless powerful secular processes – some of them directly encouraged by the projects of the EC – that will tend increasingly to homogenize environmental movement activity across Europe. Easier communication and more frequent interaction will continue to erode the distinctiveness of national cultures and aid the diffusion of political repertoires. This will, however, be a long process and one which is part of a more universal process of cultural globalization. Thus, although a gradual convergence is to be expected even among the radical sections of environmental movements, it will not be a purely European process. 'Europeanization' will very likely be compromised by the impact of linkages made between particular European movements and their counterparts outside Europe. Ease of communication and the large measure of commonality of culture and institutions among the English-speaking countries is fully reflected in the international networks of both established and new radical EMOs in Britain and these will continue to be important. In the grand scheme of globalization the EU is ambiguous; although it tends to break down barriers among Europeans, even its leading role in global environmental conventions can be represented as a pursuit of sectional interest (e.g. Kellow 2000).

Social movements cannot be wholly institutionalized and still retain the identity of social movements; as long as there is vitality in a movement, there will be those who resist institutionalization in the name of purity of purpose. This is not only an irritation to established and semi-institutionalized EMOs but often also an invaluable asset to them, for it provides them with a means of keeping in touch with grassroots opinion, and a lever on the powerful (the 'radical flank' effect). As a result, relations are often surprisingly cordial and co-operative between environmental radicals and established EMOs.

Nor is the institutionalization of the environmental movement always seen as a positive thing by EC bureaucrats. As one remarked, 'My problem is that I am not waiting for lobbies, I am waiting for movements. What I hope to have is some kind of...democratic input in my thinking'. He went on to complain that when he meets EMO people at international meetings, 'they don't bring me very much news. I know what they know, what they think, and I cannot use it'. (Ruzza 1996: 217–18). Consciousness of the EC's 'democratic deficit' as well as a genuine concern to find fundamental solutions to environmental problems encourage at least some EC officials to cultivate contacts with the more radical end of the movement. However, because environmental radicals do not present themselves in the same way as do the suited, business card carrying representatives of established EMOs and do not attend the same international meetings, the contacts such EC officials crave prove elusive. Moreover, this movement-friendly eurocrat inadvertently makes clear the relationship between the EC and the EMOs it courts; the latter are seen as sources and conduits of information but there is no suggestion that they should be partners in power (cf. Rucht 1993: 87). The officials of the Directorate General Environment may consider environmental groups as actual or potential allies, but there is no pretence that it is an alliance of equals.

Such an asymmetry of power may be pragmatically accepted by many, but it is extremely irksome to others and it serves to fuel their critique of the EC and their determination to follow an alternative, radical path. Moreover, because it will be harder for new environmental groups to gain the kind of access to Brussels that was enjoyed by their predecessors, there is more likelihood that they will regard the EC as an enemy rather than an ally, and that they will, in the name of the global interest and in reaction against the dual institutionalization of environmentalism in the EU, reject not just the EC but the EU.

To the extent that the Europeanization of environmental movements requires their institutionalization at the European level, it is never likely to be complete. The EU has been a magnet for the more institutionalized strands of European environmentalism, but even they have been constrained by their own limited resources and the restricted opportunities to effectively influence EU policy directly by action in Brussels. The likelihood that the EU will stimulate a much more extensive Europeanization of environmentalism is limited by its own character as an institution. Although secular tendencies towards globalization will, in time, erode national differences, the obstacles to the formation of a European environmental movement comparable to those of nation states such as Britain or Germany are likely to remain simply because it is unlikely that the EU will itself acquire all the attributes of a nation state. It is more likely that we shall see further evidence of the Europeanization of domestic politics than a thorough-going transnationalization of European politics (Imig and Tarrow 2001: 48). Until we can identify, at the European level, collective action based upon shared identity or environmental concern and linked by dense and active networks of EMOs and other environmental activists, talk of a European environmental movement will remain loose talk.

Notes

1 An earlier version of this chapter was published as Rootes (2002a).
2 For a more extended discussion of the issues involved in the definition of environmental movements, see Rootes (2003b).
3 EEB website (www.eeb.org) December 31, 2002.
4 Former UK Environment Secretary John Gummer's 1994 estimate that 80 per cent of UK environmental legislation originated in Brussels or Strasbourg (Lowe and Ward 1998b: 25) is probably an overestimate but, for smaller EU member states such as Spain, Portugal, Greece and Ireland, it would be an underestimate.
5 For a brief description of the TEA project (EC contract no.: ENV4-CT97-0514), see www.ukc.ac.uk/sspssr/TEA.html. The survey was conducted by means of a self-completion mail questionnaire sent to all *national* EMOs listed in *Who's Who in the Environment* (1999), excluding groups concerned only with the conservation of a single animal species and those dealing only with the built environment. Responses were received from all the large and/or well-known groups with the exception of the Socialist Environment and Resources Association and the Women's Environmental Network. See Rootes and Miller (2000) for further details.
6 Jochen Roose, personal communication based on his doctoral research, 2001.
7 Rucht (2001: 128) remarks on the small number and infrequency of such protests, and the lack of media attention they have received except when high profile personalities have been involved.
8 This observation based on perusal of the British press over recent years is supported by Rucht's (1999: 210) analysis of German newspaper reports. Of course, in a media-saturated age, token, symbolic action designed to attract the attention of press and television cameras is not necessarily any less effective than larger scale mobilization.
9 Imig and Tarrow (2001: 33–4) found that 95 per cent of all the protest they identified in EU countries from Reuters reports was domestic rather than European in character.

10 The newspapers employed were the *Guardian, Le Monde, die Tageszeitung, Eleftherotypia, La Republicca, El Pais* and *Dagens Nyheter* respectively. Reports of environmental protest events were drawn from each day's edition of the newspaper in Britain, France, Germany and Spain, and from alternate days' papers in Greece, Italy and Sweden. See Rootes (2003a) for details.
11 These figures exclude data derived solely from summary reports – reports that give minimal information about a large number of (sometimes geographically dispersed) events often (but not invariably) occurring over an extended period of time. In Britain, including summary reports, of all the 1,897 reported protests for which the level of mobilization could be determined, protests that were mobilized on an EU level comprised 6 per cent (114 protests) but all but two of these occurred as part of Greenpeace's 1995 campaign against Shell's attempt to dump the Brent Spar oil storage buoy at sea. The inclusion of data from summary reports has varied impacts on the apparent salience of EU-related protest: it increases it in Britain but dramatically reduces it in Italy. Because the amount and quality of information we are able to abstract from summary reports is so low, they have been excluded from this analysis.
  I am indebted to those of my collaborators in the TEA project – Olivier Fillieule and Fabrice Ferrier, Dieter Rucht and Jochen Roose, Maria Kousis and Katerina Lenaki, Mario Diani and Francesca Forno, Manuel Jiménez, Andrew Jamison and Magnus Ring, Sandy Miller, Ben Seel and Debbie Adams – who were responsible for assembling the data on which this discussion is based.
12 On the basis of data drawn from two other newspapers, Rucht (2001: 132; 2002: 182) reports that in Germany less than 1 per cent of pro-environmental protests reported during 1970–94 were EU-related. Rucht (2002: 183–4) presents evidence of German environmental protests for 1988–97.
13 One of these was a boycott by BodyShop of the EU's eco-labelling system, two were petitions to or attempts to lobby the EC, and the other nine were formal or procedural complaints to EU institutions about actions or inaction of the UK government.
14 This finding may appear to contradict that of Imig and Tarrow (1999, 2001) who found that, although the number and proportion of EU-related protests was very low, it rose significantly between 1983 and 1997. In fact, their data appears to show a pattern of trendless fluctuation until about 1995, with only 1997 showing a very marked increase. However, their data and ours are not comparable because their data, aggregated for 10 or 12 EU states, cover all protests whereas ours are restricted to those about environmental issues. (In their data, more than four-fifths of EU-focused protests were mounted by occupational groups, with only 88 out of 490 protests involving non-occupational groups, of which environmental groups were only some.) Moreover, their data is derived from Reuters reports, probably selected for their national/international importance and their interest to the business community, whereas ours are drawn from all environmental protests reported in one national newspaper in each country. Not only, on Imig and Tarrow's own account, is it likely that the Reuters data is biased towards the 'more important' and higher level protests, but it is likely that as the business community has become increasingly persuaded of the importance of the EU, so Reuters, as a news service selling its services primarily to business, will have become more assiduous in its coverage of EU-related protests. However, if Imig and Tarrow's data possibly exaggerates the relative incidence of EU-related protest in more recent years by comparison with earlier years, our own, because it is limited to protests occurring on the territory of just seven states, might tend to underestimate it for the

whole period. Unfortunately, we have no systematic evidence for the incidence of EU-related environmental protests in Brussels, but since there was no increase in overall EU-related protest in Belgium 1980–95 (Reising 1999, Rucht 2001: 141, n. 20), it appears unlikely that it has been sufficiently frequent to contradict our conclusions.
15 Evidence of this may be found in the low and steadily declining turnouts in European Parliament elections.
16 On Green parties in the European Parliament, see Bomberg (1998).
17 Although these protests were opposed by many in the environmental movement, they were not unambiguously anti-environmental (Doherty et al. 2002).
18 Thus, in Britain the incidence of environmental protest was relatively stable before rising significantly following the re-election of an environmentally unresponsive Conservative government in 1992 to a peak in 1995 before falling sharply in 1997, the year in which a Labour government pledged to 'put the environment at the heart of government' came to power (Rootes 2000), only to rise sharply in 1998 as new issues emerged and EMOs sought to hold Labour to its promises. In Germany, protest peaked in 1990 and fell sharply thereafter before rising again from the mid 1990s, the twilight years of the CDU–CSU government, to sustained high levels from 1995 through 1997.
19 To label concern with pollution and health as an environmentalism of personal complaint is not, however, to suggest that they were any less capable of sustaining collective action, albeit that such action was more concentrated at the local level than was environmental protest in the northern countries.
20 But sometimes with unfortunate consequences. When the EC Environment Commissioner, Carlo Ripa de Meana, intervened to try to halt the construction of the M3 motorway extension through Twyford Down, the battle was lost because then the Conservative government could only back down at the expense of apparent humiliation at the hands of Brussels.
21 In its early years, the Directorate General Environment relied heavily upon EMOs not merely for expertise but in order to defend itself (Mazey and Richardson 1992: 121).
22 Witness, for example, the Directorate General Environment's attempts to formalize its relationships with and to reduce its subsidies to EMOs (Long 1998: 116).
23 The lack of growth in these globalist EMOs may be compensated for in part by the increasing internationalization of other, more nationally institutionalized groups (e.g. the initiative of the RSPB in setting up Birdlife International) and by the broadening of the remit of more established international groups such as WWF.
24 Respondents to the 1999 survey of 86 British EMOs conducted as part of the TEA project named FoE as the EMO with which they exchanged information most often. More importantly, they indicated that they collaborated in campaigns with FoE considerably more often than with any other group (Rootes and Miller 2000). This view of FoE as the hub of the network of EMO activism is consistent with that derived from a network analysis of groups named in reports of protest events (Rootes 2000). (I am grateful to Manuel Jiménez for conducting the network analysis.)
25 It may be closing yet more, given the apparent watering down of the commitment to environmental improvement in the discussion documents produced by Giscard d'Estaing's commission on a future constitution for the EU.
26 It was attested to by representatives of Greenpeace and the Women's Environmental Network (WEN) who participated in a focus group we conducted as part of the Johns Hopkins Comparative Non-profit Sector Project in November 1998.

Bibliography

Biliouri, D. (1999) 'Environmental NGOs in Brussels: how powerful are their lobbying activities', *Environmental Politics* 8: 2, 173–82.
Bomberg, E. (1998) *Green Parties and Politics in the European Union*, London: Routledge.
Brand, K.-W. (1999) 'Dialectics of institutionalisation: the transformation of the environmental movement in Germany', in Rootes (1999a) and *Environmental Politics* 8: 1, 35–8.
Dalton, R.J. (1994) *The Green Rainbow: Environmental Groups in Western Europe*, New Haven, CT and London: Yale University Press.
della Porta, D., Kriesi, H. and Rucht, D. (eds) (1999) *Social Movements in a Globalizing World*, London: Macmillan.
Diani, M. (1992) 'The concept of social movement', *Sociological Review* 40: 1–25.
Doherty, B., Paterson, M., Plows, A. and Wall, D. (2002) 'The fuel protests of 2000: implications for the environmental movement in Britain', *Environmental Politics* 11: 2, 165–73.
Hofrichter, J. and Reif, K. (1990) 'Evolution of environmental attitudes in the European Community', *Scandinavian Political Studies* 13: 119–46.
Imig, D. and Tarrow, S. (1999) 'The Europeanization of movements?', in D. della Porta, H. Kriesi and D. Rucht (eds) *Social Movements in a Globalizing World*, London: Macmillan, pp. 112–33.
—— (2001) 'Mapping the Europeanization of contention', in D. Imig and S. Tarrow (eds) *Contentious Europeans: Protest and Politics in an Emerging Polity*, Lanham, MD: Rowman and Littlefield: 27–49.
Jamison, A. (2001) *The Making of Green Knowledge*, Cambridge: Cambridge University Press.
Jiménez, M. (1999) 'Consolidation through institutionalization? Dilemmas of the Spanish environmental movement in the 1990s' in C. Rootes (ed.) *Environmental Movements: Local, National and Global*, London and Portland, OR: Frank Cass and *Environmental Politics* 8: 1, 149–71.
Jordan, G. (2001) *Shell, Greenpeace and Brent Spar*, Basingstoke: Palgrave.
Kellow, A. (2000) 'Norms, interests and environment NGOs: the limits of cosmopolitanism', *Environmental Politics* 9: 3, 1–22.
Koopmans, R. (1996) 'New social movements and changes in political participation in western Europe', *West European Politics* 19: 1, 28–50.
Kriesi, H., Koopmans, R., Duyvendak, J.W., and Giugni, M. (1995) *New Social Movements in Western Europe*, Minneapolis, MN: University of Minnesota Press and London: UCL Press.
Long, T. (1998) 'The European lobby' in P. Lowe and S. Ward (eds) *British Environmental Policy and Europe*, London: Routledge, pp. 105–18.
Lowe, P. and Ward, S. (eds) (1998a) *British Environmental Policy and Europe*, London: Routledge.
—— (1998b) 'Britain in Europe: themes and issues in national environmental policy', in P. Lowe and S. Ward (eds) *British Environmental Policy and Europe*, London: Routledge, pp. 3–30.
—— (1998c) 'Domestic winners and losers', in P. Lowe and S. Ward (eds) *British Environmental Policy and Europe*, London: Routledge, pp. 87–104.
Marks, G. and McAdam, D. (1999) 'On the relationship of political opportunities

to the form of collective action: the case of the European Union', in D. della Porta, H. Kriesi and D. Rucht (eds) *Social Movements in a Globalizing World*, London: MacMillan, pp. 97–111.

Mazey, S. and Richardson, J. (1992) 'Environmental groups and the EC: challenges and opportunities', *Environmental Politics* 1: 4, 109–28.

—— (eds) (1993) *Lobbying in the European Community*, Oxford: Oxford University Press.

Peterson, J. (1997) 'States, societies and the European Union', *West European Politics* 20: 4, 1–23.

Reising, U. (1999) 'United in opposition? A cross-national time-series analysis of European protest in three selected countries, 1980–1995', *Journal of Conflict Resolution* 43: 3, 317–42.

Rootes, C. (1997a) 'Environmental movements and Green parties in western and eastern Europe' in M. Redclift and G. Woodgate (eds) *International Handbook of Environmental Sociology*, Cheltenham and Northampton, MA: Edward Elgar, pp. 319–48.

—— (1997b) 'Shaping collective action: structure, contingency and knowledge' in R. Edmondson (ed.) *The Political Context of Collective Action*, London and New York, NY: Routledge, pp. 81–104.

—— (ed.) (1999a) *Environmental Movements: Local, National and Global*, London and Portland, OR: Frank Cass.

—— (1999b) 'The transformation of environmental activism: activists, organizations and policy-making', *Innovation: The European Journal of Social Sciences* 12: 2, 155–73.

—— (2000) 'Environmental protest in Britain 1988–1997' in B. Seel, M. Paterson and B. Doherty (eds) *Direct Action in British Environmentalism*, London: Routledge, pp. 25–61.

—— (2002a) 'The Europeanization of environmentalism', in R. Balme, D. Chabanet and V. Wright (eds) *L'action collective en Europe/Collective Action in Europe*, Paris: Presses de Science Po, pp. 377–404.

—— (2002b) 'Global visions: global civil society and the lessons of European environmentalism', *Voluntas* 13: 4, 411–29.

—— (ed.) (2003a) *Environmental Protest in Western Europe*, Oxford: Oxford University Press.

—— (2003b) 'Environmental movements' in D. Snow, S. Soule and H. Kriesi (eds) *Blackwell Companion to Social Movements*, Oxford and Malden, MA: Blackwell.

Rootes, C. and Miller, A. (2000) 'The British environmental movement: organizational field and network of organizations', paper presented at European Consortium for Political Research Joint Sessions, Copenhagen. Available online: http://www.essex.ac.uk/ecpr/jointsessions/Copenhagen/papers/ws5/rootes_miller.pdf.

Rucht, D. (1993) '"Think globally, act locally": needs, forms and problems of cross-national environmental groups' in J.D. Liefferink, P.D. Lowe and A.J.P. Mol (eds) *European Integration and Environmental Policy*, London and New York, NY: Belhaven, pp. 75–95.

—— (1997) 'Limits to mobilization: environmental policy for the European Union' in J. Smith, C. Chatfield and R. Pagnucco (eds) *Transnational Social Movements and Global Politics*, Syracuse, NY: Syracuse University Press, pp. 195–213.

—— (1999) 'The transnationalisation of social movements: trends, causes and problems', in D. della Porta, H. Kriesi and D. Rucht (eds) *Social Movements in a Globalizing World*, London: Macmillan.

—— (2001) 'Lobbying or protest? Strategies to influence EU environmental policies', in D. Imig and S. Tarrow (eds) *Contentious Europeans: Protest and Politics in an Emerging Polity*, Lanham, MD: Rowman and Littlefield, pp. 125–42.

—— (2002) 'The EU as a target of mobilisation: is there a Europeanisation of conflict?', in R. Balme, D. Chabanet and V. Wright (eds) *L'action collective en Europe/Collective Action in Europe*, Paris: Presses de Science Po, pp. 163–94.

Rucht, D. and J. Roose (1999) 'The German environmental movement at a crossroads?', in C. Rootes (ed.) *Environmental Movements: Local, National and Global*, London and Portland, OR: Frank Cass and in *Environmental Politics* 8: 1, 59–80.

Rüdig, W. (1995) 'Public opinion and global warming: a comparative analysis', *Strathclyde Papers on Government and Politics*, no. 101, Glasgow: Department of Government, University of Strathclyde.

Ruzza, C. (1996) 'Inter-organisational negotiations in political decision-making: Brussels' EC bureaucrats and the environment', in C. Samson and N. South (eds) *The Social Construction of Social Policy*, Basingstoke: Macmillan and New York, NY: St Martin's Press, pp. 210–23.

Tarrow, S. (1995) 'The Europeanisation of conflict: reflections from a social movement perspective', *West European Politics* 18: 2, 223–51.

—— (2001) 'Contentious politics in a composite polity', in D. Imig and S. Tarrow (eds) *Contentious Europeans: Protest and Politics in an Emerging Polity*, Lanham, MD: Rowman and Littlefield, pp. 233–51.

van der Heijden, H. (1997) 'Political opportunity structure and the institutionalisation of the environmental movement', *Environmental Politics* 6: 4, 25–50.

—— (1999) 'Environmental movements, ecological modernisation and political opportunity structures' in C. Rootes (ed.) (1999) *Environmental Movements: Local, National and Global*, London and Portland, OR: Frank Cass, pp. 199–221.

Wall, D. (1999) 'Mobilising Earth First! in Britain' in C. Rootes (ed.) *Environmental Movements: Local, National and Global*, London and Portland, OR: Frank Cass and in *Environmental Politics* 8: 1, 81–100.

Ward, S. and Lowe, P. (1998a) 'National environmental groups and Europeanisation: a survey of the British environmental lobby', *Environmental Politics* 7: 4, 155–65.

—— (1998b) 'National environmental groups and Europeanisation: the British lobby and the attraction of Europe', *Working Papers in Contemporary History and Politics 21*, Salford: European Studies Research Institute, University of Salford.

Webster, R. (1998) 'Environmental collective action: stable patterns of cooperation and issue alliances at the European level', in J. Greenwood and M. Aspinwall (eds) *Collective Action in the European Union*, London: Routledge, pp. 176–95.

5 Fragmented citizenship in a global environment

Marcel Wissenburg[1]

Introduction: the environment's environment

The emergence of globalization as a topic of debate for political science has forged a link between global environmental issues on the one hand and on the other more traditional supranational issues relating to social and economic globalization (the migration of people and money (Barry and Goodin 1992), the North–South divide, the globalization of enterprise, etc.). At least in politics, however, globalization is not the only discernible form of 'regrouping'. There are also processes that can be understood as attempts to perhaps adapt to, perhaps control, perhaps even check, globalization: international regimes, more structured forms of regional co-operation or European unification. Other developments that apparently gnaw at the roots of the once 'natural' basic unit of international politics, the nation-state, point in the direction of a disintegration of states: cross-border regional co-operation, increased autonomy for national minorities, the de-nationalization of the welfare state, and so on. To describe these and similar developments I shall use the term political pluralization.

An adequate analysis of the challenges that globalization and other forms of supranational political reorganization pose for sustainability, however understood (cf. Dobson 1998), as well as of the challenges that sustainability in turn poses for these developments, must include an understanding of the nature of political pluralization. Moreover, to understand political pluralization we need to understand the role of the citizen in this new context. Citizenship is, of course, of crucial importance for environmental issues and issues of sustainability in general. Without concerned citizens, environmental issues or the interests of future generations would never have been put on the political agenda in the first place. Without at the very least passive support from citizens, no policy aimed at sustainability stands a chance of succeeding. In the context of modern (that is, post-World War I) society, these two points can be generalized: most political demands originate from within civil society, that is, from citizens, and most policies touch civil society, that is, they need to be seen as legitimate enough by enough citizens to be successful.

It is on this topic then; citizenship in a politically pluralized environment, which I want to offer some observations here. In the following section, I briefly discuss the concept of political pluralization and some of the dangers associated with it, one of these being the fragmentation of citizenship. The next section deals with traditional understandings of citizenship plus the most recent innovation in citizenship theory; environmental citizenship. I shall argue that, overall, political pluralization has a quite negative impact on the citizens' political opportunity structure (the latter to be understood in a non-traditional sense): there is little room left for the active citizen. This leads me to discuss the value of citizenship in the broader context of, or as an instance of, political representation: is it worth saving?

Given my conclusion that optimism about the power, or even existence, of the citizen seems misplaced, I turn to a relatively neglected field of study: the *ruler* as citizen. The conclusions drawn earlier on citizenship relate first and foremost to the *subject* as citizen, to the ordinary individual member of society, organized in groups or not. In a politically pluralized world, the ruler as representative of the ruled is in a totally different position. He or she is, on the one hand – relatively – free from control and interference by subjects, on the other cut off from information and support, an important source of legitimacy. I argue that, unrestrained, political pluralization tends to result in a politically realist attitude towards representation (as in Machiavellian *Realpolitik*). Building on the notion of the citizen-ruler's enlightened self-interest, I defend an alternative understanding of representation as consultative elitism, a perspective on representation and citizenship that, unlike realism, offers room for the otherwise under- and non-represented to be heard.

The (from the point of view of liberals, democrats, environmentalists and many others) rather pessimistic picture that I paint of fragmented citizenship in a global environment is based on a worst-case scenario. It deliberately leaves representative institutions and mechanisms out of the picture, for the simple reason that mechanisms ensuring democratic (or other) control of 'new' polities (from regimes and regions to the EU) presuppose a prior commitment to their creation. My argument focuses on the nature of this commitment and hence on the viability of such mechanisms. I also deliberately discount the continued importance of the nation-state both in national and international politics, and thereby the importance of national citizenship. I am not interested here in politics in a 'normal' but in an 'abnormal' context – a context which, by the way, is far more normal in the history of humankind than the brief and grossly overrated rule of the sovereign nation-state.

Political pluralization

A long series of factors contribute to what I call political pluralization (Wissenburg 1999b): the emergence of polities other than and in addition to the state. The process of political pluralization is hypothetical: it is an interpretation of political changes in the role of the nation-state since, roughly, the end of World War II. Economic globalization, for a start, means that some economic actors try and occasionally succeed in escaping the boundaries and borders of states, state laws and state taxes. It is a special case of the actual (as opposed to legal-formal) power of economic actors in politics, a power that may at times outweigh that of the state – once a popular Marxist theme but nonetheless real. Forms of international political co-operation further undermine the theoretically superior position of the state. Covenants and treaties bind states; treaty organizations monitor and occasionally discipline them. Non-elected and presumably unrepresentative non-governmental organizations (NGOs) and international non-governmental organizations (INGOs) lobby and monitor states and treaty organizations alike – giving rise to the idea of an emerging international civil society. State superiority is also called into question by border-crossing co-operation between sub-state regions and by a phenomenon like 'governance without government' (Young 1997).

Amid all this, the evolution of the European Union and its institutions plays a very special role, 'governed' as it is in most cases by a Commission supervised by Councils of Ministers who are in turn (theoretically) controlled by cabinets and who are accountable to parliaments – parliaments that are, finally, controlled every number of years by 'the people'.

Within the state, similar processes can be observed. One is 'denationalization' of the nation state, e.g. in the form of increasing independence of regions – often protected by international treaties. Another is dehierarchization, i.e. a change in the mode of governance of nation-states from direction of, to co-operation with, civil society or other actors, creating national or sub-national systems of 'governance' in which the state often plays the role of an equal partner (or even no role at all). Where this concerns the institutions of the welfare state and other public services, the term 'denationalization' is perhaps equally appropriate.

As a consequence, the nation-state's sovereignty seems to be in the line of fire as well, in a practical sense. What is undermined is the actual power[2] of state governments, not (at least not yet) the formal sovereignty of the state. Sovereignty, in this context, should be read as external independence and, slightly more unusually, as having the internal supreme authority over the distribution of rights in society (a monopoly and freedom to recognize licensed 'subcontractors'). The traditional expression of internal sovereignty as a monopoly on power is justified by, and is the means to, this end (Wissenburg 1999a). Being sovereign, the state by definition reserves for itself the legal authority to regain what it loses or delegates, but in many instances in the real world this may be or become impossible. The price of retreating from, for example, international co-operative structures may be too high, in terms of economic prosperity, reliability or viability, and the resistance from among citizens, civil society, the private initiative and/or minorities – who all stand to lose often dearly-gained freedom – may be too severe. Similar problems will make it difficult for the nation-state to regain its authority within its borders, once it has delegated enough power for long enough. Even though states are perhaps the main political actors and legal preconditions for the existence and operation of others, they no longer are the sole actors in either national or international politics.

The classical polity of the nation-state then, with its firmly controlled borders and (in practice) sovereign ruler, has disappeared – assuming it was not a mirage in the first place – and no one clearly distinguishable 'superpolity' has taken its place. Whether or not the changes in institutions, power relations, participation and policy implementation gathered under the heading of political pluralization are truly new phenomena, or at least new in some areas (environment, emancipation, unemployment policy), and whether or not such phenomena really form a pattern, remains to be seen.

Three remarks are in order here. First, not *all* political change since World War II can or need be interpreted as political pluralization. The riots surrounding World Trade Organisation meetings over the past years for instance signal a less than complete harmony in the relation between states, NGOs and civil society. Second, it is not as if the state has disappeared or lost any of its prominence. As mentioned before, I deliberately discount the continued importance of the nation-state both in national and international politics since what interests me here is not politics in a 'normal' but in an 'abnormal', new context.[3] Finally, one could argue that liberal democracies are built on the recognition of (moral pluralism and, consequently) 'state-free' social spheres (family, economy, religion, education etc.) and thereby on power sharing. The cardinal difference with political pluralization is that the latter implies something even libertarians will distrust: an increasing gap between formal sovereignty and actual power, or in other words, the deterioration of the state's monopoly on the attribution of rights and the use of power.

Political pluralization can have its advantages: with the state losing its position as the *non plus ultra* of political power, an (according to some) old and powerful enemy, instrument or cause of environmental problems will be forced to find and play a more reticent role amid other powerful actors. It can also be a source of efficiency and effectiveness when the newly created institutions are appropriately designed, particularly where complex, border-crossing, sometimes literally global problems of, for example, sustainability and sustainable development are concerned (Wissenburg 1997). Yet the down side is that new institutions, adequate or not, have to operate amidst other, older institutions that all claim their own spheres and responsibilities – particularly the sovereign nation-state. The result may be the co-existence of mutually effacing or contradictory systems of political norms. This problem is sometimes referred to as that of the *incompossibility* of rights: the attribution of rights to physically contradictory or mutually effacing ('existentially overlapping') acts of one or more agents (cf. Wissenburg 1998, 1999a, 2001a; Wissenburg and Levy 2001). In a morally and institutionally plural world, additional institutional arrangements will be insufficient to deal with global environmental problems; diverging normative conceptions of (for instance) sustainability are likely to hamper any environmental policy.

Political pluralization may also bring loss of polity and loss of identification. The emergence of political plurality implies a fragmentation of our reference group, the *polis*. What follows – hypothetically speaking – is first of all something *remotely* similar to a very diffuse market for political actors, 'regimes' rather than states alone, all relatively free to offer their services to customers formerly known as citizens or societies. What also follows is the mirror image of incompossibility: the loyalties of individuals and groups to different political entities may clash. It is on these aspects that we need to focus when discussing citizenship.

Fragmented citizenship

To understand the effects in terms of loss of identification and polity that political pluralization has on citizens, we first need a little background information on what citizenship means, particularly in the context of modern (liberal democratic) societies. Ever since Alfred Marshall (cf. Marshall 1997) it is customary to distinguish between three forms (political, economic and social) and two types of citizenship (liberal and republican). Ever since Dobson (2000), green political theorists have added ecological citizenship to the list of forms – and they will soon add postcosmopolitan citizenship to the types.

The Marshallian citizen

There is a substantial difference between the first three conceptions and the fourth – which is why I shall discuss the classic conceptions first. Marshall's citizens are constitutional citizens, victorious over tyranny: they have rights *vis à vis* a government, rights that define a border between the sphere of politics and a 'private' sphere, whereas government has duties to protect but not interfere with the private sphere. In fact, we can distinguish a number of private spheres, not just one: there is (at least) the sphere of the family where the state cannot go, the sphere of the market where it cannot go, the sphere of social activity where it cannot go and the sphere of public deliberation where it cannot go. The last two, where citizens organize themselves for recreational purposes, to represent their interests against other (groups of) citizens or the state, or simply to voice opinions, are most often grouped under the heading of 'civil society'. Since citizenship is a modern (post-1789) concept, the distinction between state, market, family and civil society or, more briefly, public and private spheres is usually, but absolutely incorrectly, associated with liberalism – these four different spheres are already explicitly present in Aristotle's account of justice and the polis in the *Nicomachean Ethics*, and from there on in virtually every account of the just society – but this aside.

Political pluralization is both good news and bad news for the Marshallian citizen, but the bad news completely outweighs the good news. On the one hand, individuals and (thereby for instance) environmental associations can profit from a *divida et impera* approach to political pluralization. It may become easier to influence distinct political institutions in a fragmented political landscape by playing them off against each other or by threatening their (relatively more sensitive) power basis among a population. In addition, the emergence of forms of 'governance' involving NGOs (market actors, civic associations or both) as more or less equal parties to governments is welcomed, albeit for different reasons under different circumstances, by proponents of deliberative and participatory democracy on the one hand and Third Way advocates on the other. In one form or another, 'governance' is heralded as promoting the exchange of information, communication, deliberation and in the end the legitimacy and effectiveness of policy – all of which can be beneficial to the protection of citizens' rights and the execution of governments' duties towards citizens.

Yet the disadvantages of political pluralization overshadow these promises of power to the people. Let me define the citizen's 'political opportunity structure' as the opportunity to influence agenda setting, deliberation, decision making and policy making. Briefer but more confusing descriptions would be 'power' (as *potentia* not *potestas*) or having a voice (being able to communicate ideas), being heard (having influence) and having a vote (having decision power). From the perspective of the individual citizen, the effects of political pluralization on his or her political opportunity structure are quite negative.

Political pluralization gnaws at the borders between the public and the private and hence at the foundations of Marshallian citizenship rights. Political pluralization brings diffusion of not only powers but also responsibilities – hence, there is a risk that no party can be singled out as accountable to the public, or responsible for or even capable of listening to and answering citizens' demands. Think, for instance, of the loss of co-ordination, power and control that often seems involved in the process of EU-unification. Think, in addition, to the concurrent fragmentation of the citizen's identity: is a citizen living in the EU supposed to identify with the interests of, and claim protection of his citizen rights from, the European community, the national government, the regional (Scottish, Catalan, etc.) government, the Council of Europe, the UN, NATO, IMF or what?

Finally, a point to which I shall return later, *divida et impera* works in two directions: parties involved in a game where no clearly dominant player exists can best reach (or approach) their objectives by creating minimal winning coalitions, coalitions that guarantee on the one hand sufficient power to effectuate the coalition's demands, on the other sufficient stability to keep the coalition together. We know such coalition formation processes, of course, from party politics – but political pluralization extends such games to more and more institutions as well as any field where institutions have to co-operate. In other words: in deliberation and decision making, policies do not necessarily need the support of all institutions involved, institutions do not necessarily need support from all associations involved, and associations do not necessarily need the support of all other associations involved, nor of that of all the citizens they represent in one way or another. In fact – it is rational to economize as much as possible on the representation of citizens, hence to exclude as many as possible.

In yet other words, political pluralization may formally offer opportunities for citizens to raise their voice, be heard and have influence – but no incentives, only disincentives. A more medieval political environment emerges with no clear ultimate wielder of political power and a reduced role for the classic instruments of representative democracy, an environment in which political institutions lose effectiveness but gain a degree of 'obstructive power'. Under conditions of political pluralization, Marshallian citizenship rights are less clearly 'automatically', constitutionally guaranteed – it is the citizens themselves who will need to become more reactive, proactive and at the very least defensive about their rights.

The ecological citizen

In green political thought, topics like deliberative, participatory and direct democracy, environmental awareness, individual responsibility, the green consumer, the role of NGOs and so on are ubiquitous. It is only fairly recently that Andrew Dobson combined these topics under one heading: that of the ecological citizen (Dobson 2000).

Dobson argued for a new conception of citizenship – not in terms of the rights of citizens against the potential tyrant called government, but in more republican terms of committed citizens fulfilling their duties to get actively engaged with the *res publica* and promote the weal of the polity. In essence, Dobson argued for an extension of the polity to include the ecology within which the polity exists.

More recently, Dobson (2002) gave ecological citizenship a totally new context as a type of *post-cosmopolitan citizenship*. Post-cosmopolitan citizenship differs fundamentally from republican citizenship by among other things including the private sphere, by rejecting territoriality as a basis of citizenship, and by regarding the obligations of citizens not as contractual but as 'historical', i.e. determined by the capacity to influence others' existence.

From a Green perspective, Dobson's original (2000) idea of ecological citizenship was refreshing and helpful; in its new post-cosmopolitan context it is even more so. The 'environment' is, after all, a necessary precondition for the existence and flourishing of humans and (in) their polity, one that has been neglected for far too long, roughly since human geography, anthropology and political science divorced – that is, post-Rousseau. Our relations with the environment are, in many ways, not unproblematic – I do not want to cry wolf like so many did in the past, but 'environment' is simply not available in unlimited quantities. Our environment consists of complicated interrelated entities and complex relations – the term ecology better expresses the appreciation of environment as not all that simple to deal with, and not bothered by artificial political borders, than the distant term environment. One does not have to become a political ecologist, let alone a deep ecologist or tree hugger to accept each and every one of these points.

Putting ecological citizenship on the research agenda is commendable for other reasons as well: ecological problems do not get solved without popular support, without virtuous citizens checking their government, stimulating it, and internalizing public values in their own lives. As a new perspective on citizenship, Dobson's post-cosmopolitan and post-republican form of citizenship adds something valuable in itself to both the Marshallian and the republican versions.

Yet there are at least five complications that call into question whether ecological citizenship of either (Dobson 2000 or 2002) type is viable and desirable. For one, arguments for extending the conception of the polity to include necessary preconditions for the flourishing of community and individual can be made on behalf of other preconditions than the ecology as well. (Indeed, this is one of the core ideas of post-cosmopolitan citizenship, one of Dobson's main reasons to 'move beyond' republican ecological citizenship.) If the polity should be extended to include the ecology because the ecology is an essential precondition, then other such conditions *must necessarily* be included as well. Thus, one could argue that a polity cannot flourish without taking into consideration the interests and roles of the now marginalized: women, hermaphrodites, bi- and homosexuals, the physically and mentally handicapped, the genetically challenged, the aged, the non-pink coloured, and so on. The next logical step then is the politically correct citizen. However, there are also politically 'incorrect' preconditions for the flourishing of a polity. There must be a free market – not for moral reasons perhaps, but, legal or illegal, because it is unavoidable; there must be science, there must be production, there must be division of labour, there must be views on whether or not there is an afterlife and who if anyone controls the outcome of horse races. We thus end up with the universally aware citizen – aware to every *res publica* that influences the weal of the world polity. We end up where we began – having added only ecological awareness and awareness to the fact that the ecology is not the only precondition of the good society, that it may have to be offset against, and sometimes sacrificed to, other needs.

This hesitation is linked to the next objection, recently voiced in another context by, among others, Mike Mills and Fraser King (2002): it seems that ecological citizenship, like eco-communitarianism (Mills and King's object of inquiry) presupposes its own conclusion. For there to be an ecologically sound polity (national, global or post-cosmopolitan), there must be ecology-minded citizens. To become ecological citizens, however, and to be aware of that and cherish it, we need a physical and political context in which it makes sense to be an ecological citizen: a context in which it is rewarding, attractive, and most of all appreciated by our equals. And this, I would argue, constitutes a circular argument. One may try to repair it, not by squaring the circle but by reinterpreting it as a spiral, a process – but there is little empirical support for that solution (admittedly, an appeal to empirical support is *always* tricky, either way). The existence of tactical co-operation between anti-globalist NGOs (Dobson 2000: 58) or of the environmental justice movement hardly constitutes proof for the emergence of a global society, nor does it indicate the rise of the kind of consciousness that comes with ecological citizenship. The existence of small protest movements can, quite to the contrary, also be construed as an indication that mainstream politics and the majority of pre-global citizens actually oppose post-cosmopolitan ideas.

Third, there is the question whether the virtues that an eco- (2000) or post-republicanism (2002) like Dobson's would like to install in the minds and hearts of citizens are desirable, and whether it is desirable to prescribe any virtues at all, thus immunizing them against critique.[4] This touches on a classical argument in favour of political pluralism, liberalism being just one practical conception of that concept: the real existence of a plurality of views on the good life (cf. Rawls 1972, 1993). It also raises the question why citizens should do the right thing (if there is such a thing) only for the right reasons (i.e. out of the correct virtue), rather than to leave room for 'deviant' motives – different moralities, religious grounds, self-interest (cf. Wissenburg 2001b). Finally, it touches on the (meta-) ethical problem that there seems to be no way to even theoretically reduce this plurality to one set of mutually compatible prescriptions.

It is not only the meta-ethical status of republicanism, eco or not, that lies under fire, but also its anthropology, sociology and political foundations. We need not repeat all classic critiques of republicanism here in detail – many of them admittedly do not even apply to post-cosmopolitan ecological citizenship. But let me just mention one point. One will not be the active and concerned citizen of the republican polity or the post-cosmopolitan polity if one does not *have* to be one – that is, if it was not a necessary condition for the flourishing of community and (*sic*) individual. Like other Arendtian interpreters of Aristotle, republicans thereby tend to rank political activity as a more worthy, more valuable existence than other occupations – not just other 'creative activities' (cf. Rawls 1993) but also and foremost the work of the common man and woman, toiling to make a living from dawn to dusk. By definition, this makes the lives of all those who run society less worthy: on any conception of the good life other than Arendt's, an unprovoked and unwarranted attack on the dignity of humanity.

Finally, the one thing that is relevant here: post-cosmopolitan and post-republican ecological citizenship do not solve the problems associated with political pluralization. Particularly republican ecological citizenship is more communitarian, in either the provincial or the global sense, than the classic conception of citizenship, hence more tied to a state of political unity that pluralization seems to be doing away with. Second, like classic citizenship, both offer citizens a quite limited and formal political opportunity structure, unlike classic citizenship they offer an incentive to participate – but again like classic citizenship they offer institutions, associations and the elites within them no incentive to bother too much with representing the citizen.

Representation and fuzzy politics

The world of political pluralization is one of multiple political institutions, NGOs, INGOs, quangos, regimes and governance-spewing bodies, operating, interacting and co-operating at multiple levels without clear jurisdiction, unifying authority or structures of accountability and representation. George W. Bush would probably prefer the term 'fuzzy politics' to political pluralization. It would seem – so far – that there is only a nominal place in this world for citizenship. There is, input-wise, room to be represented or actively represent oneself (more for some than for others, obviously), but no clear forum where to represent oneself, nor an incentive to be represented. There is in consequence, output-wise, no guarantee that citizenship can be used effectively to guarantee rights (on the Marshallian account) or (in more republican terms) to make political participation worthwhile for reasons other than the alleged intrinsic value of individual salvation or self-affirmation. Should we then mourn the passing of citizenship – and is it worth mourning? In this section, I shall address the latter question; the former will be saved for the concluding section.

The republican critique of the Marshallian conception of citizenship is absolutely correct in pointing out that there is more to citizenship than assigning rights to individuals and respecting them. Virtually every one of the rights associated with citizenship – particularly the more modern social and economic rights – can be granted to individuals by a benevolent or socialist dictator, yet we still would not call his subjects citizens, just mere subjects. Citizenship, as already indicated above, has to do with concerned citizens, people who voice concerns and want to see them addressed, and with their support for, or at the very least sufferance of, policies. It can be a way of life – several different ways, in fact – but it is always a mode of representation: a specific model for representing one's case and (it) being represented. The essence of citizenship is universal representation: the equal representation of 'all' in 'all' political affairs – both of these 'alls' to be explained in a moment.

Unlike mere subjects, citizens have a say in agenda setting, in public debate, in decision making, and in the execution of decisions. They are, in other words, involved in 'all' political affairs. They can participate (and in the republican view must participate) – but they do not, each, individually, necessarily participate everywhere all of the time. In a mediaeval city-state with citizenship limited to self-employed, independent native men, it is still theoretically possible for 'all' citizens to actively participate in 'all' of politics. The less exclusive membership of the citizenry becomes (the more 'all' becomes all), the more difficult this will be, and the greater the need for representative instruments replacing direct involvement will be. Hence, republican 'active' citizenship is inextricably linked to democracy, but only contingently linked to mass democracy. Even in mass democracies, however, citizenship comes down at its core to universal representation.

Thus, if we wish to know whether citizenship is worth saving or mourning, we need to look at least at this one thing: the role that is left for representation in a post-mass democratic society, in a politically pluralized world.

To get to the core of my argument, I shall make a few bold assumptions on the concept of representation and postpone discussion on several issues that are undeniably important but still less directly relevant to the question at hand. Hanna Pitkin distinguished three conceptions of the concept of representation (Pitkin 1967): symbolic (the flag, the crown), standing for (descriptive representation of sociological categories) and acting for (substantive representation of ideas). I shall ignore symbolic representation here, even though its importance will greatly increase in a politically pluralized world. If descriptive or substantive representation is morally valuable, its value must be:

1   intrinsic, meaning that standing for or acting for are 'absolute' goods;
2   categorical given a context or object (to be represented), that is, desirable against the background of mass democracy, but not, for instance, in a theocracy; or
3   hypothetical (instrumental) given a domain and context: desirable within representative democracy, but not always – only under circumstances, only where it is 'fitting' (cf. Cupit 1996).

I shall assume that the third option applies. Representation 'as such' has a bad reputation – if we may believe Plato (cf. Lock 1990), it is associated with falsification, cheating, insincerity; it is second-hand presence, pretending to be what one is not; it is acting – in the way an actor in a play does, or a child denying guilt after committing a transgression. It is not necessarily good, therefore not a good in itself. Nor is representation categorically valuable (to mass democracy): neither descriptive nor substantive representation is a necessary or sufficient condition for equal and universal access to power, a clear criterion for democracy. Thus, if substantive and descriptive representation through mass democracy are valuable things, they are so only hypothetically, i.e. under the right circumstances – say, when no majority wants anything immoral, and when the will of the majority poses no threat to the survival of the polity.

Finally, I shall assume that the value of descriptive representation is derivative, i.e. that what really matters is the quality of substantive representation. Problems relating to the under- or non-representation of sociological categories like race or sex are real; they make some citizens feel less equal, or even less citizens, than others, and rightly so. Substantive representation (e.g. by healthy white heterosexual Christian brethren) cannot always cure this, as experience teaches. 'Non-descriptive' representatives may for instance be physically unable to identify with the represented, and their existence may still create the impression that the non-represented are denied full membership of the polity. Yet the argument from experience is ultimately an argument in favour of a more adequate representation of ideas and interests; the argument from membership one in favour of the representation of a group's legitimate claim to full membership, i.e. another idea. They are neither arguments directly in favour of standing for, nor directly against 'acting for' – rather, they are arguments based on belief in the principal desirability of 'acting for', pointing to practical obstacles for the adequate or effective representation of ideas. If there are any positive arguments in favour of descriptive representation, they will be of a political-realist nature, arguing for a kind of representation that properly reflects the composition of a polity – though most likely not in terms of any sociological characteristic other than (ultimately) power.[5]

If citizenship is about universal substantive representation, and if the latter is only hypothetically valuable – then under which conditions is it valuable? A first answer takes a Paretian form: if it is at least as good as or better than alternatives; and when there are more criteria, if the advantage on one score outweighs the disadvantage on another. Further criteria can be normative or 'realistic'. The political realist will support substantive representation, and value citizenship, only if it contributes to stability – an argument that supports citizenship for relevant voices and ideas only, i.e. citizenship for the powerful. The powerless are of no consequence; hence their, and universal and equal, access to political decision making are redundant. Textbook descriptions of the 'functions' of democracy, citizenship and representation are in essence equally 'realistic': winning adequate information on the preferences and desires of citizens and on alternative policies, the creation of legitimacy and legitimate authority, opportunities for accountability, etc. are all functions that can be equally well performed by systems other than democracy through means other than representation and citizenship – for again, the powerless are of no consequence and universal and equal access is redundant.

Normative arguments in support of substantive representation and, indirectly, citizenship do not support universal representation or citizenship either. In the Aristotelian-Stoic tradition, the positive argument for universal membership of any group is that like cases should be treated alike – it is artificial inequality that needs to be justified. Alternatively, the anthropocentric philosophical tradition gives a negative (exclusive) argument: there is a relevant and fundamental difference between human beings on the one hand, rocks, trees and animals on the other, a difference that makes humankind superior and turns the non-human world into means to human ends. Ever since John Stuart Mill, we refer to the combination of egalitarianism and anthropocentrism as 'the plan of life', shorthand for self-consciousness, rationality, sense of future, sense of good and bad, sense of pleasure and pain, and other reasons for moral concern, the mix of which would be typical of humans only.

In an enlightening discussion of the plan of life doctrine, Robert Nozick (1974) showed the combination of the two theories to be inconclusive in one important respect: if we humans believe ourselves to be morally superior to the rest of nature due to one or more characteristic – characteristics that, since we share them, make us humans fundamentally equal – then an alien creature could claim moral superiority to us in virtue of a further, as yet unidentified, characteristic. And in fact, this – or arguments very much like it – is precisely what kept philosophers from defending mass democracy until, in the course of the twentieth century, reality had long overtaken them. On one version of the anti-democratic argument, humans may be equal in their capacity for having a plan of life (if we may reinterpret, for example, classic liberalism in such Millian terms), yet they differ in their abilities to realize this potential. Hence women, ruled as they are by dark passions, children, not yet grown to full rationality, and dependants, whose careers and lives are not of their own making, differ sufficiently from independent grown men to justify their exclusion from citizenship. An older version of anti-democracy argues that by nature, humans really differ in politically relevant respects: some are born to rule, others to grow potatoes – in other words, a special natural capacity for politics exists that either cannot be changed from potential into actual in some people, or that simply lacks in them.

Although modern science has shown obstacles to universal political participation like the female dark passions to be contingent if existent at all, and although political reality in Western liberal democracies has invalidated the old discussion, support for universal and equal access to political decision making remains contingent on the absence of convincing arguments for 'relevant' intra-human inequality – and for admissible alternatives to equal and universal access. The least we can argue for, on the basis of the plan of life doctrine, is equality of respect, 'one man, one voice': a universal and equal right to speak for one's interests, and an obligation on the side of the rulers to listen to that voice. To argue for equality in more respects – guaranteed influence, a real vote, an equal number of votes, and all other entitlements and responsibilities that come with citizenship – requires proof that one qualifies; to argue for more universality requires proof of equality.

Given mass democracy and thereby universal citizenship, the plan of life doctrine does however support the idea of substantive representation as such. Since what matters about humans is their capacity for a plan of life, it is the plans of life that need to be represented rather than the individuals themselves. Note however that even here the victory for mass democracy is limited: if it is plans of life that matter, even those of the powerless, then their preferences as such do not matter since they do not necessarily express what is 'really', on reflection and after due consideration, in the best interest of an individual's plan of life.

But mass democracy is not a given – the presumption of this paper is even that it is defunct. A politically pluralized world does not meet conditions under which citizenship can be meaningful or effective. Fuzzy politics can result in loss of community if it is no longer clear who makes and controls rules, and who controls what (state, Brussels, World Trade Organisation, Bill Gates). Loss of community goes hand in hand with loss of identity: to what unit or units do we belong, for which institution and which practices are we, or even can we, feel responsible, with which and whose issues can we be concerned? Finally, the existence of physically incompatible (systems of) rules and jurisdictions (incompossibility) takes away much of citizenship's effectiveness. Even if there can be such a thing as citizenship under these conditions – redefined and redesigned and all – we would need new arguments to defend that it would be valuable. All we have now, with the plan of life doctrine in hand, is an argument for Voice, the universal and equal right to speak for one's interests and the rulers' obligation to listen to that voice – and perhaps an intuition that citizenship is really worthwhile.

It is clear that active citizen-subjects alone cannot save citizenship or even universal substantive representation in a pluralized world – given the obstacles pluralization poses for effective citizenship, that would come down to circular reasoning. But there are other actors who can still serve the ideals of substantive representation and, if not in form then at least in content, citizenship.

Consultative elitism

In this section, I want to suggest not that we develop a new perspective on citizenship under conditions of globalization and fragmentation, but instead that we look at another, in modern times often ignored, aspect of citizenship itself: the ruler as citizen. By ruler I mean anyone who performs an executive role in a political body, that is, in a body creating, assigning and distributing rights over a collective – or more bluntly, a body determining who gets what, when, how and why.

The ruler's responsibilities towards the ruled used to be one of the main topics of debate in political philosophy – as the existence of the *Mirror of Princes* genre testifies. In democratic times, however, it has become unusual to think of politicians, ministers, governors, high-ranking civil servants or administrators of regimes or supranational organizations as 'rulers'. They are considered 'ministers' in the old sense of the word: servants, executioners of the (democratically determined) general will. Any debate on the responsibilities of rulers is usually translated into a debate on different conceptions and degrees of representativeness and responsiveness. It is acknowledged that rulers have other criteria to meet – but with the ruler turned into an employee of the people, this is seen as a matter of professional ethics. In fact, in olden times as much as today, the princes of industry are usually not even thought of as political actors even though they also determine who gets what, when and how. If they are seen as ministers at all, the people they administer are first and foremost the shareholders, although modern business ethics also acknowledges their responsibilities towards stakeholders like workers, environment and society as a whole – a point raised before the rise of capitalism as well (De Pizan 1994).

And yet the ruler still exists. No one in a position carrying political responsibility meets his or her supervisor, the people, more than once every four years or so; most never do but only meet the relatively (quite) independent delegates of the people, or the delegates' delegates. People in power wield their power autonomously most of the time – even more under conditions of pluralization and fragmentation, conditions under which no clear structures of responsibility or control exist.

The ruler is a citizen too, even if in a pluralized world it will often be unclear of what s/he is a citizen. He or she is a very special citizen: one in whom powers have been vested no ordinary citizen has and most will never have. And with power comes responsibility: the citizen as ruler has a much more extensive opportunity structure (see above) than, but is as morally accountable for his or her actions as, any other citizen.

If we care about substantive representation, about representing the plans of life of all – by definition significant – persons, we will need to devise new representative institutions and new systems of representation where there are none today. Among the side constraints for such institutions and systems are:

1   a focus on acting for (substantive representation),
2   the exclusion of no one,
3   recognition of the significance of every individual.

There are also two more controversial conditions. These new arenas of citizens' attention and activity must:

4 not require the existence of state or polity (with incorporated ideas like territory, hierarchy),
5 they must be operational wherever power is exerted.

The question before us is: if citizen-subjects are more or less powerless (as argued above) to save citizenship and its essence, which lies in substantive representation – what then can citizen-rulers do?

Let me begin by discussing a worst-case scenario. In (political) realistic terms, we would *not* expect the rise of new forms of substantive representation, but instead a continuation of classic power politics in the new context of fuzzy politics.

In fact, political fragmentation and pluralization may well increase since it can be used, or even partly caused, by existing elites to liberate themselves from control by and accountability to citizens, and to recycle their resources (organized citizens' interest groups) for future use. As Bernard Crick (2001) argued several decades ago, politics without equal and universal access is not necessarily politics without any form of representation. It is rational for any ruling elite to consult experts, powerful supporters and powerful opponents – they can provide the information needed to ensure the physical and political viability of policies. Moreover, rational rulers will be open to a dialogue with these parties, both in the hope of gaining support and in the knowledge that the dialogue may result in change or even abandonment of the original plan. This consultation model is compatible with (read: not by far necessarily identical with) what John Rawls (1999) calls a decent society: a basically just society that nevertheless lacks equal access to power. With its stress on serious consultation, it is also compatible (but again not necessarily identical) with deliberative democracy, not to mention the Third Way's version of consociationalism, associative democracy. Since in a context of political pluralization it remains rational to gather as much relevant information as possible and to be open to good suggestions, the Crickian consultation model will lose nothing of its relevance. Yet relevant information comes from relevant people only, e.g. the elites of civil society organizations as in associative democracy – the powerless will be inconsequential. Since what we may expect to be the natural course of events, the course of political realism, does not guarantee substantive representation – and that still demands in a way equal and in a way universal access to the ears of the rulers – its result can hardly count as a post-state environment beneficial to citizenship or as an alternative to mass democracy.

A first way to meet this criterion and avoid the exclusiveness of political realism is to formalize processes of consultation and deliberation and extend participation to the powerless, i.e. to translate deliberative democracy to the new context of political pluralization. In practical terms, this model would suggest more direct public control of international organizations (instead of control through representatives of states), more openness in the processes of preparation of, decision making on and implementation of policies, public debates and opportunities for consultation, responsiveness and accountability of global economic and civil actors, dialogues between NGOs and corporations, and so on. Obviously, a development in this direction will keep the classic problems of deliberative democracy theory unsolved; such as how to guarantee public interest and universal participation, how to ensure a quality of deliberative procedures sufficient to transform preferences into considered judgements, how to prevent domination by the rhetorically superior, how to reconcile political consensus as regards wishes, means and goals with viable, effective and efficient policy. In the new context of fuzzy politics, attempts at substantive representation through deliberation will also encounter a new problem: that of co-ordination. Nothing except a highly suspicious faith in an objective good guarantees that a deliberative consensus reached in one policy arena – say, Mediterranean trade – will concur with that reached in another – say, that of European environmental policy.

Unlike the deliberative strategy, the second path to substantive representation, that of consultative elitism, does not try to equate equal and universal access to power with equal and universal distribution of power. Consultative elitism is more economic in terms of formalities and institutional reforms: all it demands is that existing political institutions and those developing as a result of political pluralization extend their consultation processes as much as is needed to include anyone who is potentially excluded. It sees the existence of potentially excluded groups and ideas as a political reality and can use its willingness to represent the actually and potentially powerless as an ethical recommendation. There is also a rational motive behind this *noblesse oblige* attitude, an attitude that is difficult to foster in any time when elites are recruited through meritocracy or nepotism, and not 'raised' to be noble. In other words, consultative elitism is not totally non-self-serving: now that the twentieth century has unleashed the power of mass organization, it has become impossible to get the spirit back into the bottle (cf. Ortega y Gasset 1932). Wilfully neglecting any group can be suicidal: it can induce them to organize (and in the times of the internet, even a small organization can cause a lot of trouble) or drive them into the arms of opponents. The first politician or elite who manages to associate with an excluded but potentially powerful group usually has an advantage (albeit temporarily) over others, but also has to beware of second parties mobilizing other non-represented groups – hence, it usually pays for all rulers to include rather than exclude.

On this model consultation is not the standard operating procedure of political institutions; the initiative for consultation can also lie with the ruled and potentially excluded. This may give consultative elitism an interesting psychological and strategic advantage over the deliberative strategy: in line with Machiavelli's views on opposition, it cherishes and to a degree fosters protest, rather than filtering and perhaps suppressing it by imposing the demands of reasonable and rational debate.

The two models presented here are archetypes, and are as extrapolations of existing strategies (cf. current debates on the democratization of the European Union) inherently imperfect: they sketch options for the twenty-first century, not existing realities or historical necessities. The deliberative democratization strategy promises to save more of the traits we currently associate with citizenship, but requires either powerful citizen-subjects or incentives for citizen-rulers (or both) where neither seem to exist. If ought still implies 'can', then (realistically, not necessarily morally, speaking) consultative realism is the superior strategy. Our moral sympathies may lie with one or the other, but that would be for reasons that go beyond the value we attach to substantive representation and citizenship in a vanishing pre-pluralization context. What matters, in the present context, is that there are viable alternatives to the brave new world of political realism.

Chorus: a conclusion

The argument presented here may at first sight look rather pessimistic. After describing some of the consequences of globalization and other forms of pluralization on political institutions, I concluded that, as far as citizenship and the prospects for sustainability are concerned, the disadvantages of pluralization far outweigh the advantages. A more medieval political environment is emerging, where we find no clear ultimate wielder of political power but a reduced role for the classic instruments of representative democracy, increased ineffectiveness of political institutions and an increase in their 'obstructive power'. There is more room for citizens playing the *divida et impera* game but the institutional surroundings greatly diminish its potential usefulness. Political pluralization jeopardizes the formal bases of Marshallian citizenship rights and greatly diminishes the powers and capacities that republican and post-cosmopolitan citizens may have. In between, I also questioned the republican and post-cosmopolitan concepts of citizenship itself.

I then drew attention to an often-neglected category of citizens whose influence on politics differs from that of the average citizen: the ruler as citizen (which was not to say that the ruler can solve the problems of political pluralization – merely that s/he is a relevant factor. Again, I sketched a dark picture of the future of citizenship. If uninhibited, political pluralization will result in a 'realistic' approach to the representation of ordinary citizens by citizen-rulers, that is, to the exclusion of the powerless and therefore of inconsequential interests – and it is in this corner that we find, among others, the less human-centred and less temporarily limited demands of environmentalism. Of the two alternatives to realism that I discussed, I indicated that institutionalizing new deliberative processes stands a far worse chance of success, and of drawing the realist rulers' interest, than consultative elitism. What chances there are for sustainability on any interpretation wider than that of a global Manhattan (Wissenburg 1998) thus seem to lie in associating with elites and claiming that their enlightened self-interest will be served by the inclusion and representation of allies that are inconsequential now but may one day be mobilized by competitors.[6] It is hardly necessary to point out that the latter alternative still saves very little of the ideals associated with citizenship in the context of mass democracies and sovereign nation-states.

This is admittedly a pessimistic scenario – and that is exactly what a worst-case scenario is meant to be. It is also only part of the picture.

One conclusion that I did not draw is that citizenship is not valuable – merely that it is difficult to defend in a new and politically pluralized context. Nor can we infer that even if citizenship in its present form(s) cannot be saved, that its core cannot survive either: representation, and behind that an idea expressed by George W. Bush 'that no insignificant person was ever born' (Bush 2001). Nor can we infer that citizenship cannot survive. It can. Globalization or political pluralization is not a law of nature, not an unstoppable or unchangeable process – it is merely a hypothesis. If, and in so far as the hypothesis is adequate to reality, we can turn back the clock or stop it and reinforce the sovereign nation-state, or we can turn the clock forward and reinvent the state or move towards some other form of association and controlled concentration of power. In any of these cases, institutions need to be designed that ensure at the very least representation as acting for, the exclusion of no one, and the recognition of the significance of every individual. As I argued above, such institutions are neither logically nor contingently impossible. Moreover, and again in so far as political pluralization is a reality, I argued that in addition to the traditional focus on the ordinary citizen attention ought to be paid to the citizen in the even more traditional role of ruler. Nor, finally, can we infer that consultative elitism as an alternative to uninhibited political realism results in a desirable political landscape – it merely seems to be the best we can do under unfavourable circumstances.

There are two things worse than a worst-case scenario. One is a truly and thoroughly pessimistic scenario offering no alternatives whatsoever. And although idealism itself is a prerequisite of survival, the other is any idealistic scenario that ignores that (some) men are not angels. Prescriptive political theories that do prepare for the worst – their refutation – can never help secure sustainability of any kind, but only the end of civilization as we know it.[7]

Notes

1 The author is very grateful indeed for comments on an earlier version of this text from Marius de Geus, Andy Dobson and Yoram Levy.
2 Power is interpreted here as individual (i.e. an actor's) freedom of action, expressed in terms of the (number of) single acts that an actor is not prevented from by others. For a discussion of this conception of power see (Van Hees and Wissenburg 1999). Weberian characterizations of power, in terms of the constraints put on others, can logically be represented as instances of power as individual freedom of action. The latter concept is broader: it also includes e.g. interactions with an actor's non-human environment, and it does not require consciousness of power.
3 Although some have argued that there is nothing new about political pluralization – it would merely be a return to historical normality or to (in political-institutional terms) new Middle Ages.
4 The obvious riposte here is that one does not want to 'instal' a virtue, e.g. the ecological view, but that it is a question of 'systematically offering it and making it available. Just like mosques should be available without us all having to become Muslims' (Dobson, private communication, 2002). That is nice, but it does not work: whereas mosques are demand-based, the (in this example) ecological view is offered 'systematically' not to serve the needs of the already converted but to convert the infidels – which still does not tell us whether the truth as revealed to those 'systematically offering' it, not to mention its being offered 'systematically', is desirable.
5 Note that descriptive representation is also a lot more difficult to organize, guarantee or control in a politically pluralized world than substantive representation. Theoretically at least, any politician acting as a representative can represent any idea. Given that the fuzzy politics *milieu* leaves less room for a democratic choice of representatives, and given that it is often even unclear which part of the global collection of societies or groups a politician would represent, there is no way to guarantee that the composition of any ruling body mirrors the sociological composition of the group ruled.
6 It must be stressed that this type of inclusion still only offers 'chances' for sustainability. There is no guarantee that as yet unrepresented interests are necessarily environmentally benign (after all, twenty-third century consumers and mining corporations are unrepresented now as well); we would still need additional arguments to motivate the citizen-ruler to rule with an eye to sustainability; and even then the normative interpretation of 'sustainability' itself remains a deeply controversial issue.
7 I always wanted to end a chapter with this phrase.

References

Barry, B. and Goodin, R.E. (eds) (1992) *Free Movement. Ethical Issues in the Transnational Migration of People and of Money*, New York, NY: Harvester Wheatsheaf.
Bush, G.W. (2001) *Inaugural Address* Washington, DC, 20 January 2001. Available online: http://www.whitehouse.gov (accessed 1 April 2001).
Crick, B. (2001) *In Defence of Politics*, 2nd edn, London: Palgrave.
Cupit, G. (1996) *Justice as Fittingness*, Oxford: Clarendon Press.
De Pizan, C. (1994) *The Book of the Body Politic*, Cambridge: Cambridge University Press.
Dobson, A. (1998) *Justice and the Environment*, Oxford: Oxford University Press.

—— (2000) 'Ecological citizenship: a disruptive influence?', in C. Pierson and S. Tormey (eds) *Politics at the Edge: The PSA Yearbook 1999*, London: Macmillan.
—— (2002) *Citizenship and the Environment*, Chapters 1–2, draft manuscript.
King, F. and Mills, M. (2002) 'Eco-communitarianism: the End of Environmentalism?', paper presented at ECPR Joint Sessions of Workshops, Turin, March 2002.
Lock, G. (1990) 'The intellectual and the imitation of the masses' in I. Maclean, A. Montefiori and P. Winch (eds) *The Political Responsibility of Intellectuals*, Cambridge: Cambridge University Press.
Marshall, T.H. (1997) 'Citizenship and social class', in R.E. Goodin and P. Pettit (eds) *Contemporary Political Philosophy: An Anthology*, Oxford, Blackwell.
Nozick, R. (1974) *Anarchy, State, and Utopia*, New York, NY: Basic Books.
Ortega y Gasset, J. (1932) *The Revolt of the Masses*, New York, NY: Norton.
Pitkin, H.F. (1967) *The Concept of Representation*, Berkeley, CA: University of California Press.
Rawls, J.B. (1972) *A Theory of Justice*, Oxford: Oxford University Press.
—— (1993) *Political Liberalism*, New York, NY: Columbia University Press.
—— (1999) *The Law of Peoples*, Cambridge, MA: Harvard University Press.
Van Hees, M. and Wissenburg, M. (1999) 'Freedom and opportunity', *Political Studies* 47: 67–82.
Wissenburg, M. (1997) 'Epistemology, policy and diversity', *Episteme* 1: 123–44.
—— (1998) *Green Liberalism*, London: UCL Press.
—— (1999a) *Imperfection and Impartiality*, London: UCL Press.
—— (1999b) 'Changing shape, changing form: liberal democracy without the classical state', in K. Van Kersbergen, R.H. Lieshout and G. Lock (eds), *Expansion and Fragmentation: Internationalization, Political Change and the Transformation of the Nation State*, Amsterdam: Amsterdam University Press.
—— (2001a) 'Dehierarchization and sustainable development in liberal and non-liberal societies', *Global Environmental Politics* 1: 95–111.
—— (2001b) 'Liberalism is always greener on the other side of Mill', *Environmental Politics* 10: 23–42.
Wissenburg, M. and Levy, Y. (2001) 'Sustainable development as a policy telos: global environmental problem solving using the magic word', paper presented at ECPR Joint Sessions of Workshops, Grenoble, March 2001.
Young, O.R. (ed.) (1997) *Global Governance*, Cambridge, MA: MIT Press.

6 Sustainability through democratization?

The Aarhus Convention and the future of environmental decision making in Europe

Derek R. Bell

> Although regional in scope, the significance of the Aarhus Convention is global. It is by far the most impressive elaboration of principle 10 of the Rio Declaration, which stresses the need for citizens' participation in environmental issues and for access to information on the environment held by public authorities. As such it is the most ambitious venture in the area of 'environmental democracy' so far undertaken under the auspices of the United Nations.
>
> (Kofi Annan)[1]

The United Nations Economic Commission for Europe (UNECE)[2] *Convention on Access to Information, Public Participation in Decision-Making and Access to Justice in Environmental Matters* (otherwise known as the 'Aarhus Convention') has been hailed as 'a significant shift towards an environmentally responsible society... Europe has again confirmed the values of democracy and human rights and gives hope of sustainable development for the whole world'.[3] The Aarhus Convention was signed at the Fourth 'Environment for Europe' Ministerial Conference in Aarhus, Denmark on 25 June 1998.[4] The preamble of the Aarhus Convention makes an explicit commitment to 'sustainable and environmentally sound development' as well as 'recognizing... that every person has the right to live in an environment adequate to his or her health and well-being'. However, the Convention does not set substantive environmental standards. Instead, it adopts three procedural principles, namely, public access to environmental information, public participation in environmental decision making and public access to the courts to enforce access to information and participation in decision making.

The European Community and many of its existing members are among the 40 signatories of the Aarhus Convention. In addition, many of the future members of an enlarged European Community have already ratified the Convention.[5] The Aarhus Convention is already influencing environmental legislation in the EC and throughout Europe.[6] It seems likely that its influence will increase and its principles will constitute an important element of future environmental decision-making processes in Europe. Therefore, it is timely to consider the merits and defects of the 'Aarhus approach' to sustainability.

The aim of this chapter is not to consider all of the detailed provisions of the Convention but rather to take a broader look at the Aarhus version of the traditional 'green' ideal of 'sustainability through democratization'.[7] This chapter has two objectives. First, to analyse critically the elements of the Aarhus version of this ideal. What are the Aarhus conceptions of 'sustainability', 'democracy' and the connections between them? Second, to re-assess and develop the Aarhus version of 'sustainability through democratization' as an ideal for the future of environmental decision making in Europe and beyond.

Aarhus sustainability

We have already seen that the Aarhus Convention is intended to secure certain procedural or democratic rights. However, these procedural rights are not conceived as intrinsically valuable but rather as essential means to the production of substantive environmental outcomes. Specifically, Article 1 of the Convention makes it clear that the procedural rights are intended 'to contribute to the protection of the right of every person of present and future generations to live in an environment adequate to his or her health and well-being'.[8] In other words, the Convention is 'recognizing' a *human* right 'to live in an environment adequate to [one's] health and well-being' (Preamble, paragraph 7). It is this human right that constitutes the core of the Aarhus conception of 'sustainability'.

Any conception of 'sustainability' must provide answers to a number of questions, such as, 'What should be sustained?', 'Why should it be sustained?' and 'How should it be sustained?'.[9] The Aarhus Convention suggests that what should be sustained is an environment adequate to the health and well-being of every person of present and future generations. It should be sustained for the sake of the health and well-being of every person of present and future generations and it should be sustained by 'protect[ing], preserv[ing] and improv[ing] the state of the environment' (Preamble, paragraph 5). There are a number of interesting, controversial and problematic features of this conception.

First, the Aarhus answer to, 'Why sustainability?' is explicitly anthropocentric.[10] The aim is not to sustain an environment adequate to the health and well-being of every 'living creature' of present and future generations. More generally, there is no suggestion that we should protect the environment for the sake of other animals or for its own sake. Insofar as animals contribute to human health or well-being, we may have reason to protect their habitats. Insofar as other living and non-living entities contribute to human health or well-being, we may have reason to protect them. If something does not (and will not) contribute to human health and well-being, we have no reason to protect it. Of course, if we assume that human health and well-being are dependent on protecting the integrity of every constituent part of the global ecosystem (or, at least, every part covered by our particular non-anthropocentric conception of sustainability), there will be no practical difference between anthropocentric and non-anthropocentric sustainability.[11] However, there is no obvious reason to believe that the drafters of the Aarhus Convention would make that assumption.

Second, the Aarhus conception of what should be sustained suggests a 'negative' or 'satisficing' conception of sustainability.[12] The requirement is 'an environment *adequate*' to 'health and well-being'. It is only if an environment is *not* adequate to health and well-being that it is unacceptable. There may be many different 'states of the environment' that meet the minimum standard of being adequate to health and well-being and any of them would be satisfactory. The range of adequate 'states of the environment' will depend on how we define 'health and well-being' and the number of people who have (and will have) the right to an environment adequate to health and well-being. The more environmentally demanding the conceptions of health and well-being and the larger present and future populations of the earth, the narrower the range of adequate 'states of the environment'.

Third, the key concepts of 'health' and 'well-being' are vague and contestable. How are they related to the core concepts of the Brundtland conception of sustainable development, namely, the '*basic needs* of all' and 'the opportunity to satisfy ... *aspirations for a better life*' (WCED 1987: 44 – emphasis added)? How should we understand 'health' and 'well-being'? The 'state of the environment' is obviously inadequate when 'hundreds of thousands of people' die from air-pollution related illnesses every year in South-East Asia but would it be inadequate if there were a few days of the year when people with asthma found their symptoms aggravated by high pollution levels?[13] Or, would it be inadequate if 'wilderness' areas and 'natural landscapes' were replaced with theme parks and man-made townscapes? In particular, it is unclear what 'states of the environment' might be necessary for 'well-being'. Is there an objective or universal ideal of the 'good life' or of the components of well-being that should be considered appropriate for every person or do the components of well-being vary across cultures, places, times and even individual persons? For example, is the experience of 'wilderness' or 'natural landscapes' a necessary (or contingent) component of well-being for all (or some) persons?

Fourth, the Aarhus conception of how the environment should be sustained is unclear. The preamble refers to 'the need to *protect, preserve* and *improve* the state of the environment' (Preamble, paragraph 5). 'Protect' and 'preserve' both imply that environmental damage or degradation should be prevented while 'improve' seems to suggest that damage that has already been done should be repaired and the environment restored or renewed. The emphasis on 'protection' and 'renewal' rather than the 'substitution' of man-made for natural resources suggests that 'substitution' is not an option.[14] This might seem to imply that the Aarhus Convention is using a radically 'green' version of sustainability. However, the Aarhus 'definition' of 'the environment' suggests another explanation, namely, 'the environment' is narrowly defined to include only those 'elements' that cannot be substituted: '[Such] as air and atmosphere, water, soil, land, landscape and natural sites, biological diversity and its components ... and the interactions among these elements' (Article 2 (3a)).[15] We might interpret this as the Aarhus list of 'critical natural capital'.[16] If so, we may wonder whether it is intended to be a complete list (and other natural resources are substitutable) or a partial list. Might the shortness of the list reflect the unwillingness of the capitalist system to consider other natural resources as public goods rather than private property?

In summary, the ambiguities inherent in the Aarhus conception of sustainability raise a number of important questions that need to be answered by anyone trying to decide what it is they are aiming at when they try to promote 'Aarhus sustainability'. Moreover, Aarhus sustainability as an ideal does not tell us what to do when we live in a world that does not even begin to approximate to the ideal. In today's world, millions of people do not live in an environment adequate to health and well-being (on any plausible conception of this ideal). If we cannot solve all of their problems simultaneously (and ensure the same right for future generations), which elements of health and well-being should be prioritized? How should providing an environment adequate for health and well-being be ranked against providing non-environmental (e.g. economic, political, social) conditions necessary for health and well-being? If our ultimate concern is for the health and well-being of present and future generations, non-ideal theory must address the relative contributions of such things as economic growth, technological progress, social and political forms and environmental conditions to the various elements of health and well-being of present and future generations.[17] In short, non-ideal decisions based on 'Aarhus sustainability' may be even more contestable than ideal interpretations of 'Aarhus sustainability'.

Aarhus democracy

The Aarhus Convention prescribes three rights: 'the rights of access to information, public participation in decision-making, and access to justice in environmental matters' (Article 1). These three rights enable citizens to participate directly in environmental decision making. They introduce an element of participatory democracy to the environmental decision-making process. However, the aim of the Aarhus convention is not to replace but rather to supplement representative democracy. The Aarhus ideal is not the traditional 'green' vision of autonomous local communities making collective decisions in a non-discriminatory version of the Athenian assembly. Indeed, the Aarhus notion of democracy is hardly any closer to the traditional 'green' position than the Aarhus conception of 'sustainability' is to the 'green' ideal of small, self-sufficient agrarian communities.[18]

The primacy of representative institutions and the constrained role of public participation are evident throughout the Convention. The participation process is convened and managed by the appropriate public authorities. The 'public' is not given the right to initiate a participation process, organize its format or set its timetable.[19] The institutions of representative democracy are the authoritative decision makers. They must follow the consultation procedure and they must 'ensure that in [their] decision due account is taken of the outcome of the public participation' (Article 6 (8)). However, they are not bound to accept or act on the comments of any of the participants: 'In general, it can be said that taking account of the outcome of public participation ... does not require the relevant authority to *accept* the substance of all comments received and to change the decision according to every comment' (Stec *et al.* 2000: 109). The public authorities should treat comments from the public as 'information' to be added to the information that they have from other sources (Stec *et al.* 2000: 109). Their decision should be based on all of the information available to them and they should explain how that decision is supported 'all things considered' by the information.

The Aarhus Convention prescribes participation 'in decisions on specific activities' (Article 6), 'concerning plans, programmes and policies relating to the environment' (Article 7) and 'during the preparation of executive regulations and/or generally applicable legally binding normative instruments' (Article 8). However, its emphasis is firmly on specific local decisions rather than strategic regional, national or international decisions. Article 6 sets out detailed provisions for public participation in decisions on a long list of specific activities specified in Annex 1 and other 'proposed activities ... which may have a significant effect on the environment' (Article 6 (1b)). The emphasis here is not only specific and local but also 'reactive' and 'defensive'. The public has the opportunity to react to and defend themselves against proposals for activities with significant environmental impacts. Articles 7 and 8 are much less detailed and set less demanding standards for the participation process. For example, Article 7 does not require that 'the reasons and considerations' supporting a plan or programme are published (compare Article 6 (9)). Similarly, no specific mechanisms for participation concerning plans and programmes are mentioned (compare Article 6 (7)) and no detailed 'provision of information' requirements are set out for plans and programmes (compare Article 6 (6)).

Moreover, the strength of the participatory requirements diminishes further as we move from plans and programmes (which are often regional) to policies and executive regulations (which are often national). Article 7 devotes only one sentence to policies: 'To the extent appropriate, each Party shall endeavour to provide opportunities for public participation in the preparation of policies relating to the environment'. The institutions of representative democracy are required to consult only 'to the extent appropriate' and have no obligation to take 'due account' of any public comments. Similarly, Article 8 requires only that 'the result of the public participation shall be taken into account *as far as possible*' in the preparation of executive regulations and legally binding normative instruments (emphasis added). Policies, executive regulations and laws provide the context in which plans, programmes and decisions about specific activities are made. The greater 'freedom' allowed to the institutions of representative democracy with respect to policies, executive regulations and laws[20] confirms that the 'democratization' envisaged by Aarhus is not a radical 'attack' on representative democracy. At most, it is an attempt to tackle the democratic deficit in local politics with respect to concrete environmental matters and a small step toward 'opening up' the elite dominated policy-making processes.

It is important to emphasize that the procedural rights prescribed by the Aarhus Convention are not trivial.[21] They offer a genuine opportunity for real participation. The 'access to information' (Articles 4 and 5) and 'access to justice' (Article 9) rights guaranteed by the Convention help to make the consultation process more than *pro forma*. Article 4 requires the provision of environmental information on request. It offers a broad definition of 'environmental information', sets time limits for dealing with requests for information and qualifies a standard list of excuses for not providing information with a 'public interest' test. Article 5 requires public authorities to be proactive in the 'collection and dissemination of environmental information'. It stresses the importance of both ensuring that 'there is an adequate flow of information to public authorities' (Article 5 (1b)) and of making that information 'effectively accessible' to the public (Article 5 (2)).[22] Article 9 provides for access to 'a review procedure before a court of law and/or another independent and impartial body' when a member of the public considers that rights guaranteed under articles 4 (requests for information) or 6 (participation in decisions on specific activities) have been violated. The rights to information and justice guaranteed by articles 4, 5 and 9 provide a basis for informed, effective participation that can be enforced.

We should note four additional features of the Aarhus conception of democracy. First, the commitment to informed participation is supported by the provision that 'Each Party shall promote environmental education and environmental awareness among the public' (Article 3 (3)). Second, the Convention recognizes that national borders do not constitute impermeable environmental barriers by insisting that the prescribed rights apply to all persons 'without discrimination as to citizenship, nationality or domicile' (Article 3 (9)). This is a particularly interesting provision because it challenges the conventional idea that the demos is made up of citizens of a single state. Of course, the demos of the representative democracy that frames the participatory opportunities provided by Aarhus is still made up of the citizens of a single state. The novelty (and the tension?) comes with the recognition that if environmental decisions have transboundary (and even global) effects, the people affected should have the right to participate in those decisions.[23]

Third, the international dimension of environmental decision making is also recognized in the commitment to 'promote the application of the principles of this Convention in international environmental decision-making processes and within the framework of international organizations in matters relating to the environment' (Article 3 (7)). This provision requires Aarhus parties to begin to tackle the democratic deficit associated with the negotiation of international treaties and, especially, the operations of international institutions, such as the World Bank, the World Trade Organization and the European Bank for Reconstruction and Development, which are 'infamous' for their secrecy and their remoteness from the public.[24]

Fourth, the Aarhus Convention emphasizes the role of Non-Governmental Organizations (NGOs) as participants in environmental decision making.[25] In addition to having the same rights to information, participation and justice as any other 'legal' or 'natural' person (Article 3 (9)), NGOs 'promoting environmental protection' are given special consideration (Article 2 (5)).[26] They should always be counted among the 'public concerned' (Article 2 (5)) for the purposes of Article 6 and should, therefore, be informed of new proposals for specific activities. They should also be deemed to have 'sufficient interest' under Article 9 'to challenge the substantive and procedural legality of any decision... subject to the provisions of article 6' (Article 9 (2)). The attribution of special status to NGOs appears consistent with a concern that ordinary citizens may often be ill equipped to participate effectively. Ordinary citizens might not have the time, money, knowledge or inclination to become informed and effective participants committed to enforcing their rights. NGOs can represent citizens' interests in the decision-making process and are more likely to have the resources to participate (or even 'compete') effectively in a process that will also include powerful stakeholders, such as businesses, local government and other executive agencies. Insofar as the Aarhus Convention makes environmental governance a competitive struggle among stakeholders, the special status of NGOs may help to address the inequalities of power among the competing interests. However, many NGOs may not represent citizens' understandings of their own interests. In this sense, NGO participation may be more about influencing than representing the views of ordinary citizens.

In this section, I have highlighted some of the key features of the Aarhus conception of democracy. It is fundamentally a representative democracy with elements of participation designed to overcome some of

Sustainability through democratization? 101

the problems of democratic deficit. The Aarhus conception of democracy offers more than *pro forma* participation by adding information and enforcement rights to participation rights. Finally, Aarhus democracy is notable for its international dimensions and the role it gives to NGOs.

Aarhus on the connection between democracy and sustainability

So far, we have looked at the Aarhus conceptions of sustainability and democracy. In this section, I consider the Aarhus conception of the connection between democracy and sustainability. How do rights to information, participation and justice help to promote a world in which the human right to an environment adequate to health and well-being is never violated? Unsurprisingly, the Aarhus Convention as an international treaty does not offer a detailed explanation of the connection between democracy and sustainability. However, there are two paragraphs in the Convention preamble that address this issue and those paragraphs are further elaborated in the 'Implementation Guide' for the Convention.

Paragraph 8 of the preamble expresses what we might call the 'protective' role of democracy:

> *Considering* that, to be able to assert this right ['to live in an environment adequate to his or her well-being'] and observe this duty ['both individually and in association with others, to protect and improve the environment for the benefit of present and future generations'], citizens must have access to information, be entitled to participate in decision-making and have access to justice in environmental matters.[27]

The procedural rights enable a citizen to 'protect' his or her own substantive right to live in an environment adequate to his or her health and well-being ('self-protection'). They also enable citizens (individually and in associations) to 'protect' the human right of any present or future person(s) to live in an environment adequate to health and well-being ('other-protection').

There is no doubt that the right to participate in decision making gives people opportunities to protect their own and others' interests that they would not have if they did not have that right. However, the nature of the connection between self- and other-protection and sustainability needs clarification. First, a person will use democratic procedures to protect his or her own interest in an environment adequate to his or her health and well-being only insofar as that interest outweighs other relevant interests, including his or her interest in doing something other than participating.[28] Empirical studies of public attitudes to 'the environment' suggest that for many people environmental concerns are outweighed or 'balanced' by economic concerns.[29] For example, people may not oppose a 'polluting' factory that might compromise their right to health and well-being but would also provide jobs for the local community.

Second, differences in participation rates and resource inequalities among social groups are likely to lead to unequal protection of the right to live in an environment adequate to health and well-being. Some social groups (notably, low income and racial minorities) are likely to suffer worse environmental conditions than other groups because they do not make such effective use of their rights to participate.[30] Poorer communities may not have the 'economic freedom' to oppose the location of polluting facilities in their area.[31] They are less likely to engage in any form of 'political' participation or to possess the confidence, skills, knowledge and financial resources necessary to participate effectively.[32] Aarhus procedural rights might help rich and poor to protect their right to live in an environment adequate to health and well-being but they may help the rich (who already live in a better environment) more than they help the poor.

Third, an individual will use democratic procedures to protect others' interests in an environment adequate to health and well-being only insofar as the individual's concern for the others' interests and, in particular, their interest in an environment adequate to health and well-being, outweighs other relevant interests of that individual, including the interest in doing something other than participating. Humans are not purely self-interested creatures but we are not good at persistently pursuing the interests of anonymous and/or remote others. Most people are unlikely to be sufficiently concerned about the interests of future generations and people in distant places to attempt to protect their interests through participation in environmental decision making.[33] Prima facie, the degree of protection that non-participants will gain from participants is likely to be (roughly) inversely proportional to the 'distance' – in space, time, culture and religion (among other things) – between them. In short, democratic rights may facilitate self-protection and other-protection but they will only promote sustainability insofar as people are willing and able to use them for their intended purpose.

Paragraph 9 of the Convention preamble offers several other reasons for believing that more democracy will promote sustainability: '*Recognizing* that, in the field of the environment, improved access to information and public participation in decision-making enhance the quality and the implementation of decisions [and] contribute to public awareness of environmental issues'. The assumption of paragraph 8 was that the public needs participation rights to protect itself from the institutions of representative democracy. The assumption of paragraph 9 is that the institutions of representative democracy need public participation to achieve better outcomes.[34] The principal benefits of participation are that it can improve the 'quality' of decisions and the 'implementation' of decisions. In addition, participation has an 'educative' effect that will have a positive recursive impact through future participation on the 'quality' and 'implementation' of decisions.

Sustainability through democratization? 103

The Convention does not explain how public participation will improve either the 'quality' or the 'implementation' of decisions but the 'Implementation Guide' makes some suggestions. On the 'quality' of decisions it says:

> The quality of decisions can be improved by the public's provision of additional information, as well as through the influence that advocacy of alternative solutions can have on the careful consideration of possible solutions. Members of the public will often have a special knowledge of local conditions and of the practical implications of proposed activities.
>
> (Stec *et al.* 2000: 18).

The role of the public is to provide 'additional information' (probably, based on local knowledge) and to advocate 'alternative solutions'. More information and a clear account of the (claimed) advantages of different options should provide a better evidence base from which the relevant public authority can make its decision.

This seems a relatively limited conception of the role of the public. It is not part of their role to address the question, 'What should we sustain?' Instead, their role is to provide information and ideas that will help the relevant public authorities to assess the environmental effects of the activities, plans, programmes or policies under consideration. The role of public participation is to contribute to the 'technical' assessment of the alternatives so that the public authorities can accurately determine which of the alternatives is the best 'means' to the pre-defined 'end'. On this account, the only (relevant) disagreements among the public or between the public and the public authorities are factual or empirical disagreements. The participation process is not a place for normative discourse: it is not a place to which participants bring their values for deliberation in the hope of achieving consensus or even compromise.

The idea that the public has a contribution to make to the 'technical' assessment of the environmental impacts of alternatives takes seriously the criticisms that have been made of the 'technocratic' approach to environmental decision making.[35] It is simply not true that the 'experts' know everything and the public knows (more or less) nothing. However, the idea that public participation should 'enhance the quality' of decisions but not set the criteria for a 'good' decision retains the 'technocratic' model's exclusive focus on 'techniques' and information at the expense of norms and values. Moreover, unless we assume that there is already consensus on values, the putative benefits of public participation for the 'implementation' of decisions may be undermined.

The 'Implementation Guide' to the Convention explains that:

> The implementation of decisions can be improved where the members of the public most interested in the result have been

included in the process and have had their concerns considered. In such cases they can be expected to support the decision more strongly.

(Stec *et al.* 2000: 18)

If people participate in the decision-making process, they are more likely to conceive of the outcome of that process as 'legitimate' even if they disagree with it. However, the 'degree' to which people conceive of the outcome as 'legitimate' is likely to depend on their perception of the fairness and appropriateness of the decision-making process. For example, if they believe that their experiential knowledge of local conditions has not been taken seriously or that their normative beliefs about the relative importance of different 'health' or 'well-being' issues are considered irrelevant, they may consider neither the decision-making process nor its outcome as legitimate. Participation will only increase support for decisions if participation is meaningful. Taking 'due account' of information and ideas goes some way to making participation meaningful but a process that takes 'due account' of competing ideals and conceptions of what should be sustained and of the relative importance of different environmental (and 'non-environmental') goods may also be necessary.

In this section, I have drawn on the limited discussion in the Aarhus Convention (and the 'Implementation Guide') of the connection between democracy and sustainability. I have argued that the Convention suggests two connections: democratic rights help the public to protect itself from 'unsustainable' policies and activities; and democratic rights facilitate public participation, which makes outcomes more sustainable by improving the evidence-base for decisions and increasing the perceived legitimacy of decisions. I have raised some doubts about these connections but my intention has not been to suggest that these are not genuine connections between 'Aarhus democracy' and 'Aarhus sustainability'. Indeed, I would claim that 'Aarhus democracy' will make *some* contribution through these connections (and others[36]) to 'Aarhus sustainability'. However, the Aarhus ideal of 'sustainability through democratization' is incomplete and might be improved in a number of ways.

Reconsidering the ideal of sustainability through democratization

'Aarhus democracy' is the future of environmental decision making in Europe. However, 'Aarhus democracy' is not constrained to work only through the 'Aarhus connections' or to produce only 'Aarhus sustainability'. There are no real constraints on the kinds of considerations that might be introduced by participants in the environmental decision-making process. The participation process can become the place for normative deliberation that addresses the question, 'What should be sustained?' alongside 'technical' deliberation about how it can be sustained.

Ordinary citizens, NGOs and other participants come to the decision-making process with very different priorities. They value different things and even when they value the same things, they rank them differently. They have different conceptions of 'health' and 'well-being'. In short, the participation process has to deal with 'the fact of reasonable pluralism': in liberal societies reasonable people disagree about 'ideals' or values.[37] If the public authorities that 'manage' the participation process do not allow the explicit discussion of these competing ideals, they undermine the perceived legitimacy of the process, foster misunderstandings and obfuscate empirical evidence by not revealing its 'ideological' context.[38]

The recognition of normative disagreement raises the question of how to take 'due account' of different (and competing) ideals of what should be sustained. The standard liberal answer is that the state should be 'neutral' among 'reasonable' ideals or 'doctrines' – it should not seek to promote some doctrines or undermine others. In the context of public participation in environmental decision making this would seem to require that public authorities do not make decisions based on their own ideals. It is not just that individual officers should not allow their personal ideals to determine or influence their decisions but also that there should not be an 'official' ideal that determines or influences their decisions. The only plausible way of achieving that kind of neutrality is for participation to go beyond consultation to become genuine participatory democracy where the decision is made by the participants rather than the public authority (or, more accurately, public institution).

Of course, to be neutral the rules for inclusion in the process, the framework for the participants' deliberations and the procedure for making a decision when consensus cannot be achieved should meet appropriate standards of fairness. Would self-selection supported by targeted invitation be fair or do we need to ensure that the participants are statistically representative of all the stakeholders? What is a fair format for deliberation?[39] If voting is to be used, who votes, and should votes be weighted to reflect different 'stakes' in the decision? There are no straightforward answers to these questions (or the many others), but the possibility of 'participant control' rather than 'representative control and participant consultation' should be part of the post-Aarhus agenda. Indeed, the issue should not be whether the public should ever have direct control over environmental decisions but how, when and within what limits they should have direct control over environmental decisions.

If the idea of democracy is that the people make decisions for themselves, the complete reliance on representative democracy is unjustified in modern societies where the connection between voting at elections and the decisions of appointed officials are so tenuous and the democratic deficit is so great. However, unless we want to reject the whole idea of voting for representatives and replace it with something different (but, in some sense, representative), such as Burnheim's idea of 'demarchy', the complexity and scale of modern societies and environmental issues makes representative democracy indispensable.[40] The question that we need to address is, 'How do we balance indirect control through representative democracy and direct control through participatory democracy in environmental decision making?'

We have seen that the Aarhus Convention emphasizes participation in local decisions on specific activities while paying less attention to participation in strategic regional, national and international decisions. Insofar as we accept the Aarhus conception of participation as consultation, this emphasis is misguided. However, if participation involves direct control (or some degree of direct control), the emphasis on local decision making seems more appropriate (although, not necessarily the emphasis on 'defensive' responses to specific activities). Generally, national decisions are likely to affect more people than local decisions and assessment of their consequences is likely to be more difficult for many people. If we hand over control of national decisions to people who are not elected as representatives by the whole people, we must either be prepared to make the numbers involved unwieldy or we must be prepared to leave most people with no control (direct or indirect) over those decisions.

In principle, the same problem arises with local decisions but it is less significant because the numbers are smaller. If the decision affects fewer people, it is more likely that people who want to participate can be accommodated and it is more likely that those who do not participate can exercise some indirect influence over the decision through informal contacts with participants. Moreover, people may be more likely to participate (directly or indirectly) in local decisions because the effects of decisions have a more immediately visible impact on their local environment and they have a clearer understanding of the issues through previous experience and local knowledge.[41]

The most appropriate model of public participation in environmental decision making should seek to give some direct *control* to the public on local matters while ensuring that public *consultation* is an essential feature of all environmental decision making. Control and consultation both reflect the ideal of democracy and may both promote sustainability under the right conditions. They are both essential elements of a post-Aarhus conception of the ideal of 'sustainability through democratization'.

Participation as control reflects a fundamental commitment to democracy and the related ideal of liberal neutrality. It offers people the opportunity to make decisions about their own environment. Formally, direct control might be established by making the outcome of an appropriately constituted participation process legally binding, by requiring that there be a presumption in favour of the outcome chosen by participants, or by allowing the public to directly veto some options. However, direct control cannot be without limit even in local matters because environmental issues cannot be completely separated from other issues and local issues cannot be completely separated from national issues. Instead, direct control must operate within limits set indirectly by the whole demos through representative institutions. In this way, it is the responsibility of the society as a whole to decide how much autonomy should be given to smaller communities with respect to any particular issue. Similarly, it is the responsibility of the society as a whole to decide what is a fair distribution of environmental (and other) benefits and burdens among communities. For example, it is up to the society as a whole to decide when or if a community should have the right to veto a chemical factory that would contribute to national economic goals or a windfarm that would contribute to national (and international) goals for the reduction of carbon dioxide emissions.

Of course, participation as control may not produce 'sustainable' results insofar as participants' decisions are guided by an ideal of the good life that cannot be sustained over time. However, participation as control may help to promote decisions that show more awareness of (at least) local environmental 'limits'. Direct control may bring with it a feeling of empowerment such that individuals develop a sense of personal control and responsibility for the community and the environment.[42] Moreover, if people conceive of themselves as belonging to a community, they identify with a temporally extended 'entity' that will exist after they have died.[43] The environmental benefits of this kind of extended conception of the self and increased sense of responsibility are likely to be felt beyond the decision-making process in an increased sense of legitimacy and community 'ownership' of decisions. The Aarhus hope of 'enhanced implementation' is likely to be realized and the increased sense of responsibility might even have the more general effect of promoting 'green consumerism'.

The concern for the local environment and its sustainability that might be fostered by participation as control is less likely to extend to 'global limits' or the very long term. A sense of community does not necessarily bring with it a more general concern about the 'ecological footprint' made by that community in other areas of that nation, in other areas of the world or in the distant future.[44] Participation as direct local control might through 'green communitarianism' promote short-term sustainability of a shared (or negotiated) ideal of the local environment. A more ambitious ideal of sustainability (such as the Aarhus conception) may also need to draw on the environmental benefits of participation as consultation in the development of programmes, policies, executive regulations and laws by the institutions of representative democracy.

The Aarhus Convention is right to point to the benefits of additional information and advocacy of options that consultation brings to the decision-making process. However, it may be the discussion of values and the opportunity to encounter and reflect on other ideals that is most important. The real value of participation as consultation in the context of representative democracy may lie in the promotion of a 'deliberative democracy' in which ethical issues are reflectively discussed in the public sphere. If it is *right* to promote sustainability (or, more accurately, some specific conception of sustainability), ethical reflection should make that apparent.[45]

If voters, representatives and appointees all live in a society where ethical reflection is facilitated in formal consultative forums, encouraged in civil society and taught in schools, there is a real chance that their decisions will reflect their ethical beliefs. Many people may still find it difficult to be concerned about future generations or remote strangers on a day-to-day basis in all of their consumption decisions but they may find it less difficult to vote for a representative who is committed to a sustainable ideal and the policies it implies. It is often more difficult psychologically to make a voluntary sacrifice than it is to accept sacrifices when they are required of us and there is a guarantee that others will make them too.[46] Moreover, if we only have to reaffirm our commitment to those sacrifices infrequently and under special circumstances that encourage reaffirmation, democratic support for sustainability might be maintained.

Of course, the 'educative' effect of participation as consultation and deliberative democracy will only influence societies in the long term. Moreover, it will only have a significant effect if it becomes 'normal' for people to participate in forums such as citizens' juries. The Aarhus conception of participation is that the public and NGOs provide information, defend their own interests and advocate their own solutions. On the proposed conception of participation as consultation, the role of NGOs is unchanged except that they are conceived as defending particular normative ideals, which may or may not represent public opinion. However, the essence of participation as consultation for ordinary citizens is rather different. Their primary role is to reflect on the information, interests, solutions and values involved so that they can contribute to ethical deliberation about the available options. The proposed conception of participation as consultation aims to 'enhance' the *ethical* quality as well as the technical quality of environmental decisions.

To summarize, the first three sections of this chapter have offered a critical analysis of the Aarhus conception of 'sustainability through democratization'. I have highlighted major features of the constituent parts of that conception and offered some comments on particular features. My conclusion was that 'Aarhus democracy' will make *some* contribution through the 'Aarhus connections' to 'Aarhus sustainability'. In this section, I have considered how we might go beyond Aarhus to a conception of democracy that can make a more significant contribution to the promotion of sustainability in Europe and beyond. I began by claiming that the Aarhus conception of 'sustainability through democratization' does not pay sufficient attention to values. I have argued that if we take seriously the 'fact of reasonable pluralism' and the Aarhus commitment to taking 'due account' of public views, we should adopt a more radical model of participation. I have suggested that we distinguish 'participation as control' from 'participation as consultation'. The Aarhus idea of 'participation as consultation' should be broadened (beyond the local and the technical) to help create the conditions for a deliberative representative democracy that can deliver (ethically right or just) sustainable decisions. In addition, the post-Aarhus idea of 'participation as control' should be introduced for some local environmental decisions to address the problem of democratic deficit and promote 'green communitarianism'.

Notes

1 Quoted in UNECE (2001).
2 UNECE is a regional organization of the UN founded in 1947 to promote 'economic dialogue and co-operation'. The region covered extends beyond geographical Europe to include Turkey, Israel, the Central Asian Republics of the former Soviet Union, the United States and Canada. See http://www.unece.org/oes/eceintro.htm.
3 Professor Laszlo Miklos, Slovak Minister of the Environment quoted in UNECE (2001).
4 On the history of the Convention and its place in the history of international environmental treaties see Petkova and Veit (2000: 2–3), Brady (1998a: 69), Stec *et al.* (2000: 1–4) and Shelton (2002).
5 The Convention has 22 parties (at 30 August 2002) including just 3 EU members; namely Denmark, France and Italy. Many EU countries, including the UK, are promising ratification in the near future. For full list of signatories and parties see http://www.unece.org/env/pp/ctreaty.htm.
6 See, for example, Rose-Ackerman and Halpaap (2001: 33) and Tuesen and Simonsen (2000).
7 For a clear 'article-by-article' critique of the Convention see Ebbeson (2002). The connection between democracy and sustainability has been much discussed in green political theory. See, especially, Goodin (1992: chapter 4), Mathews (1995) and Doherty and de Geus (1996).
8 The Convention text is available at http://www.unece.org/env/pp/documents/cep43e.pdf. References to the Convention follow the article and section numbers used in the Convention text.
9 See Dobson (1998, chapter 2 (especially, p. 39)).
10 On anthropocentric conceptions of sustainability see Dobson (1998: 44–5).
11 The most notable advocate of the 'convergence' thesis is Bryan Norton (1991). Adopting a sufficiently expansive notion of human 'well-being' or human interests (see, e.g. Hayward 1998) might also eliminate the practical gap.
12 On 'negative' conceptions of sustainability see Meadowcroft (1997: 171).
13 The 'figure' (based on a UNEP report) is from Pearce and Edwards (2002).
14 The terms are from Dobson (1998: 45–6).
15 No explicit definition of 'the environment' is given in the Convention. The quotation is drawn from the definition of 'environmental information'. See Stec *et al.* (2000: 35–6).
16 For a clear definition of 'critical natural capital' see Dobson (1998: 43–4).
17 For example, how seriously should we take Wilfred Beckerman's claim that our priority should be preventing 'human-induced suffering' and promoting 'justice and decent behaviour' rather than tackling environmental degradation (Beckerman 1999: 89–90)?

18 See, for example, the list of industrial activities 'regulated' by the Convention (Annex 1).
19 For details of Aarhus requirements on these matters see Article 6.
20 On legislative independence and the role of the executive in drafting laws see Stec *et al.* (2000: 119).
21 Most countries have already amended or will have to amend their legislation and practice to meet the demands of Aarhus. See, for example, Tuesen and Simonsen (2000: 299–302) on Denmark, which is one of the most progressive countries in this area.
22 Among the requirements are freely accessible public registers (Article 5 (2)), the provision of information in electronic format (Article 5 (3)) and state of the environment reports every 3–4 years (Article 5 (4)). There is also a commitment to make progress towards 'pollution inventories' (Article 5 (9)).
23 Petkova and Veit argue that 'the mobilization of local actors across borders' is an appropriate response to the 'processes of economic globalization' (2000: 7). For general discussion of the principle underlying this provision see Dobson (1996: 128–31).
24 The examples are from Stec *et al.* (2000: 46). For further examples, see Petkova and Veit (2000: 7–9).
25 NGOs played a major role in the development of the Convention and even organized a full session at the Aarhus Convention. For details of their involvement see Petkova and Veit (2000: 5–6) and Brady (1998b).
26 See also Article 3 (4) and the 'Resolution of the parties' (in Stec *et al.* 2000, 179–80).
27 The quotations in square brackets are from paragraph 7 of the Preamble.
28 For a concise discussion of the 'costs' and 'benefits' of participation see Rydin (2000: 10–13).
29 See, for example, Bush *et al.* (2002: 129–30) and Burningham and Thrush (2001: 23–4).
30 'Environmental injustice' has been the topic of much research in the USA but has received less attention in Europe. However, recent studies in the UK suggest that there are significant inequalities in the distribution of environmental benefits and disbenefits. See Friends of the Earth (2001) and Stephens *et al.* (2001).
31 For a good example, see Lake (1996: 161 and 165–7).
32 The Aarhus Convention attempts to tackle some of these problems through environmental education (Article 3 (3)), free access to information (Article 5 (2c)) and inexpensive access to the courts (Article 9).
33 The Aarhus emphasis on the role of NGOs might help to alleviate this problem because they may be more likely than individual citizens to defend anonymous or remote strangers.
34 The two assumptions are not mutually exclusive but might be seen as different perspectives on the same process (although, not if protection is against illintent rather than ineptitude or imperfect knowledge).
35 See Dryzek (1997: 79–82), Irwin (1995: esp. chapters 3–5), Petts (1997: esp. 378) and Tytler *et al.* (2001: esp. 359).
36 See next section.
37 See Rawls (1993: 36–7).
38 See, for example, Davies (2001: 97–8).
39 For general discussion of the fairness of different forms of participation see Renn *et al.* (1995).
40 See Burnheim (1985).
41 See, for example, Lowe *et al.* (2001: 82–3).
42 See Hawthorne and Alabaster (1999: esp. 27 and 40) for a 'model' of the factors promoting 'environmental citizenship'.

43 See de-Shalit (1995: esp. 14–15) on 'transgenerational community'.
44 See de-Shalit (1995: 62).
45 This claim is not necessarily tied to any particular metaethical conception of 'rightness' (e.g. realist or constructivist) but it does assume some kind of ethical 'objectivity' and the capacity of humans (in general) to 'reason' towards the 'objective'. In the context of a standard representative democracy – as opposed to one that is 'constitutionally' extended to include formal representation for future generations or the environment – very long-term sustainability requires more than the recognition of a common or 'generalizable' interest (Dryzek 1987: 203). Instead, there must be a (widespread) ethical belief that it is right (or just) to make certain provisions for future generations (despite their absence from the deliberative forum).
46 See Nagel (1995: 146–7).

References

Beckerman, W. (1999) 'Sustainable development and our obligations to future generations', in A. Dobson (ed.) *Fairness and Futurity*, Oxford: Oxford University Press.
Brady, K. (1998a) 'New convention on access to information and public participation in environmental matters', *Environmental Policy and Law* 28/2: 69–75.
—— (1998b) 'Aarhus Convention signed', *Environmental Policy and Law* 28/3–4: 171–90.
Burnheim, J. (1985) *Is Democracy Possible?*, Cambridge: Polity Press.
Burningham, K. and Thrush, D. (2001) *'Rainforests are a Long Way from Here': The Environmental Concerns of Disadvantaged Groups*, York: Joseph Rowntree Foundation.
Bush, J., Moffatt, S. and Dunn, C. (2002) 'Contextualisation of local and global environmental issues in north-east England: implications for debates on globalisation and the "risk society"', *Local Environment* 7: 2, 119–33.
Davies, A. (2001) 'What silence knows – planning, public participation and environmental values', *Environmental Values* 10: 77–102.
de-Shalit, A. (1995) *Why Posterity Matters*, London: Routledge.
Dobson, A. (1996) 'Representative democracy and the environment', in W. Lafferty and J. Meadowcroft (eds) *Democracy and the Environment*, Cheltenham: Edward Elgar Publishing.
—— (1998) *Justice and the Environment*, Oxford: Oxford University Press.
Doherty, B. and de Geus, M. (eds) (1996) *Democracy and Green Political Thought: Sustainability, Rights and Citizenship*, London: Routledge.
Dryzek, J. (1987) *Rational Ecology*, Oxford: Basil Blackwell.
—— (1997) *The Politics of the Earth*, Oxford: Oxford University Press.
Ebbeson, J. (2002) *Information, Participation and Access to Justice: The Model of the Aarhus Convention*, Background Paper No.5 for the Joint UNEP-OHCHR Expert Seminar on Human Rights and the Environment, Geneva, 14–16 January. Available online: http://www.unhchr.ch/environment/bp5.html (accessed 18 July 2002).
Friends of the Earth (2001) *Pollution and Poverty – Breaking the Link*, London: Friends of the Earth.
Goodin, R. (1992) *Green Political Theory*, Cambridge: Polity Press.
Hawthorne, M. and Alabaster, T. (1999) 'Citizen 2000: development of a model of environmental citizenship', *Global Environmental Change* 9: 25–43.

Hayward, T. (1998) *Political Theory and Ecological Values*, New York, NY: St Martin's Press.

Irwin, A. (1995) *Citizen Science*, London: Routledge.

Lake, R. (1996) 'Volunteers, NIMBYs, and environmental justice: dilemmas of democratic practice', *Antipode* 28: 2, 160–74.

Lowe, P., Murdoch, J. and Norton, A. (2001) *Professionals and Volunteers in the Environmental Process*, Newcastle: Centre for Rural Economy.

Mathews, F. (guest ed.) (1995) *Environmental Politics* 4: 4 (Special Issue: Ecology and Democracy).

Meadowcroft, J. (1997) 'Planning, democracy and the challenge of sustainable development', *International Political Science Review* 18: 2, 167–89.

Nagel, T. (1995) 'Nozick: libertarianism without foundations', in his *Other Minds*, Oxford: Oxford University Press.

Norton, B. (1991) *Toward Unity Among Environmentalists*, Oxford: Oxford University Press.

Pearce, F. and Edwards, R. (2002) 'Forest fires fuel pollution crisis', *New Scientist* 17 (August): 8–9.

Petkova, E. and Veit, P. (2000) *Environmental Accountability Beyond the Nation – State: The Implications of the Aarhus Convention*, Washington, DC: World Resources Institute.

Petts, J. (1997) 'The public-expert interface in local waste management decisions: expertise, credibility and process', *Public Understanding of Science* 6: 359–81.

Rawls, J. (1993) *Political Liberalism*, New York, NY: Columbia University Press.

Renn, O., Webler, T. and Wiedemann, P. (eds) (1995) *Fairness and Competence in Citizen Participation*, London: Kluwer Academic Publishers.

Rose-Ackerman, S. and Halpaap, A. (2001) 'The Aarhus Convention and the politics of process: the political economy of procedural environmental rights', paper presented at *The Law and Economics of Environmental Policy: A Symposium*, Faculty of Law, University College London, September 5–7.

Rydin, Y. (2000) *The Public and Local Environmental Policy: Strategies for Promoting Public Participation*, London: Town and Country Planning Association.

Shelton, D. (2002) 'Environmental rights in multilateral treaties adopted between 1991 and 2001', *Environmental Policy and Law* 32: 2, 70–8.

Stec, S., Casey-Lefkowitz, S. and Jendroska, J. (2000) *The Aarhus Convention: An Implementation Guide*, New York, NY: United Nations.

Stephens, C., Bullock, S. and Scott, A. (2001) *Environmental Justice: Rights and Means to a Healthy Environment for All*, ESRC Briefing Paper No. 7, London: Economic and Social Research Council. Available online: http://www.foe.co.uk/resource/reports/environmental_justice.pdf.

Tuesen, G. and Simonsen, J. (2000) 'Compliance with the Aarhus Convention', *Environmental Policy and Law* 30: 6, 299–306.

Tytler, R., Duggan, S. and Gott, R. (2001) 'Public participation in an environmental dispute: implications for science education', *Public Understanding of Science* 10: 343–64.

UNECE (2001) 'Environmental rights not a luxury: Aarhus Convention enters into force', UNECE press release. Available online: http://www.unece.org/pp/press.releases/01env15e.html (accessed 29 April 2002).

WCED (1987) *Our Common Future*, Oxford: Oxford University Press.

Part II
Policy

7 Social inclusion, environmental sustainability and citizenship education

Andrew Dobson

There is a European Union directive that calls for heavy cuts in the amount of household waste sent to landfill sites in Britain – currently about 1,400 of them. This leaves the British government with the tricky task of working out how best to wean the public off its habit of throwing stuff away. Downing Street has a 'Performance and Innovation Unit' charged with suggesting answers to such questions, and its proposals in this case shed interesting light on the prevailing view of how to get people to do environmentally beneficial things when their inclination is not to do them.

A principal suggestion is to charge people for taking sacks of rubbish away – say £1.00 per sack, or £5.00 per month (Strategy Unit 2002: 13). From one point of view the logic is impeccable: people will want to avoid paying the rubbish tax and so will reduce the amount of waste they throw away. The proposal is rooted in the 'self-interested rational actor' model of human motivation, according to which people do things either for some gain or to avoid some harm to themselves. Critics of the proposed scheme immediately pointed out that this model contains the seeds of its own demise. People uncommitted to the idea behind the scheme will take the line of least resistance in a way entirely consistent with the model of behaviour on which the scheme depends – but entirely at odds with its desired outcomes. As a *Guardian* leader pointed out, 'Rather than pay up, the public are likely to vote with their cars and take their rubbish and dump it on the pavement, in the countryside or in someone else's backyard' (12 July 2002).

At no point in this debate was an alternative approach canvassed, admirably captured in the following from Ludwig Beckman:

> The fact that the sustainability of the consumerist and individualist lifestyle is put in question undoubtedly raises a whole range of questions about how to reconstruct our society. What new economic and political institutions are needed? What regulations and set of incentives are necessary in order to redirect patterns of behaviour in sustainable directions?

However, the question of sustainable behaviour cannot be reduced to a discussion about balancing carrots and sticks. The citizen that sorts her garbage or that prefers ecological goods will often do this because she feels committed to ecological values and ends. The citizen may not, that is, act in sustainable ways solely out of economic or practical incentives: people sometimes choose to do good for other reasons than fear (of punishment or loss) or desire (for economic rewards or social status). People sometimes do good because they want to be virtuous.

(Beckman 2001: 179)

Beckman is gesturing here towards a conception of environmental or ecological citizenship, and I propose to fill this out a little in what follows (I have offered a more detailed account in Dobson 2003: Ch. 2). Then, assuming that people are not already environmental or ecological citizens (if they were then the EU's waste directive would be unnecessary), the problem arises of how the required changes in value and behaviour are to come about. Inevitably, although not of course exclusively, the issue of citizenship education arises at this point, an idea that has a long and chequered history, running (at least) from Rousseau's *Emile* to the civics classes of the United States of America. Can environmental or ecological citizenship be taught? What would the syllabus look like? These are appropriate questions for any country with a citizenship education programme – and they are perhaps especially germane in the British context, since citizenship education has been a statutory requirement in secondary education from September 2002. I shall say more about environmental or ecological citizenship education in general, and the British case in particular, later in the chapter, but first we need to be clearer about what environmental or ecological citizenship is, and why the issues with which we are dealing here can be talked of in terms of citizenship at all.

In this context I am especially keen to draw a distinction between obligations of citizenship and obligations of a more general humanitarian type. I believe that the obligation to recycle and reduce waste (for example) can be expressed in terms of citizenship, and that the way to do this is to show that these obligations are rooted in justice, which is, after all, a specifically political notion and thus entirely appropriately predicated of citizenship. In this regard, I take it that justice is to citizenship as charity is to humanitarianism, or to make the same point in a different way, that justice is to the Good Citizen as charity is to the Good Samaritan. I am interested in the former rather than the latter. Let me begin, then, by drawing a distinction between environmental and ecological citizenship and along the way try to substantiate the view that they are both grounded in the discourse and practice of justice. Given that I introduced this chapter with an example from New Labour, let me increase the parochialism quotient still further by using a favourite bit of New Labour language as a cipher for social justice: inclusion and exclusion. I hope to show that sustainability can be linked to the inclusion/exclusion debate, and this, I reiterate, is what makes it appropriate to talk of the rights and obligations associated with sustainability as those of citizenship rather than of some other kind of non-political relationship.

We are used to thinking of citizenship in two different but related kinds of ways. On the one hand there is the liberal tradition according to which citizenship confers upon citizens certain *rights* that they claim against the constituted political authority – usually the state. Then there is a tradition of citizenship that stresses its *obligations* – usually obligations to the state (to pay taxes, to do military service where required, to vote, for example). But sometimes these obligations are regarded more generally as responsibilities to work towards the public good (for more on models of citizenship see Dobson 2003: Ch. 1). Both of these dimensions of citizenship are connected with environmental sustainability and social inclusion in important ways, as I hope to show in what follows. I propose to reserve the term 'environmental citizenship' for *rights* – based thinking, and 'ecological citizenship' for *obligations* relating to sustainability.

Citizenship rights and environmental justice

In liberal democratic societies such as the United Kingdom, rights-based notions of citizenship have been dominant for some time – and certainly since the Second World War. In part this is because of the influence of T.H. Marshall who gave a series of lectures in 1949 and then published a book entitled *Citizenship and Social Class and Other Essays* in 1950. Marshall's thesis, which has come to colour so much of our thinking about the nature of citizenship, is that the idea has passed through a number of phases, all of which can be characterized in terms of the acquisition of different types of rights. The phases he identifies are: civil rights (the right to associate, to speak freely and so on), political rights (the right to vote and run for election) and finally welfare rights (the right to social security). None of these sets of rights was achieved without great political and social struggle, and none of them has been achieved permanently.

The connection between citizenship, rights and inclusion should be obvious. Civil, political and welfare rights are desirable, and anyone who does not possess them must be regarded as excluded from society's basic infrastructure. *Membership* is a crucial issue here. Membership of the political community automatically confers these rights on members, and they are so valuable that the governments of wealthy countries spend a lot of time and money determining who shall and who shall not be granted membership – the issue of 'illegal immigration'. The unprecedented flows of people from poorer to wealthier countries can be regarded in this sense as movements from 'citizenship-poor' to 'citizenship-rich' states – states where the benefits attached to membership are low to states where such benefits are high. Migrants may regard some of these benefits, or rights, as more important than others. Seekers after political asylum, for example, may be especially attracted to the rights to free speech and association denied in their country of origin. Economic migrants, on the other hand, are more likely to be moved by the promise of the rights to social security granted to citizens of wealthy countries. In neither case, though, is the set of rights fully assured until citizenship is granted, for only membership of the community of citizens confers such rights by right, as it were. In this sense, the boundary between inclusion and exclusion is the boundary between the possession and non-possession of the rights of citizenship.

Recently, the existence of another set of rights has come to be canvassed: environmental rights. Bart van Steenbergen, for example, has argued the need for '*ecological* citizenship as an addition, but also as a correction, to the three existing forms of citizenship: civil, political and social' (van Steenbergen 1994: 142). If such rights could be established, both in theory and in constitutional practice, this would simultaneously open up another front on which citizenship battles with the state could be fought and erect yet another boundary for inclusion and exclusion – between those entitled to certain environmental rights, and those not entitled to them. Not all those entitled to environmental rights will necessarily have them realized, of course, and this is the basis for another type of social exclusion on which I shall say more a little later, in the context of what has come to be known as 'environmental justice'.

As I remarked above, we are used to refugees seeking the comparative luxury of European political and social rights. It may not be too far-fetched to think of additional waves of refugees seeking asylum in countries relatively rich in *environmental* rights. And environmental rights do exist – constitutionally at least. As Tim Hayward has remarked:

> Globally, more than 70 countries have constitutional environmental provisions of some kind, and in at least 30 cases these take the form of environmental rights... No recently promulgated constitution has omitted reference to environmental principles, and many older constitutions are being amended to include them.
>
> (Hayward 2000: 558)

What is an environmental right, though? Hayward goes on to say that

> The scope of the right under discussion is basically that proposed in the Brundtland Report: 'All human beings have the fundamental right to an environment adequate for their health and well-being'... Its most obvious application would be with respect to pollution, waste disposal, and other sorts of toxic contamination.
>
> (Hayward 2000: 558)

This will serve as a working definition for now.

The mention of toxic contamination points us in an important direction. As I said above, the idea of environmental rights also erects a boundary *within* the community of environmental rights-holders, between those whose environmental rights are upheld (the included) and those whose environmental rights are not upheld (the excluded). I want to explore this in more detail now in the context of the movement for 'environmental justice'. The environmental justice movement has been – and is – particularly important in the United States of America. This is significant for us because the environmental justice battle there has been fought within the civil rights context, a context with great salience in US political history. In the terms of our subject here, environmental justice is about inclusion and exclusion: whether one's 'right to an environment adequate for... health and well-being' is upheld or not. It has become increasingly apparent in the US – and elsewhere – that environmental *in*justice abounds.

Perhaps the most well-known case of environmental injustice in the US has come to be known as 'Love Canal', and it is representative of most of the issues raised in other cases. On 2 August 1978 CBS and ABC networks first carried news of the effects of toxic waste on the health of the people of a place called Love Canal (Szasz 1994: 42). It turned out that decades earlier Hooker Chemical had dumped thousands of drums of waste into an abandoned navigation canal which was subsequently (in 1952) filled in. In 1953, Hooker sold the land to the Niagara Falls Board of Education. A school was built, houses were erected in the neighbourhood, and people moved in. Twenty or so years later heavy rains washed the chemicals to the surface and alarming health problems – including birth defects – began to emerge.

The link between the relative poverty of many of the inhabitants of Love Canal and the poisoned environment in which they lived was immediately apparent, and in the months and years that followed, more and more similar cases came to light. So the environmental justice movement was born, based on the simple and not very surprising observation that 'Toxic victims are, typically, poor or working people of modest means. Their environmental problems are inseparable from their economic condition. People are more likely to live near polluted industrial sites if they live in financially strapped communities' (Szasz 1994: 151). Victims of environmental injustice have their environmental citizenship right 'to an environment adequate for... health and well-being' denied. This amounts to systematic exclusion from a fundamental prerequisite for a decent life, and indicates quite clearly the relationship between environmental sustainability and the inclusion/exclusion debate.

Nor is environmental injustice confined to the United States of America. Some key findings of a Friends of the Earth (England, Wales and Northern Ireland) investigation into the unequal distribution of pollution

(Friends of the Earth 2000) were that '662 of the UK's largest factories occur in areas with average household incomes of less than £15,000 and only five occur in areas where average household incomes are £30,000 or more' (Agyeman 2002). Further, 'those with household incomes below £5,000, ie the poorest families, are twice as likely to be in a neighbourhood with a polluting factory as the most wealthy families, ie those with a household income of £60,000' (Agyeman 2002). As Agyeman comments, this 'is social exclusion of an extreme nature' (Agyeman 2002).

Similarly, environmental racism is as much a feature of the British political landscape as it is in the USA. The Black Environment Network was set up in 1987 to address a perceived inequality of access to the countryside between white and ethnic minority communities. More recently, Capacity, whose director is on the New Labour government's Roundtable on Sustainable Development, has set about co-ordinating a UK Environmental Justice Network to clarify the links between environmental injustice and social exclusion, and to persuade the government that environmental injustice is a priority area.

I hope that all this shows that the links between citizenship, sustainability and social inclusion and exclusion are clear, systematic and important. To the existing list of civil, political and social citizenship rights we can add another set of rights – environmental rights. Such rights amount to the right to live in a society that is developing in an environmentally sustainable fashion. The environmental justice movement has shown that some people – usually poor people and/or people of colour – are systematically excluded from having this right made good. In this sense, movements for environmental sustainability are movements for social inclusion, using the idea of environmental citizenship both to establish the existence of environmental rights, and to have them made good. It should also be clear from the themes of this section of the paper that environmental citizenship could be an excellent vehicle through which to teach the rights-based aspects of citizenship, and I shall say more about this possibility in the chapter's final section.

Citizenship obligations and ecological footprints

All of this comes about through regarding citizenship in terms of the articulation of certain rights. I pointed out at the beginning, though, that there is an alternative way of thinking about citizenship – as the meeting of obligations or the exercise of responsibilities. This is a subordinate tradition in citizenship theory and practice – or at least it is subordinate when looked at from today's liberal democratic vantage point, since the so-called 'republican' idea of citizenship, archetypally associated with the period of the French Revolution, was once dominant itself. This idea has it that citizenship is more about duty than rights – duty to the Republic, either in whatever way is deemed appropriate by the Republic or, in the best light, in ways mutually agreed upon by citizens themselves.

Talk about the duties or responsibilities of citizenship is usually reluctant talk, for a number of reasons which it is inappropriate to detail here (see Dobson 2003: Ch. 1). In part it has to do with the liberal emphasis on freedom rather than obligation, and in part with the way in which citizenship duty – as an idea – has most recently been endorsed by the American New Right. This has made it difficult for progressive politics to talk about itself in the language of obligation, duty, or responsibility. There used to be signs that New Labour was prepared to take on the challenge of articulating citizenship in these terms, but this seems not to be as central to 'the project' as it used to be. Anthony Giddens, for example, widely regarded as Tony Blair's favourite intellectual, homed in on the rights/responsibilities theme as the key defining feature of 'Third Way' politics:

> [O]ne might suggest as a prime motto for the new politics, *no rights without responsibilities*. Government has a whole cluster of responsibilities for its citizens and others, including the protection of the vulnerable. Old-style social democracy, however, was inclined to treat rights as unconditional claims.
>
> (Giddens 1998: 65)

Similarly Geoff Mulgan, of the Number 10 Policy Unit, has written of a general 'unease that the left's ideas about citizenship should end up as nothing more than a package of rights without obligations, a programme for a loose society in which relationships are contingent and undemanding' (Mulgan 1991: 41).

There is, though, still some embarrassment on the left – even the soft-left – as far as talking about citizenship duties is concerned. Very many people are worried about the apparent decline in political commitment in contemporary, so-called advanced industrial societies, for example. It is a matter of hand-wringing grief in the political class that only 59 per cent of eligible voters exercised their right to vote in Britain's last General Election. Very few people, though, have dared to refer to voting as a citizenship duty, and the idea of putting voting booths in supermarkets only seems to underline the dominant view that voting is a right to be consumed rather than a duty to be exercised. Professor Bernard Crick was commissioned to report on citizenship as part of the government's drive to raise political literacy and awareness, and we have yet to see just how schools will take up the challenge of teaching the subject at secondary level, beginning in 2002. I shall say more on this shortly, but let me say now that I, for one, hope that both environmental and ecological citizenship will be regarded as an essential part of the curriculum, not only as a form of citizenship in its own right, but also as a way of discussing the themes of citizenship more generically.

If, as I suggested at the end of the previous section, environmental citizenship is a good way of introducing school pupils to rights-based citizenship, then *ecological* citizenship is an excellent expression of a citizenship that has the idea of obligation at its heart – as I now hope to show. This is another way of connecting citizenship with the inclusion/exclusion debate, but this time on a much broader canvas than the usually local focus of the environmental justice movement.

We all know that environmental problems cannot be confined to the boundaries of nation-states. Environmental pollution, for example, has an annoying propensity for international travel, as is attested by fisher folk in those Scandinavian lakes affected by acid rain produced by industrial practices in Britain. The question arises whether, in cases such as this, we have international environmental obligations, and if so, whether these obligations can be regarded as obligations of citizenship. This raises all sorts of awkward technical questions, such as whether states can be regarded as 'citizens', and it would be inappropriate to detail these questions and potential answers here. For the sake of argument let us assume that individuals are to some degree or another implicated in the environmental behaviour of the wider political communities to which they belong. More explicitly, let me refer to the environmental *impact* of individuals in these communities and beyond them.

It is self-evident that the environmental impact of individuals' habits and practices varies throughout the world. Inhabitants of resource-intensive and waste-producing states will generally make a greater impact on the environment's productive and absorptive capacities than inhabitants of societies that recycle and reuse resources (I say 'generally' because some people in very wealthy societies make minimal demands on the environment, because they are prevented from doing so through poverty or other forms of exclusion).

One evocative and suitably earthy way of referring to the environmental impact of individuals and communities is through the notion of the 'ecological footprint' (Wackernagel 1995). The notion assumes that the earth has a limited productive and waste-absorbing capacity, and a notional and equal 'land allowance' – or footprint – is allocated to each person on the planet, given these limits. The footprint size is arrived at by dividing the total land available, and its productive capacity, by the number of people on the planet, and the figure usually arrived at is somewhere between 1.5 and 1.7 hectares. Inevitably, some people have a bigger impact – a bigger footprint – than others (median consumers in 'advanced industrial countries' are generally reckoned to occupy about 5 hectares of ecological space), and this is taken to be unjust, in the sense of a departure from a nominal equality of ecological space.

This approach to determining environmental impact is of course open to all the standard objections to 'limits to growth' and other Malthusian-type analyses of the relationship between human beings and their natural environment. Thus, it will be argued that such an approach underestimates the resources available, the capacity for doing more with less through technological advances, the possibility of substituting one resource for another with the same function, and that it ignores the historical evidence suggesting that resource availability is more elastic than 'finitude' analyses would have us believe. Its implicitly egalitarian view of distributive justice is also open to the objection that departures from the norm of equal shares are often justifiable.

I cannot fully review these criticisms here, and nor, I think, do I need to for present purposes. The relevance of the ecological footprint notion to ecological citizenship – broadly unaffected by the criticisms to which I have just alluded, unless we believe in a totally cornucopian world in which infinite substitutability of resources is possible – is that it contains the key spatial and obligation-generating relationships that give rise to the exercise of specifically citizenly virtues. The *nature* of the obligation is to reduce the occupation of ecological space, where appropriate, and the *source* of this obligation lies in remedying the potential and actual injustice of appropriating an unjust share of ecological space. The idea recognizes that some countries, and some people within some countries, systematically affect the life chances of others in this generation and future generations. Obligations are owed by those in ecological space debt, and these obligations are the corollary of a putative environmental right to an equal share of ecological space for everyone.

How does all this relate to our themes of social inclusion, environmental sustainability and citizenship? Plainly, on anything other than a cornucopian view of possibilities, anyone making too large an ecological footprint is living unsustainably. Further, those who put down large footprints leave less ecological space for others to inhabit, thereby excluding them from their rightful share of the basic ecological necessities that make a dignified life possible to live. The duty of the ecological citizen, then, is to live more sustainably so that others can live well.

A key point is that we must regard this is an obligation of *citizenship*, rather than an obligation owed generally to humanity. It is not the same kind of obligation as that which moved the Good Samaritan to help the stricken man by the side of the road. The Good Samaritan is not motivated to act for reasons of justice, but the ecological citizen *is* so motivated. The Good Samaritan is not responsible for the condition of the stricken man. His or her actions, therefore, are not actions of justice. Overoccupation of ecological space, though, leaves less ecological space for others, and this is unjust. The obligation to occupy less space is therefore a political obligation which it would be wrong not to fulfil as a matter of justice, as opposed to simply desirable to fulfil as a matter of benevolence.

If the idea of ecological space is not convincing, then focus solely on the issue of the differential environmental impact that people across the world make. Most countries can only act locally, but some can act globally – and this asymmetry is particularly true in the context of global warming. It is increasingly pointed out that many so-called 'natural' disasters may in fact have anthropogenic origins. Climate scientists are fairly confident that although the disaggregated impacts of global warming are very hard to predict, we are likely to experience an increased incidence of extreme weather events – so-called 'strange weather'. When floods devastate large areas of developing countries, we congratulate ourselves on the generous quantities of aid we offer to alleviate the suffering. From the 'closed earth' point of view, though, the campaigning issue is not so much about how generous aid should be, but whether 'aid' is the appropriate category at all. If global warming is principally caused by wealthy countries, and if global warming is at least a part cause of strange weather, then monies should be transferred as a matter of compensatory justice rather than as aid or charity. Once again this points us towards the Good Citizen rather than the Good Samaritan. The ecological citizen's obligations are born of justice, not charity.

Towards environmental and ecological citizenship education

Whichever way we look at it, then, environmental sustainability and social inclusion are intimately linked – particularly if we talk about the links in terms of citizenship. We have seen that citizenship can be regarded as the possession of rights. We have also seen that increasing numbers of countries are either including environmental rights in new constitutions, or interpreting clauses in old constitutions in an environmental fashion. This gives rise to two axes of inclusion and exclusion. First, there are those who possess the environmental rights that go with being a citizen of a particular state or collection of states, and those who do not. Citizenship is always an exclusionary category, and the environmental case is just one instance of this practice of exclusion and inclusion at work. Second, there is the exclusion of those who may *formally* possess environmental rights from their *actual* enjoyment of them. The environmental justice movement has shown us that this is a reflection of other types of cleavage in society – the rich and the poor, for example, and ethnic majorities and minorities.

The other dimension of citizenship concerns the responsibilities and obligations it confers on citizens. It is suggested that people in wealthy countries – most of them, anyway – have an environmental impact that amounts to a form of injustice as far as people in other countries, and in future generations, are concerned. There was a time when the actions of wealthy people in dominant societies had little effect further afield. Think of the Roman Empire, for example. But in this globalized world, members of wealthy societies have an 'always already' impact on people far away – even on people yet to be born. The citizenship obligation here is, as I said above, for the minority to live sustainably so that the majority can live well.

Both citizenship rights and citizenship duties, then, point in the direction of 'environmental inclusion', and both build on the well-established truth that inequality is the fundamental cause of present patterns of environmental exclusion. Now what are the implications of all this for citizenship education in the environmental and ecological contexts? Well, we now have a rough-and-ready template for a citizenship curriculum in the environmental context. Our exploration of environmental citizenship pointed up the importance of rights and justice, so any curriculum that fails to broach these questions will be incomplete. Second, justice is also a key component of ecological citizenship, but this time with an explicitly transnational and responsibility-oriented component. Citizenship curricula must therefore raise the issue of *international obligations*.

Similarly, I have made it plain elsewhere (Dobson 1998) that I consider sustainable development to be at least as much about values as about techniques and technologies. Science might be able to tell us what the threshold tolerances of nitrogen in the atmosphere are for any given species, but it cannot tell us which species we should be concerned about. The key questions, then, are not technical – they are *normative*. Values are key in a number of ways. One way of seeing this is to ask the classic sustainability question: what kind of a world do we want to pass on to future generations? This raises questions of value related to environmental protection: do we want *Blade Runner* or *The Waltons*? Or something else entirely? Is it possible that future generations will want electronic birds and plastic trees? It also obliges us to think about the relationship between sustainability for the future and justice and democracy in the present. Is there a trade-off between them, or can we have them all at the same time? How much might future generations legitimately ask us to sacrifice for the sake of their well-being? And who in the present generation should bear the greatest burdens? VAT on domestic fuel might lead to a reduction in greenhouse gas emissions, for example, but it is a regressive tax, and so hits the poor hardest. Bearing all this in mind, we have to say that we will be short-changed by any ecological citizenship curriculum that does not confront normative questions of this sort.

As I said earlier, Britain provides an interesting point of departure for once (for once, I mean, in the context of citizenship education which has largely passed the British education system by in recent times). Almost immediately after the election of the first New Labour administration in 1997, the then Secretary of State for Education and Employment, David Blunkett, pledged to 'strengthen education for citizenship and the teaching of democracy in schools' (*Education for Citizenship and the Teaching of Democracy in Schools*: 4). He set up an Advisory Group with the following terms of reference: 'to provide advice on effective education for citizenship in schools – to include the nature and practices of participation in democracy; the duties, responsibilities and rights of individuals as citizens; and the value to individuals and society of community activity'. The Chair of the Advisory Group was political scientist Professor Bernard Crick, and his team duly produced a report, *Education for Citizenship and the Teaching of Democracy in Schools,* in 1998. The main conclusion and recommendation ran as follows:

> We unanimously advise the Secretary of State that citizenship and the teaching of democracy, construed in a broad sense that we will define, is so important both for schools and the life of the nation that there must be a statutory requirement on schools to ensure that it is part of the entitlement of all pupils.
> (*Education for Citizenship and the Teaching of Democracy in Schools*: 7)

And so education for citizenship as part of the national curriculum for 11–16-year-olds was born. I do not propose to offer a detailed analysis of either the process that led to the curriculum guidelines being set up, or of the content of the guidelines themselves. I plan, instead, to refer only to those aspects of the curriculum requirements that bear upon our topic: environmental and ecological citizenship.

And perhaps that is the first surprise: that there *is* content that refers either explicitly or implicitly (but in germane ways) to environmental and ecological citizenship. Specifically, the curriculum asks for:

> education for sustainable development, through developing pupils' skills in, and commitment to, effective participation in the democratic and other decision-making processes that affect the quality, structure and health of environments and society and exploring values that determine people's actions within society, the economy and the environment.
> (Department for Education and Employment and the Qualifications and Curriculum Authority: 8)

This reference to 'sustainable development' opens the door to a systematic exploration of the relationship between this objective and citizenship. One fear, though, might be that sustainable development education will be delivered as a series of largely technical moves. There is a welcome determination, though, in both the Crick Report and in the curriculum guidelines to avoid teaching citizenship as if it were a matter of learning the institutional nuts and bolts of politics. Crick himself said recently that, 'We have tried to construct a curriculum that will not bore the kids, as old-fashioned civics did. Rather than learning facts about institutions, it encourages discussion of "events, issues and problems"' (Crick 2002: 17). In fact, the subject matter is much closer to political theory than to British government – and this is a promising starting-point for environmental and (particularly) ecological citizenship. Our template, earlier, contained reference to norms and values, so it is good to see the curriculum containing the instruction to teach: 'spiritual development, through fostering pupils' awareness and understanding of meaning and purpose in life and of differing values in human society' (Department for Education and Employment and the Qualifications and Curriculum Authority: 7). This may seem a rather grandiose objective, and citizenship purists may feel it goes way beyond the classical remit of rights and responsibilities to the constituted political authority. I believe, though, that it provides the ideal statutory context within which to teach what is perhaps admittedly the rather unusual idea of environmental or ecological citizenship, precisely because it contains the injunction to learn about, and negotiate, questions of value.

This is underscored by the requirement to teach 'moral development, through helping pupils develop a critical appreciation of issues of right and wrong, justice, fairness, rights and obligations in society' (Department for Education and Employment and the Qualifications and Curriculum Authority: 7). I said earlier that the citizenship curriculum has the merit of cleaving more to political theory than to political institutions, and references to 'justice, fairness, rights and obligation' merely confirm that impression. The triumvirate of 'justice, fairness and obligation' is particularly important given everything I have said about environmental and ecological citizenship being underpinned by notions of justice. The presence of the triumvirate indicates that a key part of the curricular framework is in place for these types of citizenship to feature prominently in secondary school citizenship education in England. This is especially the case if we add in the references to values, noted above, which are such a crucial element in determining what sustainability might be.

I also referred earlier to the way in which ecological citizenship has an irreducibly transnational dimension – ecological footprints cannot be confined to national boundaries. In this context it is encouraging to see the curricular obligation to learn about

> the work of community-based, national and international voluntary groups... the importance of resolving conflict fairly... the world as a global community, and the political, economic, environmental and social implications of this, and the role of the European Union, the Commonwealth and the United Nations.
> (Department for Education and Employment and the Qualifications and Curriculum Authority: 14)

There is even the possibility for a spot of direct action, since the curriculum at Key Stage 4 (age 15–16) requires that pupils be taught 'the opportunities for individuals and voluntary groups to bring about social change locally, nationally, in Europe, and internationally' (Department for Education and Employment and the Qualifications and Curriculum Authority: 15).

All this suggests that contrary to what one might expect from a citizenship curriculum, given its likely institutional orientation, the requirements of the English curriculum are pretty well suited to the specific cases of environmental and ecological citizenship. We might go further. A case could be made that the entire curriculum be taught *through* these citizenships – practically every theme in the curriculum is importantly present in them. I fear, though, that teachers will regard this as a luxury. There has already been some resistance in the teaching profession to the inclusion of citizenship in the National Curriculum because there is already too much to teach. One way of alleviating the pressure is to teach citizenship through other subjects – rather different to teaching citizenship through environmental and ecological citizenship. In a recent debate in *Prospect* magazine between the architect of the citizenship curriculum, Bernard Crick, and the shadow secretary of state for education and skills, Damian Green, Crick responded to Green's concern that citizenship would overload already busy teachers with this response:

> The guidance on teaching citizenship (from the Qualifications and Curriculum Authority) says that while a school may choose to deliver it as a separate subject, most of it can be delivered through other subjects with only minor adjustments. Geography stresses environmental and resource problems; History deals with conflicts of interests and values; English literature deals with moral problems of the use and abuse of power.
>
> (Crick 2002: 16)

This is an entirely understandable response, but from an environmental or ecological point of view the strategy runs the risk of diversion and dilution. Diversion, because it is unlikely that Geography, History and English literature are presently geared up to deal with the issues raised by environmental and ecological issues 'with only minor adjustments'. Dilution because 'resource problems', 'values' and 'power' are linked in quite specific ways in the environmental/ecological context – ways which are unlikely to emerge from separate treatments of them without unprecedented and probably unrealistic levels of co-operation between subject teachers.

New Labour prides itself on 'joined-up government', but it has missed a trick here. It should be clear by now that governments cannot meet all their environmental obligations without the backing, support and actions of citizens. Policy advisers seem incapable of seeing their way beyond financial sticks and carrots as a way of transforming behaviour. New Labour has presented itself with an alternative in the guise of the citizenship curriculum, but there are absolutely no signs that the government realizes this. I hope I have shown that citizenship is an appropriate discursive vehicle for environmental and ecological transformation, and that the new curriculum for England has the makings of a context within which environmental and ecological citizenship can be fomented.

References

Agyeman, J. (2002) 'Constructing environmental (in)justice: transatlantic tales', *Environmental Politics* 11: 3, pp. 31–53.
Beckman, L. (2001) 'Virtue, sustainability and liberal values', in J. Barry and M. Wissenburg (eds) *Sustaining Liberal Democracy: Ecological Challenges and Opportunities*, Houndmills: Palgrave.
Crick, Bernard (2002) 'Should citizenship be taught in British schools?', *Prospect*, (September): 16–19.
Department for Education and Employment and the Qualifications and Curriculum Authority (1999) *The National Curriculum for England: Citizenship*, London: Department for Education and Employment and the Qualifications and Curriculum Authority.
Dobson, A. (1998) *Justice and the Environment: Conceptions of Environmental Sustainability and Dimensions of Social Justice*, Oxford: Oxford University Press.
—— (2003) *Citizenship and the Environment: aux arbres citoyens!* Oxford: Oxford University Press.
Friends of the Earth (2000) *Pollution Injustice*. Available online: http://www.foe.co.uk/pollution-injustice/2000 (accessed June 27, 2001).
Giddens, A. (1998) *The Third Way: The Renewal of Social Democracy*, Cambridge: Polity.
Hayward, T. (2000) 'Constitutional environmental rights: a case for political analysis', *Political Studies* 48: 3, 558–72.
Marshall, T.H. (1950) *Citizenship and Social Class and Other Essays*, Cambridge: Cambridge University Press.
Mulgan, G. (1991) 'Citizens and responsibilities', in G. Andrews (ed.) *Citizenship*, London: Lawrence and Wishart.
Strategy Unit, The (2002) *Waste Not, Want Not: A Strategy for Reducing the Waste Problem in England*, London: Cabinet Office. Available online: http://www.cabinet-office.gov.uk/innovation/2002/waste/report_menu.shtml (accessed January 28, 2002).
Szasz, A. (1994) *Ecopopulism: Toxic Waste and the Movement for Environmental Justice*, Minneapolis, MN and London: University of Minnesota Press.
van Steenbergen, B. (1994) 'Towards a global ecological citizen', in B. van Steenbergen (ed.) *The Condition of Citizenship*. London, Thousand Oaks and New Delhi: Sage.
Wackernagel, M. (1995) *Our Ecological Footprint: Reducing Human Impact on the Earth*, Gabriola Island, BC Canada and Philadelphia, PA: New Society Publishers.

8 The Europeanization of national environmental policy:
A comparative analysis[1]

Andrew Jordan, Duncan Liefferink and Jenny Fairbrass

Introduction

The European Union (EU) affects domestic politics, policies and administrative structures. Even ten years ago, this statement might have generated controversy in some quarters. But today, it is almost axiomatic that the EU 'matters', sometimes hugely, in the daily political life of its citizens. This shift in perceptions about the EU's importance has helped to open up a new and important research frontier in social sciences. The 'Europeanization turn' is exciting because it provides a fresh perspective on some very old debates within European studies. Traditionally, the EU has been researched and taught using the theoretical models and organizing principles of International Relations. It was, as Stephen George explains, entirely logical to have proceeded in this way because 'what was taking place ... was an experiment in putting *inter-state* relations on a new footing' (1996: 11). The primary aim of the work was to understand the development of institutions and policies at the *European* level. The steadily growing size and importance of the EU policy competences in fields ranging from trade and finance, through to energy and the environment, has now prompted scholars to investigate the rebound effect of European integration (that is the process through which decision-making powers are pooled in the EU) on the Member States. In particular, there is a growing awareness that European integration is not simply something which occurs at the European level, 'above the heads' of states, but has developed to the extent where it now impacts on the basic building blocks of the EU; that is the very states that initially created it. In other words, the EU has, it is widely claimed, begun to 'Europeanize' national cultures, legislatures and policy systems.

The aim of this chapter is to document the Europeanization of national policy in 10 Member States, namely Austria, Ireland, Finland, France, Germany, Greece, the Netherlands, Spain, Sweden and the UK, since 1970. Given that our aim is to explore how common policies adopted by the EU are refracted by national institutional forms, we have opted to focus on one sector, namely environmental policy, rather than looking at the Europeanization of many sectors in one single country. Our selection of countries constitutes a representative sample of 'new' (i.e. post-1995) and older Member States, environmental 'leaders' and 'laggards', and northern and southern states, to understand the main dynamics at work. By national 'policy' we mean the content of policies (the paradigms of action, the objectives and the policy instruments), the legal and administrative structures that have been established to oversee them, and the dominant style in which policy is made and implemented. The chapter builds upon ten country studies first presented at a three day workshop held in Cambridge (UK) in the summer of 2001.[2]

An obvious question to ask is: have some national environmental policies been more Europeanized than others? It seems reasonable to expect that states that are relatively good at nationalizing or 'domesticating' (Wallace 2000: 369–70) EU policy, i.e. exporting ideas and standards to Brussels, will be little touched by Europeanization, whereas net importers will have to significantly adjust their policy systems under the influence of Europeanization. Similarly, which aspects of national activity have been most significantly Europeanized: structures, styles or policies? Has Europeanization proceeded faster and further in some sub-sectors (e.g. water) than others and what are the causal factors? Furthermore, has Europeanization affected the relationship between different national actors, both vertically (i.e. between levels of governance – European, national and sub-national) and horizontally (i.e. between environment and cognate policy sectors such as transport and energy)? Finally, who have been the main losers and winners to emerge from the Europeanization process?

This chapter proceeds as follows. The next section discusses some basic aspects of our research approach, such as the definition of Europeanization we utilize, the reasons for taking environmental policy as our case, and the basic categories for 'measuring' the degree of Europeanization. The main findings of our comparative analysis of the Europeanization of national environmental policy in ten EU Member States are presented in the next section and then further analysed in the following section. Finally, we draw together the main conclusions and consider their implications for the study of Europeanization.

What is Europeanization?

Definitions of Europeanization

To date, there is no single, all-encompassing 'theory' of Europeanization, and even its basic meaning remains contested (see Radaelli 2000). However, the mainstream opinion is that Europeanization research should seek to understand the domestic impacts of European integration. For instance, Heritier *et al.* define it as 'the process of influence deriving from European decisions and impacting member states' policies and political and administrative structures' (2001: 3). Boerzel simply describes it as a 'process whereby domestic policy areas become increasingly subject to European policy making' (2002a: 6). According to this view, Europeanization concerns the process through which European integration penetrates and, in certain circumstances brings about adjustments to, domestic institutions, decision-making procedures and public policies. Of course, this definition begs many more questions than it answers, some of which we return to below.

In adopting this particular interpretation of Europeanization, we are consciously choosing *not* to frame our research in order to explore two other possible interpretations of that term. The first holds that Europeanization is really about the accumulation of policy competences at the EU level. This particular definition was particularly popular in early studies of member state-EU dynamics (e.g. Rehbinder and Stewart 1985: xx), but it was recently resurrected by Cowles *et al.*, who defined Europeanization as 'the emergence and development at the European level of distinct structures of governance' (2001: 2). The main problem with this particular definition is that it risks eliding Europeanization with the source of domestic change – European integration.

The second interpretation views Europeanization as a 'two way street', in which states affect the EU at the same time as the EU affects states (e.g. Boerzel 2002a, b). While the argument that the flow of influence between states and the EU is reciprocal and continuous is essentially unimpeachable, it is nonetheless difficult to fashion it into a rigorous research strategy (i.e. where does the analyst start to look for the causes and consequences of change if they are reciprocally interconnected?) (but see Boerzel 2002a, b; Jordan 2002a). In the language of more positivistic social science, a two-way definition of Europeanization lacks a set of dependent and independent variables.

Why environmental policy?

There are three good reasons for taking environment policy as a case of Europeanization, two of them theoretical, the third pragmatic. First, it is one of the EU's most well developed areas of competence. Most of the early measures of the 1970s were tied quite closely to the logic of creating an internal market in goods. However, EU environmental policy soon broke free of the legal and political constraints that linked it to the internal market, to encompass areas that had never been comprehensively regulated at the national level before such as access to environmental information, the protection of natural habitats and systems of environmental impact assessment (Liefferink *et al.* 1993; Jordan 2002b). Consequently, many have claimed that national systems have been deeply and irreversibly Europeanized as a result of their involvement in EU policy making (Haigh 1984; Lowe and Ward 1998). The 30-year time period thus spanned gives a sufficiently long timeframe to comprehensively assess the impacts of Europeanization. It would be much more difficult (though no less important) to study Europeanization in sectors where the EU does not have such a long and intensive history of involvement such as defence or foreign affairs.

Second, *contra* Moravcsik (1994), national policy *was* already relatively well developed when the EU started to develop its own environmental powers. This allows us to construct a policy 'baseline' for the ten countries for the year 1970, against which we can measure any subsequent EU induced effects. It will be much harder (though not impossible) to study Europeanization in sectors where EU and national policy have co-evolved.

Finally, a huge amount of good empirical work has already been conducted on the implementation of EU environmental policy in national contexts. The purpose of this paper and its underlying country studies is to build upon that substantial empirical base, by looking for broad patterns in the national adaptations to the EU (i.e. Europeanization) and searching for causal mechanisms.

The Europeanization of national environmental policy

How then, does Europeanization take place in the environmental sector? Throughout the history of the EU environmental policy, states have tried to shape European rules to ensure they are aligned with their own national approaches and practices. By working to ensure a 'goodness of fit' (Cowles *et al.* 2001) between the two, states hope to reduce adjustment costs, achieve 'first mover advantages' and reduce political and legal uncertainty by minimizing the extent of Europeanization. The 'regulatory competition' (Héritier *et al.* 1996) between the fifteen Member States to set the 'rules of the game' at the European level, defines the scope of European integration. Crucially, this process inevitably creates instances of institutional 'misfit' when European requirements conflict with the way in which states have traditionally organized their domestic environmental affairs – i.e. the structures, style and philosophy of national policy. It is commonly argued that these 'misfits' are pre-requisite for Europeanization (Cowles *et al.* 2001).

The logical implication of this argument is that more proactive states can forestall Europeanization by exporting, uploading or projecting (Bulmer and Burch 1998) their preferred national policy approach to the EU. After all, if (as has often been the case with the more environmentally progressive states such as the Netherlands (Liefferink 1996) and Germany (Weale 1992)) European rules are based on the core features of national rules, the misfit is likely to be low and the degree of Europeanization correspondingly weak. By contrast, states that consistently download EU policies which are modelled on alien institutional systems, will find themselves under European and domestic pressure to fall into line. The gradual accumulation of misfits will eventually produce serious implementation problems, significant political crises and, possibly, sudden domestic transformations (Risse *et al.* 2001: 8). To summarize the argument thus far, 'policy shapers' in the EU seek to ensure that the two logics of action – the European and the national – are as closely aligned as possible, whereas as 'policy takers' struggle to achieve such a fit. Consequently, they find themselves under pressure from national actors such as environmental pressure groups, as well as EU bodies such as the Commission and the European Court of Justice (ECJ), to adapt their policy systems to EU requirements. Generally speaking, the larger the 'misfit' the greater the likelihood of domestic change (see Table 8.1).

However, several observers have correctly pointed out that the presence of a 'misfit' is only ever a necessary but an insufficient condition for Europeanization (i.e. domestic change). This is because EU policy is a complex amalgam of different national approaches (i.e. a 'patchwork' (Rehbinder and Stewart 1985: 254)). Weale claims that EU environmental standards are:

> neither a reflection of a dominant coalition of countries pushing their own national style of regulation, nor a merry go round, in which different countries have a go at imposing their own national style in a sector that is of particular importance to them. Instead they are the aggregated and transformed standards of their original champions modified under the need to secure political accommodation from powerful veto players.
>
> (2002: 209–10)

Table 8.1 Degrees of domestic policy change

	Extent of policy 'misfit'	*Amount of domestic change*
Absorption	Small: EU and national policy similar	Small: States are able to incorporate/domesticate EU requirements without substantially modifying national policies
Accommodation	Medium: EU and national policy differ	Medium: states accommodate/mediate EU requirements by adapting existing policy while leaving its core features intact
Transformation	High: EU and national policy markedly different	High: domestication fails; states forced to replace or substantially alter existing policy to satisfy EU requirements

Source: Based on Boerzel and Risse 2000.

The obvious implication of this is that no state can ever be perfectly aligned to every requirement listed in a single Directive, let alone every Directive in the whole *acquis* – that is, there will *always* be some misfits. Somehow, other intervening variables need to be included in the analysis to account for the specific patterns of Europeanization that we see unfolding in different Member States (see Cowles *et al.* 2001; Boerzel 2002a). These variables include, among others: the extent to which features of national policy are institutionally rooted (Knill and Lenschow 2000; Knill 2001); the number of 'veto points' that have to be passed at the domestic level (Haverland 2000); the presence of national pressure groups able and willing to 'exploit' misfits; the national societal support for environmental protection and the national societal support for European integration.

Measuring the Europeanization of national environmental policy

In this chapter, the combined effects of Europeanization and domestication will be assessed along three distinct but subtly interrelated variables, namely *policy content*, *policy structure* and *policy style*.

Following Hall (1993), policy content can be divided into three different levels. The first relates to the precise setting of policy instruments, e.g. the level of emission standards or taxes, the chemicals included in 'grey' and 'black' lists, etc. The second is the instruments or techniques by which policy goals are attained, e.g. direct regulation, fiscal instruments, or voluntary agreements. The third level comprises the overall goals that guide policy. These goals operate within a policy paradigm or a 'framework of ideas and standards that specifies not only the goals of policy and the kind of instruments that can be used to attain them, but also the very nature of the problems they are meant to be addressing' (Hall 1993: 279).

The concept of policy structure is potentially very broad, which raises some problems defining its boundaries, not least in relation to policy style. National institutional structures range from the basic building blocks of the state (departments, agencies, etc.) through to policy co-ordination networks, codes, guidelines, and 'ways of working' (Peters, 1999: 28, 146; Bulmer and Burch 1998, 2000).

The more cultural aspects of national policy structure – the norms and values associated with administrative work (e.g. Bulmer and Burch 1998, 2000) – will be dealt with here separately as policy style. Following Richardson, Gustafsson and Jordan, a society's 'standard operating procedures for making and implementing policies' (Richardson *et al.* 1982: 2) can be characterized along two axes:

1   a government's approach to problem solving, ranging from anticipatory/active to reactive,
2   a government's relationship to other actors in the policy-making and

implementation process, characterized by their inclination either to reach consensus with organized groups or to impose decisions.

With the help of these two axes, dynamic changes in national policy styles due to Europeanization can be 'mapped'.

Findings of the comparative study

This section presents a comparative analysis of the Europeanization of national environmental policy in ten EU Member States (namely, Austria, Ireland, Finland, France, Germany, Greece, the Netherlands, Spain, Sweden and the UK) on the basis of detailed country studies to be published in full elsewhere (see Jordan and Liefferink 2004).

Policy content

Table 8.2 summarizes the main impacts of Europeanization on environmental policy content in the ten countries. The single most obvious point is that the EU has affected some aspect of policy content in all 10 states, even the most environmentally progressive or 'leader' states such as Germany, Sweden and the Netherlands. At a very general level it is possible to identify instances where the EU has Europeanized all three levels of policy content as well as the overarching policy paradigms of national action. In terms of policy paradigms, the EU has undeniably promoted a more preventative, source-based approach to policy making, which fitted neatly with common practice in countries such as the Netherlands and Germany, but clashed with (and required changes to be made to) everyday practice in, for example, Ireland and the UK. A raft of water and air pollution Directives dating back to the 1970s have also helped to bring about a fundamental shift in the goals of national policy. Countries such as the UK, Finland, France and Greece have had to adapt their domestic arrangements, which contained relatively few explicit emission standards or focused on attaining pre-determined levels of environmental quality through the setting of environmental quality objectives (EQOs). However, the environmental *acquis* also contains some EQOs and environmental quality standards (e.g. the Directives relating to bathing water, freshwater fish and shellfish, as well as to air quality, and the application of sewage sludge to agricultural land), which have disrupted arrangements in countries such as Germany and Sweden which had traditionally relied upon emission limits.

The EU has also introduced entirely new policy instruments in some countries (e.g. air quality standards for SO_2 and smoke, lead and NO_2 in many Member States including the Netherlands and the UK; 'emission bubbles' and restrictions on the total production of certain chemicals such as CFCs). It has also altered the manner in which existing tools are

Table 8.2 Policy content in c.2000 as compared to 1970

	Goals	Dominant instrument(s)	Calibration of instruments: additional EU effect
Austria	Still source-based	Still mostly regulation, but various NEPIs/procedural instruments	Little overall change
Finland	Increasingly source-based	Still mostly regulation, but some NEPIs	Tighter standards
France	Increasingly source-based	Still mostly regulation, but various NEPIs	Tighter standards
Germany	Still mainly source-based	Still mostly regulation, but various NEPIs/procedural instruments	Little overall change
Greece	Increasingly source-based	More regulation but also more procedural instruments	Significantly tighter standards
Ireland	More source-based	More regulatory, but several NEPIs	Tighter standards (but implementation problems)
The Netherlands	Still mainly source-based	Still mostly regulation, but several NEPIs	Little overall change
Spain	More source-based	Still mostly regulation, but various NEPIs/procedural instruments	Significantly tighter standards
Sweden	Still mainly source-based	Still mostly regulation, but more procedural instruments	Little overall change
The UK	More source-based	Mostly regulation, but some NEPIs	Tighter standards

Source: Country studies, see note 2.

applied (e.g. the use of environmental impact assessment (EIA) in Sweden). The tools that have caused the most disruption are those that belong to the new generation of less interventionist, 'bottom-up' instruments, sometimes referred to as 'new environmental policy instruments' (NEPIs) (Jordan and Worzel 2003; cf. Knill and Lenschow 2000). Many of them are mainly procedural in nature, for example the Directives on access to environmental information, environmental impact assessment and environmental management. Although these have been fairly comfortably accepted in countries such as the UK, they have misfitted with everyday practice in states such as Sweden, Germany and Austria. In these states, environmental policy objectives have traditionally been implemented through the setting of strong, source-based controls and the adoption of the 'best available technology' (BAT).

Finally, the EU has tightened the level at which these instruments are formally calibrated or 'set'. In some countries the overall extent of domestic adaptation has been relatively limited (e.g. the Netherlands, Austria, Sweden and Germany), whereas in others it has been quite dramatic (namely Greece, Ireland and Spain). The rest (e.g. France, Finland and the UK) have been forced to raise their standards by an intermediate amount.

In fact, the EU's influence extends well beyond the three main levels of our definition of policy content. For instance, the EU has introduced entirely new policy issues in some countries. The best examples are probably Ireland (waste management), and Spain (fisheries), though the EU could also be said to have championed a formalized system of biodiversity protection that is alien to several member states (namely France, the UK, Sweden and Ireland among others). The EU has also forced member states to alter the importance that they place on particular sub-categories of environmental protection. For instance, the EU forced the UK, which had a well developed corpus of policy relating to land use planning and nature conservation, to pay much more sustained attention to controlling industrial pollution at source.

Policy structure

As in the case of policy content, the single most obvious point to make about the Europeanization of environmental policy structures (Table 8.3) is that the EU *has* affected some aspect of policy structure in all 10 countries, including the most environmentally progressive or 'leader' states. It is immediately obvious that the policy pressures arising from membership of the EU, have forced all states to develop new environmental policy coordination mechanisms. These take the form of committees or networks at the domestic level, whose purpose is to ensure that national negotiators present one, single coherent point of view or position in EU negotiations. Similar arrangements have had to be created in, or involving the national permanent representations to co-ordinate the national position in,

Brussels. The most striking feature of these arrangements is that while they are 'new', they often represent only a very slight modification of the pre-existing networks that traditionally linked different departments. The degree and suddenness of these changes has been greatest in countries which joined the EU only very recently (e.g. Sweden and Finland), or had traditionally relied upon a much less co-ordinated approach to EU policy making (e.g. Germany and the Netherlands). The need for better co-ordination has not been nearly so pressing in hierarchically structured states such as the UK, which have simply fine-tuned their existing arrangements to respond to EU pressures.

Similarly, most states have created new institutional procedures to consult with their national parliaments throughout the course of a negotiation on a particular dossier. Again, many of these are new, but they do not represent a dramatic or wholesale break with the past; they are a modification of existing practices and structures. However, there is a common perception among many of the country study authors that the highly technical nature of much environmental decision making and the EU, the speed at which dossiers are moved through the EU system, and the physical remoteness of Brussels and Strasbourg, have combined to reduce national parliamentary scrutiny of EU policy making.

The Europeanization of the content of national policy has also vastly increased the workload in most national environmental departments. Consequently, some have grown in size relative to less-Europeanized cognate departments (e.g. the UK). Membership has also created new political opportunities and points of leverage for national environmental departments to exploit. In less strongly co-ordinated national governments, the Europeanization of environmental policy making allows national environment ministries to agree to ambitious proposals in the Environment Council, which can then be presented to cognate departments as a *fait accompli*. In more tightly co-ordinated national systems (e.g. the UK), Europeanization has strengthened the arm of environment ministries in inter-departmental conflicts with cognate departments which set the agreed, cross-governmental position (Jordan 2001, 2002a).

In addition to that, the country studies confirm that Europeanization has helped to centralize policy making responsibilities into the hands of central government departments (e.g. the UK), and technical agencies (e.g. Sweden) at the expense of sub-national pollution control bodies, and local or regional government (e.g. Germany). Finally, Europeanization has generally increased opportunities for environmental NGOs. The possibility to lodge formal complaints with the Commission against imperfect implementation of EU law has created an important additional route for them to 'fight' their own national governments (Fairbrass and Jordan 2001). Most well-known in this context are cases where NGOs have tried to stop building projects in natural areas with reference to EU directives (e.g. the UK, Spain and the Netherlands).

Table 8.3 Policy structure in c.2000 as compared to 1970

	Arrangements for EU and foreign environmental policy co-ordination	Importance of national parliament in environmental policy	Strength of national environment ministry	Importance of sub-national level in environmental policy
Austria	+ Some new structures added	− Weaker	++ Significantly stronger	−− Länder and 'social partners' weaker
Finland	++ Strengthened domestically and in the EU	−	+	??
France	++ New co-ordination structures created; attempt to be more pro-active	−− Increasingly marginalized	+ Empowered	− Weaker
Germany	++ Strengthened domestically and in the EU	+/−	+	+/− Länder initially weaker, later partly reclaimed
Greece	++ Strengthened domestically and in the EU	+/−	++ Creation of Environment Ministry	??
Ireland	+ Some new co-ordination structures	+/−	+/− More powerful but still relatively small	+/−
The Netherlands	++ Strengthened domestically and in the EU	− Still low	+ Growing c.f. MFA	+/− Still low
Spain	++ Strengthened domestically and in the EU	+/−	++ Creation of Environment Ministry	+/−
Sweden	++ Strengthened domestically and in the EU	+/− New consultation procedures added	+/−	+ Increased importance of technical agencies
The UK	+ Existing structures strengthened	−	+	−− Significantly lower

Source: Country studies, see note 2.

Notes
Meaning of signs
++ significantly more; + slightly more; +/− unchanged; − slightly less; −− significantly less.

Europeanization of national environmental policy

The overall pattern is one of slow and steady adaptation, with very few obvious discontinuities or sudden step changes. The two most dramatic changes to arise from EU membership are as follows. The first is probably the creation of integrated environmental ministries in Greece and Spain, and larger technical enforcement and monitoring agencies in the UK, France and Spain. However, in none of these cases was the EU the only motivating factor. The second is the deep Europeanization of national legal structures, which is of course, a general feature of many policy areas, not just the environment. In the case of Regulations the extent of Europeanization is effectively total, because EU law is directly applicable and in effect automatically becomes national law. With Directives the extent of Europeanization is not nearly so great as each country usually relies upon its own approach to transposition. However, nowadays, the Commission is usually very quick to commence infringement proceedings against states that do not adapt their national legal systems to fit EU legislative requirements. The practice of using administrative circulars to transpose Directives, which was common in Germany, Ireland and France, has been outlawed by the ECJ. In effect, the Commission has succeeded in preventing states from evading or otherwise masking the Europeanization of legal structures.

Finally, our study identifies the same overall pattern of winners and losers as that identified by other analysts (e.g. Rometsch and Wessels 1996). Of the main winners, the most prominent in the environmental sectors are national environmental departments, sub-national technical agencies (e.g. France and Sweden) and environmental pressure groups. The main losers are national parliaments, which have seen their importance further denuded by the centralization of policy making, foreign ministries (which are no longer solely responsible for determining the content of national foreign policy), and local and regional government.

Policy style

In sharp contrast to the content of national policies, national policy styles appear not to have changed that much under the EU's influence (see Table 8.4). On the whole the dominant style remains consensual rather than adversarial, and has become more proactive in a number of member states. The latter appears to be restricted mainly to some of the environmental 'leader' states; such as Germany, the Netherlands, Sweden and France. However, this suggests that there has been an autonomous trend rather than an EU effect. In Finland, by contrast, the increasing role of the EU in agenda-setting seems to have led national policy actors to behave in a more reactive way. The basically reactive style of Greece, Spain, Ireland and the UK, moreover, appears to be hardly affected by Europeanization. This is intriguing because the aim of many EU environmental policies (and established principles of several Action Programmes)

Table 8.4 Policy structure in c.2000 as compared to 1970

	Active (precautionary) versus reactive (curative)	Adversarial versus consensual
Austria	More anticipatory/strategic	More adversarial
Finland	More reactive	Somewhat more adversarial
France	More anticipatory	More adversarial
Germany	More anticipatory	Still consensual
Greece	Still reactive	Still state-led
Ireland	Still reactive	Still consensual
The Netherlands	More anticipatory	Still consensual
Spain	Still reactive	Still consensual
Sweden	More anticipatory	More adversarial
The UK	Still reactive	Still consensual

Source: Country studies, see Note 2.

is to prevent environmental problems before they appear and become serious, and to promote public consultation and public participation. We speculate on possible explanations below.

One other anomaly is worthy of note, namely the shift towards a more adversarial style of politics in countries that have traditionally been highly consensual. The two most obvious examples here are Austria and Sweden and, to a lesser extent, Finland. The explanation offered by the respective authors is that the deadlines governing EU policy making have speeded up the domestic policy process, reducing the scope for extensive consultation with affected interests.

Apart from the latter, quite specific change, the overall impact of the EU on national policy style appears to have been quite limited; or at least it is very difficult to disentangle the 'EU effect' from other domestic and/or socio-economic causes of change. These include the post-industrial demand among national publics for higher environmental standards, financial budgetary pressures (Austria, Ireland, Germany and Finland), domestic political change (namely the election of right wing governments promoting variants of new public management, e.g. the UK) and long-term economic transformations (e.g. the rapid development of the tourist industry in Greece and Spain)

The Europeanization of national environmental policy: general patterns and processes

Table 8.5 summarizes these general patterns of Europeanization in the ten countries using the measures introduced above (Table 8.1). It reveals that the impact of the EU is indeed differentiated between sectors and between countries. The EU effect on the content of policy appears to have been the deepest and most profound, whereas policy structures and policy

Table 8.5 The overall extent of Europeanization

	Policy structures	Policy content	Policy style
Austria	Accommodation	Accommodation	Absorption
Finland	Absorption	Accommodation	Absorption
France	Accommodation/ transformation	Accommodation	Absorption
Germany	Accommodation	Accommodation	Absorption
Greece	Accommodation	Transformation	Absorption
Ireland	Accommodation	Transformation	Absorption
The Netherlands	Accommodation	Absorption	Absorption
Spain	Accommodation	Transformation	Absorption
Sweden	Accommodation	Absorption	Absorption
The UK	Absorption	Transformation	Absorption

Note
For meaning of terms, see Table 8.1.

style appear to have been much less affected. In general, the effects of Europeanization can be identified at the level of policy paradigms, policy goals, policy tools and the calibration of those tools. The impact on structures has been less dramatic, incremental and mostly path dependent. With some exceptions (see above), the basic building blocks of the state remain remarkably untouched. In fact, recent research even on the most 'Europeanized' parts of state structures (i.e. those co-ordinating EU policy within Brussels) (Kassim *et al.* 2000, 2001) has found that each country essentially retains its own, distinctive approaches and procedures. Thus, national co-ordination mechanisms come in very different sizes, have very different ambitions and interface with national actors in markedly contrasting ways. The really big 'machinery of government' changes have arisen because of domestic and mostly 'non environmental' political demands. Finally, it is very difficult to make firm statements about the Europeanization of policy style, given the difficulties of disentangling the 'EU effect' from the many other causal factors.

The most obvious explanation for this pattern is related to the *modus operandi* of the EU. First and foremost, the EU disseminates policy content, not policy structures and a policy style. To use Alberta Sbragia's apt phrase, the EU has taken a 'vow of poverty'; it steers by issuing regulations (Sbragia 2000). Some policy instruments may, of course, imply a change in policy style (e.g. the dissemination of emission limits and EIA procedures is supposed to promote more anticipatory policy style), but do not of themselves directly require it. The EU has in fact very little ability to dictate the operation or structure of national public administrations (Bossaert *et al.* 2001: 3; Goetz 2001: 1040), or directly influence the policy style of a country. Directives (the main instrument of EU environmental policy) are, of course, mainly output orientated – they specify the ends to be achieved, but not the means of doing so. European integration is, at the end of the day, a legal process, enshrined in and underpinned by written legal texts. Therefore, it is not at all surprising to find that national legal systems have been the most Europeanized (Alter 2001; Snyder 2001).

Another aspect of Europeanization we sought to understand was the overall geographical pattern of change. Simplifying greatly, the well-known 'pioneers' (Andersen and Liefferink 1997) in our sample (i.e. Germany, the Netherlands and Sweden), have had to adapt the least, whereas some aspects of policy in Spain, Greece and Ireland have been completely transformed by EU membership. These two groups could be crudely labelled as policy 'shapers' and policy 'takers'. The UK initially belonged to the group of heavily Europeanized policy 'takers' but started to adopt a more active stance in EU environmental policy from the 1990s. An intermediate grouping of states comprising France, Finland and Austria have neither consistently 'shaped' nor 'taken' EU policy since joining. They have nevertheless been able to limit the impact of the EU on national environmental policy as compared with the group of policy 'takers'. The overall pattern is shown in Figure 8.1, which provides a 'snapshot' of the situation around 2000.

At a very general level it is possible to explain this pattern in terms of the regulatory competition between states to set the European 'rules of the game'. Every single country has at times – alone or together with other states – sought to upload aspects of policy content to the EU. The Netherlands has been conspicuously concerned with promoting long-term strategic planning, environmental impact assessment and 'good governance'. These are very similar to the UK's priorities. Germany in particular sought to promote uniform emission limits and the use of BAT, as well as measures to reduce car pollution. France and Germany on the other hand were early advocates of stronger water pollution controls. Still other states have tried to upload generic issues rather than specific approaches, for example chemicals (Sweden), transport (Austria), water supply (Spain and Greece). Finally, deeply Europeanized states (i.e. Spain, Greece and Ireland) have not consistently uploaded anything, although Ireland has long standing reservations about nuclear power (especially in the UK), and Greece and Spain have successfully argued for EU cohesion funding (i.e. a subsidy for fitting domestic pollution control facilities). If anything, Figure 8.1 suggests that those countries that have been engaged most consistently in uploading policies to Brussels have generally been least Europeanized. However, this by no means suggests a direct link between the two. With the exception of the UK's shift from the late 1980s, perhaps, countries do not decide to invest in uploading only or mainly in order to limit the degree of Europeanization. There are many variables intervening in this process. To mention just a few: a generally positive attitude towards European integration is likely to increase the willingness to put considerable effort in uploading (or 'constructive pushing', cf. Liefferink and

	EU policy taker	EU policy maker
Weakly Europeanized	Austria, France, Finland	The Netherlands, Germany, Sweden
Strongly Europeanized	Ireland, Greece, Spain	The UK

Figure 8.1 Patterns of domestic action and domestic impact in c.2000.

Andersen 1998; e.g. in Germany and the Netherlands), whereas a high public and political profile of environmental issues 'at home' may have a similar effect (e.g. Sweden and the UK since the late 1980s). On the other hand, those countries that have generally set their priorities on other issues of European integration than the environment are more likely passively to 'take' policies suggested by the EU in this particular field (the Mediterranean countries, Ireland and, to a lesser extent, Finland). The figure thus shows an end effect rather than a direct causal relationship (for an alternative discussion of essentially the same relationship, see Boerzel 2002b).

However, these very broad patterns mask a number of interesting subdynamics. The first relates to the timing of change. Generally speaking, the element of national policy to be Europeanized first is policy content. Much later, states react to the emergence of politically embarrassing or financially costly misfits by making structural and tactical changes to better 'shape' EU policy. The best examples are to be found in the Netherlands and Germany (which improved their respective internal coordination capacities) and the UK (which took a strategic decision to domesticate the EU by uploading national 'success stories'). Similarly, traditional policy styles in Austria, Germany and Sweden are coming under pressure to adapt to cope with the Europeanization of their respective national policies.

The second relates to specific items of legislation which, in certain circumstances, can have anomalous impacts. It is obvious that specific Directives can and often do provoke significant national adaptations even in those countries that have been much less Europeanized than the norm. A number of Directives stand out as having caused problems in almost all states. These include the drinking and bathing water Directives, the nitrates Directive, and the habitats and wild birds Directives. This suggests that there are some Directives that misfit with most, if not all, national policies – that is, almost all states find them deeply problematic. This finding has potentially important implications for the continuing debate about which actors exert the strongest control in the EU (see below). Moreover, even the original champions of these particular Directives have been Europeanized to an important extent. There are various examples of an uploaded policy 'backfiring' in unexpected ways, causing much more domestic change (i.e. Europeanization) than the original champion originally intended, e.g. in the UK (IPPC), the Netherlands (nature conservation), and Germany (various air pollution Directives). These and other sub-dynamics cannot be properly understood without more detailed comparative empirical research.

Third, as touched upon above, the extent to which states 'take' or 'shape' policy has varied over time. The UK is a good example of a 'taker' that has transformed itself into much more of a 'maker'. Germany on the other hand has shifted in the other direction, 'making' important areas of EU policy in the 1980s only then to lapse into a more passive mode of behaviour in the 1990s which has culminated in a significant 'proceduralization' of national policy. The behaviour of other states has remained much more constant, be they 'shapers' (the Netherlands) or 'takers' (Greece, Ireland and Spain). There are country-specific reasons for these changes, but the important overall point is that they cannot be understood simply as a response to 'outside pressures' from the EU, or 'inside out' pressure exerted by states on the EU (e.g. by uploading successful national policies). Rather, they demonstrate the intricate interrelationships between European integration and Europeanization. For example, European integration may lead to a series of politically and economically costly domestic adaptations. One way states seek to circumvent future 'misfits' is to adopt a more proactive mode of behaviour, although uploading policies to the EU may still result in unforeseen 'rebound effects' at some future point. When viewed over longer periods of time, it is possible to appreciate that national and EU policy systems are, in fact, mutually co-evolving. However, above we identified the difficulties that mutual causality poses for the design of EU research.

It has been suggested above that Europeanization is the outcome of an external pressure (or combination of pressures) exerted on member states by the EU. When states adapt to that external pressure by adjusting their domestic policy arrangements then Europeanization has occurred. Therefore, a discontinuity or 'misfit' between what the EU requires and pre-existing national policy arrangements, has to be a necessary (though not a sufficient) condition for Europeanization to take place. If this view is correct, what additional, intervening variables might predict whether that change actually occurs or not?

A reasonable predictor of national change appears to be the level of domestic political support for environmental protection. Thus the most Europeanized states in Table 8.5 (namely Spain, Greece, Ireland and the UK) have generally exhibited lower than average levels of political support for environmental protection. On the other hand, 'leader' states with more environmentally demanding publics such as Germany, Sweden, the Netherlands and Austria have been far less Europeanized across all three domains of policy. There are two possible flaws in this line of argument. The first is that although levels of environmental ambition are negatively correlated with the depth of Europeanization, one is still left to explain the differential Europeanization of the three components of national policy, or, indeed, the variations within any one component (e.g. policy content). Second, levels of environmental ambition may simply be another way of measuring the level of misfit (i.e. more environmentally progressive societies tend to have more progressive environmental policies which fit with what the EU demands).

A more important intervening variable is the presence of actors who are sufficiently well motivated to exploit any misfit between EU and national policy. At this point, it becomes very difficult to identify *a priori* the precise conditions under which a misfit will translate into domestic change. Much depends on what is being Europeanized. Clearly, some changes (e.g. the amendment of national legal structures) are fairly easy for states to make, or are patently in their self-interest to make (e.g. the improvement of internal co-ordination arrangements). Others (e.g. the wholesale re-organization of national permitting systems or the commitment of large amounts of new investment in environmental improvement) require harder choices and are less likely to occur without sustained political pressure. This explains why the EU appears to have succeeded rather better at Europeanizing (i.e. harmonizing) national legal systems, than national polities or policy outcomes (see below). Clearly, national actors do have to exploit misfits to exert political pressure on states. Environmental pressure groups served this purpose in the UK and, to a much lesser extent, Spain, Greece and Ireland. Interestingly, also producers of environmental technology or 'progressive' industries with a competitive interest in strict environmental policies have at times played this role (so-called 'helpers interests', cf. Prittwitz 1990). However, there must also be personalities in EU institutions willing to respond to these demands. The most important locus for these conflicts is the Commission's infringement procedure. Often, unless and until this process is triggered, 'paper' misfits will not translate into domestic change (cf. the 'pull-and-push' model of implementation, developed by Boerzel 2000). It is very difficult to generalize because in the final analysis Europeanization (or, to be more precise, EU demands) are often just an input to domestic political processes, of which there is no single, commonly agreed model.

Conclusions

The main finding of this chapter is that each and every state has been Europeanized to some extent. Overall, the EU has had a much deeper impact on the content of national policy than policy structures or the style in which they function. The impact is, of course, highly differentiated across countries and the three dimensions of national policy because states began from different starting positions. The level of 'fit' or 'misfit' between the EU and national policies provides a crude predictor of the overall level of Europeanization. Thus states such as the Netherlands, Sweden and (until recently) Germany have always been quite closely aligned to EU policies and have not been that deeply Europeanized. However, conscious human agency also plays an important part in modulating the long-term effect of any misfit. The most obvious action a state can take to circumvent misfits is to upload policies of its own to the EU. The UK has employed this strategy to particularly good effect since the early 1990s. However, the relationship between the depth of Europeanization and the eagerness to 'make' (rather than 'take' EU rules) is not clear cut (Figure 8.1). There are, for instance, deeply Europeanized states such as Spain, Greece and Ireland that continue to 'take' policy from the EU; i.e. they show little willingness to circumvent Europeanization by uploading national policy models to the EU. At the same time there are very weakly Europeanized states such as the Netherlands and Sweden that continue to pursue a highly proactive environmental stance in the EU.

Do these findings imply that studying Europeanization is somehow unimportant or unnecessary? Our response is emphatically 'no'. First, even though the EU has not completely overturned domestic structures and policy styles, its influence has been hugely significant over such a comparatively short period of time. National politics (as distinct from policy) has been deeply transformed by EU membership and to that extent cannot be properly understood outside of an EU framework of analysis. Future analysis might seek to describe and explain the patterns of Europeanization in other, non-environmental sectors, in order that cross-sectoral comparisons can be made. Such research might explore how far the depth of Europeanization in various sectors can be related to the length of the EU's involvement (i.e. is it less significant in policy areas where the EU's competence is less well or more recently developed?), or the mode of the EU's action (i.e. positive or negative integration?)

Second, there are many instances where the EU has directly affected national policy. These provide fairly clear-cut symptoms of Europeanization at the national level (and particularly on the content of national policy), and their timing and distribution deserve to be documented empirically, not least because they provide such an important trigger of national policy and politics. However, having looked in some detail at Europeanization in the ten countries, one is struck by the extent to which states and the EU are involved in a highly dynamic set of two-way interactions. It is more meaningful, we would argue, to use the term 'Europeanization' to describe national adaptations to EU requirements, and use other terms (e.g. benchmarking, policy transfer etc.) to describe and explain the horizontal (i.e. predominantly state to state) flows of influence which occur in the EU. Having said that, future Europeanization research now needs to question whether it is appropriate to bracket off the 'inside out' impact of states on the EU, and treat the EU as an independent variable. To the extent that states use the EU to upload their preferred policies (and thereby circumvent Europeanization), the EU is at best only an intervening variable.

Finally, irrespective of these new debates, Europeanization research is worth pursuing because it sheds much new light on the old debate about European integration. The old debate between intergovernmentalism and its critics reached an impasse in the 1990s. By studying Europeanization it is possible to better understand the extent to which states genuinely do achieve their objectives in the EU, although this feedback effect on integration is not always that well developed in the existing literature on Europeanization. One of the striking findings of this chapter is that for many countries (and not just the weakly co-ordinated, policy 'takers'), Europeanization has been a hugely unexpected, unpredictable and, at times, chaotic process. This casts doubt on the intergovernmentalist claim that states are remote from (and largely in firm control of) the integration process (e.g. Moravcsik 1998). Our conclusion is that such an argument imputes to Member States far more autonomy and human agency than everyday experience suggests they actually have.

Notes

1 This chapter presents the preliminary findings of a three-day workshop held in Cambridge (UK) in the summer of 2001. We would like to thank the participants as well as the European Science Foundation, the UK Economic Research Council (R000237870) and the University of Nijmegen for kindly providing joint funding.
2 This chapter draws upon a series of national case studies written by: Volkmar Lauber (Austria), Brendan Flynn (Ireland), Rauno Sairinen and Arto Lindholm (Finland), Henry Buller (France), Rüdiger Wurzel (Germany), Maria Kousis and Joseph Lekakis (Greece), Mariëlle van der Zouwen and Duncan Liefferink (the Netherlands), Susana Aguilar Fernández (Spain), Annica Kronsell (Sweden) and Andrew Jordan (the UK) (for details, see Jordan and Liefferink 2004).

References

Alter, K. (2001) *Establishing the Supremacy of European Law*, Oxford: Oxford University Press.
Andersen, M.S. and Liefferink, D. (eds) (1997) *European Environmental Policy: The Pioneers*, Manchester: Manchester University Press.
Boerzel, T.A. (2000) 'Why there is no Southern problem: The implementation of EU environmental policy in Germany and Spain', *Journal of European Public Policy* 7: 141–62.
—— (2002a) *States and Regions in the European Union*, Cambridge: Cambridge University Press.
—— (2002b) 'Pace setting, foot dragging and fence setting: Member State responses to Europeanisation', *Journal of Common Market Studies* 40: 193–214.
Boerzel, T. and Risse, T. (2000) *When Europe Hits Home: Europeanisation and Domestic Change*, Paper RSC 2000/56. EUI Working Papers: Florence.

Bossaert, D., Demmke, C., Nomden, K. and Polet, R. (2001) *Civil Services in the Europe of the Fifteen*, Maastricht: European Institute for Public Administration.

Bulmer, S. and Burch, M. (1998) 'Organizing for Europe', *Public Administration*, 76: 601–28.

—— (2000) 'The Europeanisation of British Central Government', in Rhodes, R.A.W. (ed.) *Transforming British Government*, London: Macmillan.

Cowles, M., Caporaso, J. and Risse, T. (eds) (2001) *Transforming Europe*, Ithaca: Cornell University Press.

Fairbrass, J. and Jordan, A. (2001) 'Making European Union biodiversity policy: national barriers and European opportunities', *Journal of European Public Policy* 8: 499–518.

George, S. (1996) 'The EU: approaches from international relations', in Kassim, H. and Menon, A. (eds) *The European Union and National Industrial Policy*, London: Routledge.

Goetz, K. (2001) 'Executive governance in Central and Eastern Europe', *Journal of European Public Policy* 8: 863–1051.

Haigh, N. (1984) *EEC Environmental Policy and Britain*, London: ENDS.

Hall, P. (1993) 'Policy paradigms, social learning and the state', *Comparative Politics* 25: 275–96.

Haverland, M. (2000) 'National adaptation to European integration: the importance of institutional veto points', *Journal of Public Policy* 20: 83–103.

Héritier, A. *et al.* (1996) *Ringing the Changes*, Berlin: De Gruyter.

Heritier, A., Kerwer, D., Knill, C., Lehmkuhl, D., Teutsch, M. and Douillet, A.-C. (2001) *Differential Europe*, London: Rowman and Littlefield.

Jordan, A.J. (2001) 'National environmental ministries: managers or ciphers of European environmental policy?', *Public Administration* 79: 643–63.

—— (2002a) *The Europeanisation of British Environmental Policy: A Departmental Perspective*, London: Palgrave.

—— (ed.) (2002b) *Environmental Policy in the European Union: Actors, Institutions and Processes*, London: Earthscan.

Jordan, A.J. and Liefferink, D. (eds) (2004) *Environmental Policy in Europe: The Europeanization of National Environmental Policy*, Routledge: London.

Jordan, A., Wurzel, R. and Zito, A.R. (eds) (2003) *New Instruments of Environmental Governance?*, Frank Cass: London.

Kassim, H., Peters, B.G. and Wright, V. (eds) (2000) *The National Coordination of EU Policy: The Domestic Level*, Oxford: Oxford University Press.

Kassim, H., Menon, A. Peters, B.G. and Wright, V. (eds) (2001) *The National Coordination of EU Policy: The European Level*, Oxford: Oxford University Press.

Knill, C. (2001) *The Europeanisation of National Administrations*, Cambridge: Cambridge University Press.

Knill, C. and Lenschow, A. (eds) (2000) *Implementing EU Environmental Policy*, Manchester: Manchester University Press.

Liefferink, D. (1996) *Environment and the Nation State*, Manchester: Manchester University Press.

Liefferink, D. and Andersen, M.S. (1998) 'Strategies of the "Green" Member States in EU environmental policy', *Journal of European Public Policy* 5: 2, 254–70.

Liefferink, D., Lowe, P.D. and Mol, A.P.J. (eds) (1993) *European Integration and Environmental Policy*, Chichester: John Wiley.

Lowe, P. and Ward, S. (1998) (eds) *British Environmental Policy and Europe*, London: Routledge.
Moravcsik, A. (1994) *Why the EC Strengthens the State*, Centre for European Studies Working Paper 52. Cambridge, MA: Department of Government, University of Harvard.
—— (1998) *The Choice for Europe*, Ithaca, NY: Cornell University Press.
Peters, B.G. (1999) *Institutional Theory in Political Science*, London: Continuum.
Prittwitz, V. von (1990) *Das Katastrophenparadox. Elemente einer Theorie der Umweltpolitik*, Opladen: Leske und Budrich.
Radaelli, C. (2000) Whither Europeanisation? *EiOP online working paper series* 4, 8 (http://eiop.or.at/eiop/).
Rehbinder, E. and Stewart, R. (1985) *Integration Through Law, Volume II: Environmental Protection Policy*, Berlin: Walter de Gruyter.
Richardson, J., Gustafsson, G. and Jordan, G. (1982) 'The concept of policy style', in Richardson, J. (ed.) *Policy Styles in Western Europe*, London: George Allen & Unwin, pp. 1–16.
Risse, T., Cowles, M. and Caporaso, J. (2001) 'Europeanisation and domestic change: introduction', in Cowles, M. *et al.* (eds) *Transforming Europe*, Ithaca, NY: Cornell University Press.
Rometsch, D. and Wessels, W. (eds) (1996) *The EU and Member States: Towards Institutional Fusion?*, Manchester: Manchester University Press.
Sbragia, A. (2000) 'The EU as coxswain: governance by steering', in Pierre, J. (ed.) *Debating Governance*, Oxford: Oxford University Press.
Snyder, F. (ed.) (2001) *The Europeanisation of Law*, Oxford: Hart.
Wallace, H. (2000) 'Europeanisation and Globalisation', *New Political Economy* 5: 369–82.
Weale, A. (1992) *The New Politics of Pollution*, Manchester: Manchester University Press.
—— (2002) 'Environmental rules and rule making in the European Union', in Jordan, A. (ed.) *Environmental Policy in the European Union: Actors, Institutions and Processes*, London: Earthscan.

9 Ecological modernization, globalization and Europeanization

A mutually reinforcing nexus?

Debra Johnson

> There is still, in many places, a general perception that eco-efficiency means higher cost, lower profit – a sort of sacrifice you must make with respect to shareholder interests. However, if you look at the real world you find among companies a strong and positive correlation between being at the forefront of eco-efficiency and being profitable and generally successful. It is not a contradiction, it is a correlation.
> (Percy Barnevik, former President and CEO, ABB 1995)

Globalization and environmental quality remain incompatible in the eyes of many environmental NGOs and activists. Indeed, the dynamics of globalization are frequently cited as a root cause of environmental degradation. These arguments mirror those presented in the 1960s and 1970s that economic growth and environmental protection were incompatible. It was the emergence of ecological modernization (EM) ideas in Western Europe in the 1980s that helped undermine the argument regarding the antagonism between growth and environmentalism.

This chapter argues that the application of ecological modernization to the concept of globalization potentially makes globalization more palatable to environmentalists. Given the emergence of ecological modernization as a guiding policy principle within the European Union and its member states; the parallels that can be drawn between the process of Europeanization and globalization and the introduction of EM compatible policies within and by the EU, the chapter also argues that EM, globalization and Europeanization are potentially mutually supportive ideas and that the EU policy experience may act as a bellwether for future international environmental policy.

The first section discusses the globalization-environment interaction without incorporating EM ideas. The second section examines the interaction between globalization and the environment, taking EM ideas into account. The following section identifies common features underpinning the processes of globalization and Europeanization before tracing the emergence of EM principles and policies within the EU. The chapter concludes by speculating that the lagging of globalization behind Europeanization could give the EU a leadership role and/or a competitive advantage in future international environmental initiatives.

Globalization and the environment – general considerations

Through its elimination of effective borders and the subsequent emergence of multinational corporations (MNCs) as networks of globally integrated production, globalization clearly alters the context in which environmental regulation occurs, resulting in the recasting of environmental issues and the creation of new configurations of interests around these issues. However, this new context has also led to a re-run of earlier anti-growth arguments – this time with an anti-globalization theme. This section examines these arguments before introducing ecological modernization into the picture.

To the extent that globalization increases production, consumption and trade flows, it is held responsible for an accelerated rundown of the earth's natural resources and a general increase in environmental degradation. Increased trade flows, for example, involve more journeys over longer distances, thereby increasing fuel consumption and the release of greenhouse gases. The primacy of market forces fostered by globalization and the accompanying deregulation and liberalization trends, it is argued, intensifies competition. The resulting competitiveness concerns make attention to environmental issues an unaffordable luxury both for government and for the corporate sector.

In addition, globalization critics point to the diminished ability of local and national regulators to implement environmental regulations given the borderless nature of much pollution, the mobility of MNCs and the alleged priority given to economic and trade matters over environmental concerns by policy makers generally. As such, globalization raises policy issues concerned with links between trade and the environment, technology, corporate competitiveness and governance and institutions.

The pollution havens and the so-called 'race to the bottom' hypotheses are both concerned with the impact of differential environmental standards in a world of globalization-driven free factor mobility. More specifically, the pollution havens hypothesis states that in order to avoid the costs of complying with higher environmental standards in their current location, firms will relocate to countries (pollution havens) where standards, and therefore costs, are lower, resulting in the loss of jobs and investment in the country with higher standards. In this scenario, higher standards, ironically, lead to greater environmental damage as firms liberate themselves from environmental constraints in their new location. Pollution havens can also trigger off a 'race to the bottom' by increasing pressure to lower standards to prevent such migration occurring. In essence, so the argument goes, open markets undermine national environmental policies and create intense pressure to weaken regulations in order not to deter foreign investment, to make exports uncompetitive or, in line with the pollution haven hypothesis, to remove the incentive to relocate in countries with lower standards. The outcome is a downward spiral of environmental standards.

The pollution haven hypothesis ignores the increasing tendency of MNCs to standardize their technology across locations: this strategy increases compatibility between different parts of the production chain, yielding cost benefits in the process. According to the US International Trade Commission

> much research indicates that multinational firms tend to replicate the technologies employed in their home markets when operating in developing countries. Indeed the ability to duplicate technology in a number of countries is deemed central to the competitive strategy of most multinationals.
>
> (Vaughan and Nordström 1999)

Furthermore, if the home market has stricter environmental regulations than the host country, thereby requiring integration of pollution control into its technology, foreign direct investment (FDI) will be less polluting than domestic plants in the host country.

Both the 'pollution havens' and the 'race-to-the-bottom' hypotheses depend on the assumption that environmental regulations impose compliance costs that are sufficiently high to become a determining factor in business location. The limited evidence that exists indicates that environmental compliance costs are no more than 2 per cent of total costs, even for the most polluting industries. US Bureau of Census data published in 1996 indicates that, on average, US industry spent no more than 0.6 per cent of its revenue on pollution abatement. For the vast majority of sectors, the figures were lower than this, as the average was pulled up by higher figures for the most polluting industries (petroleum and coal products, chemicals, primary metal industries and paper and pulp products). This phenomenon has also been noted by the OECD, the WTO, and by the US non-governmental organization (NGO) the Worldwatch Institute (Renner 2000).

However, the additional costs incurred as a result of environmental regulation can be a determining factor in relocation, especially when profit margins are tight and the economic environment is generally unfavourable. Furthermore, it is possible that it is not actual increased costs or job losses that results in governments backing off from higher standards or lowering of standards, but the threat or fear of such effects. Again, there is some, albeit limited, evidence that fears of job losses arising from environmental regulations are much bigger than actual job losses and that the cost burden imposed by regulation turns out to be less onerous than originally envisaged (Marx 2000). Nevertheless, it can be difficult to gather support for new regulations if the general perception is that the cost of proposed regulations will bear down heavily on domestic industry. It is certainly the case that business often appeals to competitiveness concerns in its lobbying efforts against proposed new regulations.

Although examples of companies moving to 'benefit' from lower environmental compliance costs exist, there is scant evidence that this occurs in any systematic and sustained way. Analysis of trade and FDI patterns does not reveal a relative shift of 'dirty' industries from developed to developing industries. Indeed, such a move would go against the Heckscher-Ohlin principle of neo-classical trade theory that it is differences in factor endowments, namely capital and labour, which determine trade patterns. Accordingly, capital-intensive industries should be attracted to developed countries and labour intensive industries to developing countries. Trade encourages specialization, implying an increase rather than a decrease in pollution in developed countries, given their specialization in more polluting, capital-intensive industries.

Globalization and the environment after ecological modernization

As the previous section shows, even before ecological modernization ideas are brought into the debate, the trade-off between environmental quality and economic factors such as growth, investment and trade, is far from simple. It was the emergence of EM ideas (even if they were not always explicitly acknowledged as such) that helped reclaim economic growth – and also have strong resonance for the environmental quality-globalization debate.

Contemporary environmental concerns have their roots in the 1960s when many proponents of greater environmental protection were on the political margins, arguing that only a profound transformation of the political, social and economic systems would protect the planet. By the early 1970s, environmental issues were becoming more mainstream, but the title of the Club of Rome's landmark report, *Limits to Growth*, published in 1972, summed up the continuing assumption of growth-environmental incompatibility. Another 1972 publication, *Blueprint for Survival*, reinforced this view, arguing that continuation of existing trends of production and consumption would lead to 'the breakdown of society and the irreversible disruption of life-support systems on this planet'.

However, a rethink of the supposed incompatibility between growth and environmental protection began in the early 1980s, driven in part by the failure of traditional regulatory 'command-and-control' measures to deal with environmental degradation. Social scientists like Martin Jänicke, Joseph Huber and others in Germany; Gert Spaargaren, Maarten Hajer and Arthur Mol in the Netherlands and Albert Weale and Joseph Murphy in the UK were instrumental in developing EM theory as an alternative approach to environmental problems. The emphasis shifted to prevention and to the resolution of environmental problems through utilization of market forces – the essence of ecological modernization (and of globalization). This shift was reflected in the OECD and various UN agencies and was supported by less radical NGOs like the International Union for the Conservation of Nature and the World Wildlife Fund. In 1987, the Brundtland Report *Our Common Future* emphasized that environmental considerations were not peripheral but central to economic concerns and linked economic growth, social welfare and ecological sustainability.

EM developed as social theory, but the emphasis in this chapter is on the application of EM to policy and as a potential resolution of environmental-globalization conflicts. As such, the following assumptions of EM are highlighted:

1 **The reconciliation of environmental and economic objectives**
   In other words, economic growth and environmental protection are mutually beneficial. Given the incorporation of environmental features into technology, economic growth will be qualitatively different from the past. The integration of growth and environmental objectives results in a 'win-win-win' situation for the environment, the economy and business. The integration of the environmental dimension into all policy areas was a key aspiration of the EU's Fifth Environmental Action Programme (1992–2000) – an aspiration that was incorporated into the 1997 Amsterdam Treaty and which was implemented in a number of practical ways towards the end of the 1990s (see below).

2 **Technocentricism or 'Vorsprung durch Technik'**
   This is the emphasis on innovation and technology (modernism) to deliver both growth and environmental benefits by emphasizing prevention and a Schumpeterian adherence to competitiveness through innovation and market size. Accordingly, stricter environmental regulations and policies act not as a cost burden for industry but as an incentive to innovate and compete. This is reflected in the so-called 'Porter hypothesis': this states that not only are growth and environmentalism compatible but also that competitiveness depends on this link. Porter and Linde's 1995 study (Porter and Linde 1995), for example, found that of major process changes at ten manufacturers of printed circuit boards, environmental staff were behind 13 out of 33 major changes. Of these 13 changes, 12 contributed to cost reduction, eight to improvements in quality and five in extended product capabilities.

3 **The primacy of the market**
   The market is a key feature in EM. For most writers, however, the emphasis is not on pure market forces – that is, the removal of the

state or other forms of governance from the market place – but on utilizing intervention to correct for market failure and on creating an enabling framework for a positive interaction between economic development and the environment. This represents a rejection of the rigid command-and-control regulations and standards used to regulate and constrain business activities in the early days of environmental policy activism. Instead, policy makers increasingly see their role as enablers and guardians of the market, using economic or market-based instruments such as taxation, eco-labelling and emission trading schemes that work with the market to achieve their goals. This reliance on the market renders ecological modernization compatible with the dominant neo-liberal economic philosophy that has driven globalization and which underpins many of the integrative initiatives within the EU. It is the complete antithesis of the radical ecologist view that environmental protection requires systemic transformation. Indeed, 'ecological modernization can best be understood as a late twentieth-century strategy to adapt capitalism to the environmental challenge, thus strengthening it' (Young 2000). In addition, ecological modernization also offers potential for job creation.[1]

In short, the essence of EM is the assumption that innovation, stimulated by the pressures of a market economy and facilitated by an enabling state, can contribute to economic prosperity and reduce environmental degradation. These characteristics make EM attractive to several stakeholders. In the political sphere, ecological modernization has transformed the environmental debate from one of confrontation to one of consensus and co-operation – that is, it has been captured by, or adapted to, the needs of the market economy and capitalism. Ecological modernization thus holds out the possibility of resolving environmental problems within existing social, political and economic systems. As such, it has marginalized the more extreme critics of the status quo and co-opted its more moderate critics who see opportunities to bring pragmatic, technical solutions to bear on environmental problems and to bring environmental issues into the political mainstream. Ecological modernization has not only made environmental protection much less threatening to business (see Barnevik quotation at the head of chapter), but has also encouraged companies to regard the search for greater environmental protection as a positive factor in competitiveness and profitability.

That is not to say that ecological modernization is accepted wholesale – far from it. Many ecologists continue to regard reductions in consumption and the cultivation of self-sufficiency as the only long-term sustainable option. These and other less radical critics argue that ecological modernization is effectively a 'business as usual' ploy used to head off legitimate environmental concern and to ignore demands for a fundamental reassessment of approaches to environmental degradation.

Many businesses also continue to lobby against environmental measures on cost grounds. The EU's failure to reach agreement on a carbon energy tax in the early 1990s and a more general energy tax a few years later is attributable to the reluctance of member states to agree such measures unilaterally without similar action by the US and Japan. MNCs and some governments have also acted determinedly and to a degree successfully against aspects of the global climate change initiatives.

EM is also subject to a critique that is often applied to globalization – that is, that it applies to and brings benefits to developed countries but has little to offer the developing world that accounts for almost 80 per cent of the world's population.

Developing countries argue that development remains their overriding priority, that they cannot afford to embrace costly environmental measures and that, given the responsibility of the developed countries for much of the world's environmental degradation, it is the developed world that should take and pay for the necessary corrective measures.

However, a concept closely related to ecological modernization, the Environmental Kuznets Curve (EKC), supports the view that growth will ultimately also provide the solution for environmental problems in the developing world. The EKC derives its name from the original U-shaped Kuznets curve that posited that as growth increases, income distribution becomes more uneven, stabilizes at middle-income levels and then starts to even out again. In the case of the EKC, as growth gets underway, environmental degradation and pollution grow. It then stabilizes at middle-income levels and starts to decline with prosperity. Once basic needs are met, so the explanation goes, priorities shift towards improvement of the quality of life. If this hypothesis is correct, the emphasis of developing countries on attaining growth is compatible with environmental protection and in line with the philosophy of ecological modernization.

The, albeit limited, available evidence suggests that the EKC applies more to local pollution issues like urban air quality and freshwater pollutants than to degradation resulting from global phenomena like greenhouse gases (Vaughan and Nordström 1999). A possible explanation for this is that in local issues, there is a much more explicit link between cause and remedy. It is also conceivable that the EKC effect may not be so easily attainable for the least developed countries if the EKC effect experienced by developed countries occurred as a result of the migration of polluting industries to developing countries – that is, if the pollution havens hypothesis stands – as in this case, there will not be any countries to which the least developed countries can pass on their own polluting industries. However, evidence supporting the pollution havens hypothesis is not strong.

On the other hand, the EKC effect may occur if developing countries can utilize technologies that were not available to developed countries when they were at a similar stage of development. In short it is likely that economic growth is a necessary but not sufficient condition for pollution to decline with higher levels of growth. The downward turn of the U-shaped curve also requires the implementation of appropriate polices and has occurred more readily in democratic countries according to the WTO (Vaughan and Nordström 1999), which has claimed that in countries with similar income levels environmental degradation tends to be worse where greater income inequity is greatest, literacy levels are lower and there are few political and civil liberties.

Globalization and Europeanization

Many of the arguments regarding globalization and the environment and globalization and ecological modernization apply to Europeanization and the environment and to Europeanization and EM. Indeed, these arguments apply even more so in the case of Europe, given that the degree of economic and market integration is greater within the European than within the global context. Furthermore, policy initiatives within Europe provide learning opportunities regarding policy and policy implementation within a wider context.

Europeanization and globalization are both expressions of economic integration – that is, the removal of barriers to the movement of goods, services, labour, capital and communications. Achievement of this barrier-free world frees up and liberates the market and creates opportunities for the restructuring of industries and their value chains to maximize scale economies in production and distribution. In short, it is essentially a means whereby resources are allocated according to market signals that are no longer muted or even obliterated by state-led regulations and policies. As alluded to above, it is the freeing up of the market which enables innovation-led growth and the forces of competitiveness (the prime movers of ecological modernization) to come to the fore.

However, there are differences between Europeanization and globalization that render Europeanization more advanced than globalization. Europeanization is a deliberate, shaped attempt at integration. Europeanization is essentially, although not entirely, a political project with political objectives. Although its objectives are political, the methods by which European leaders have chosen to achieve these objectives are essentially economic – that is, through the construction of first a customs union, then a single market and finally economic and monetary union – and rely on closer and closer economic interdependence and integration. This is not to downplay the importance of institution and coalition building but rather to reclaim the importance of informal integration that has been rather neglected within mainstream integration literature.

Globalization is a more spontaneous process. In others words, unlike Europeanization where the explicit intention was to create 'an ever closer union',[2] there has not been, despite the conjectures of conspiracy theorists, an explicit commitment to create a globalized economy. The trade-liberalizing agenda of GATT/WTO has undoubtedly made a major contribution to globalization, but, unlike the case of Europeanization, the objectives of this policy option were apolitical and limited to forestalling the downward economic spiral that began with the pre-war surge in protectionism. It is the interaction of trade liberalization with the subsequent growth of economic liberalism in all economic spheres and technological developments, especially in the field of information and communications technology, which have contributed to the intensification of the globalization process. In short, it is the coming together of a diverse array of forces that has underpinned globalization. Europe is subject to the same forces, but its integrating momentum is reinforced by its explicit unifying agenda and as such integration is therefore more advanced within the European context. This means that, although many barriers remain within the European market place, the market is freer within EU boundaries than in the wider world, thereby providing a potentially more favourable environment in which EM ideas can work themselves out.

Europe is also the birthplace of EM. It was in the Netherlands and Germany, countries frequently regarded as environmental leaders, that EM ideas were originally articulated and it is within northern Europe in particular that new environmental ideas and policies often receive their first try-out. Unlike the international community[3] and other regional trading organizations,[4] the EU also has a governance structure that facilitates the introduction of cross-border environmental policy. Indeed, EU Treaty revisions firmly establish the legitimacy of such policy.

Europe and the emergence of EM principles and policies

Ecological modernization ideas permeate EU environmental policy. The Sixth Environmental Programme, which runs until 2010, is driven very much by the view that 'high environmental standards are also an engine for innovation – creating new markets and business opportunities' (Commission of the European Communities 2001: 9). It links environmental policy into the Lisbon process of making Europe the world's most competitive knowledge-based economy, claiming 'if we can support and encourage the development of a greener market place, then businesses and citizens will respond with technological and management innovations that will spur growth, competitiveness, profitability and job creation' (Commission of the European Communities 2001: 11).

This EM conversion has evolved over many years. The Treaty of Rome contained no direct reference to environmental issues. Indeed, given that it was drafted and agreed in the 1950s, it would have been surprising if it had. However, the Paris Summit of EC Heads of State and Government in October 1972 followed on closely from the landmark UN Conference on the Human Environment in Stockholm and resulted in the EC's First Environmental Action Programme.

The rationale for an EU environmental policy gathered pace with the beginning of the campaign to create a Single European Market (SEM) in the 1980s. The pressure came partially from the more environmentally aware member states of West Germany and the Netherlands and partially from the possibility that differences in national environmental regulations could result in the persistence of fragmented markets. There were also concerns that open markets would result in a 'race to the bottom' as described above. In other words, it was not only environmentalism but also the need to engage with the market and the spread of neo-liberal ideas that underpinned the early stages of EU environmental policy.

The 1987 Single European Act (SEA), the first reform of the EU's treaties, was passed primarily to facilitate the introduction of the SEM. However, it gave the Community explicit powers in the environmental field for the first time and determined that Community action in the environmental field should be based on the principles of polluter pays, policy integration, prevention and the rectification of damage at source. These principles had been included in earlier Environmental Action Programmes – the SEA gave them even greater import. Significantly, these principles are compatible with EM ideas: the 'polluter pays' principle (PPP) requires polluters to pay the full cost of the environmental damage they cause. In this way, the PPP provides an incentive to make products less polluting and/or to reduce the consumption of polluting goods – that is, the PPP corrects for market failure, requiring the use of market-based, policy instruments to do so. In other words, the PPP is entirely consistent with EM principles.

The 'prevention' principle involves changes to products and processes to prevent environmental damage occurring rather than relying on remedial action to repair damage after it has taken place. This implies the development of 'clean technologies'; minimal use of natural resources; minimal releases into the atmosphere, water and soil; and maximization of the recyclability and lifespan of products – developments which again are in line with the innovatory element of EM. The prevention principle also implies a move away from the regulatory command-and-control system of early environmental policy.

Policy integration involves the integration of environmental considerations into all other policy areas. Insofar as these other policy areas are directed towards the removal of barriers among member states, including barriers to investments in innovation and technology diffusion, the principles of policy integration and ecological modernization are mutually supportive. Policy integration tries to end the separation between sectoral and environmental policies, a situation that means that environmental concerns can become an add-on and can be perceived as a burden or restrictive, perhaps resulting in end-of-pipe solutions rather than preventive or anticipatory responses. In addition, the embedding of environmental considerations in sectoral policy development at the outset as a matter of course implies the compatibility of environmental considerations and economic development and should result in joint problem solving regarding environmental and sectoral matters.

The Maastricht Treaty added the precautionary principle to the list of principles guiding environmental policy and the Amsterdam Treaty incorporates sustainability as a core EU objective. Debate about the nature of environmental policy at international level increasingly incorporates the polluter pays and prevention principles.

It is all very well developing policy principles, but these principles need to be implemented. The Fifth Environmental Action Programme (EAP) (1992–2002) represented a concerted attempt to do just that. In particular, it advocated the use of a broad range of policy tools, including economic instruments and voluntary measures, and policy integration.

Previous environmental action programmes had been dominated by legal instruments. Although these remain important, the Fifth EAP envisaged the use of EM-compatible, market-based instruments such as environmental charges and taxes to avoid pollution and waste through the internalization of external costs in line with the polluter pays principle. These instruments included fiscal incentives (subsidies) and disincentives (taxes), application of the principle of environmental liability, voluntary agreements, environmental accounting, and so on. The 1993 White Paper *Growth, Competitiveness, Employment* extended this debate onto a broader policy agenda by advocating the substitution of environmental taxes for taxes on labour, resulting in a positive sum game which would enhance the Community's environmental position while increasing the number of jobs by lowering the tax on employment.

In practice, attempts to institute Community-wide environmental tax policy have not been overly successful (apart from the tax differential on lead/unleaded gasoline). The Commission's proposals in the early 1990s to introduce a carbon energy tax ran aground: member states were keen to retain their tax raising sovereignty and a conditionality clause in the proposal that the tax would not be applied until the Community's main OECD competitors, namely the US and Japan, introduced measures with equivalent effect effectively killed off the proposal. In 1997, the Commission proposed to extend excise duties to cover all energy products to end distortion between fuels and to implement the aspirations of the 1993 White Paper. Such wide-ranging, comprehensive proposals met with no success. The EU's current emphasis is on the introduction of a Directive enabling Member States to apply reduced excise duties to biofuels. Significantly, this initiative is an enabling Directive rather than a proposal for an EU-wide initiative and therefore stands a better chance of success.

Member States are reluctant to yield sovereignty to the EU for tax purposes but they have shown themselves prepared to embrace eco-taxes across a wide range of areas: energy taxes, for example, are common at Member State level as are taxes on waste and on specific products such as the recent Irish tax on plastic bags. Despite the reluctance at Union level to adopt eco-taxes, market-based instruments remain an important part of the EU's environmental strategy. The Sixth Environmental Action Programme argues 'in the right circumstances, environmental taxes can be highly effective in both cost and environmental terms... They also provide incentives for companies to research and invest in more environmentally friendly or less resource intensive technologies' (Commission of the European Communities 2001: 15).

The EU is also keen to develop initiatives to improve collaboration between environmental authorities and industry and to encourage voluntary actions by the corporate sector to improve their environmental performance. Environmental management and audit schemes fall into this category. Some large multinationals have conducted environmental audits of sorts since the early 1970s. By the late 1980s, environmental audits, especially in Europe were beginning to take on a broader and more pro-active scope. In 1993, the European Community's Environmental Management and Audit Scheme (EMAS) was adopted: it was intended not to dictate the details of audits, which were voluntary, but to create a common framework. Involvement in the scheme required external verification of the audit's findings, thereby conferring greater legitimacy on the audit.

As one of the first attempts to develop a cross-border environmental management scheme, EMAS led the way. In 1996, the International Organisation for Standardisation (ISO) made available the ISO 14000 family of standards: ISO 14001 is the only standard in the 14000 series that can be certified and is concerned with the environmental management process.[5] It is a voluntary standard that commits registered companies to introduce a systematic approach to the improvement of environmental management: it incorporates the principle of continuous improvement and has strict requirements in terms of a policy statement, document control, management review, internal audit, record keeping and training. Companies registering under ISO 14001 must also make a commitment to compliance with environmental regulation, the prevention of pollution and a formal process of planning environmental improvement and control.

By scrutinizing their processes and products, and the processes and products of their suppliers, to ensure they deliver their goods and services in a way that enhances their cost and production efficiency, companies adopting EMAS and increasingly ISO 14001 are effectively endorsing the principles of ecological modernization. More specifically, companies are increasingly recognizing that pollution represents an inefficient and incomplete use of resources, involving them in activities like waste disposal that create no added value. Effective environmental management systems (EMS) are therefore seen as a way of boosting the bottom line and of yielding competitive advantage. Indeed, Jochim Kruger, Celanese director for Europe and Asia, reportedly said, 'it's like a windfall profit having ISO 14001'[6] (Scott 1999).

In the first six years of its existence, 36,000 ISO 14001 schemes were registered, an impressive registration rate and indicative of growing and widespread acceptance of the scheme. Its acceptance has been particularly marked in the EU and Japan. Indeed, by January 2002, almost 15,500 ISO 14001 registrations (43 per cent of the total) had been made for EU sites. This compares to almost 4,000 registrations for EMAS, a scheme that now appears geographically limited and overly prescriptive compared to ISO 14001.[7]

This move towards common international auditing standards and practices has been accelerated by globalization, driven by the possibility that the persistence of different standards and regulations will act as non-tariff barriers or market fragmenting mechanisms that regulate and limit access to particular markets. The adoption of international standards by companies both facilitates access to markets across the globe and the global integration of production networks and contributes towards successful international tendering.

As alluded to above, the integration of environmental policy is a principle enshrined in the EU's treaties. The Fifth Environmental Action Programme identified five sectors – agriculture, energy, industry, tourism and transport – for which environmental policies were to be developed and promoted the idea of policy integration generally (Commission of the European Communities 2001: 13–22). The European Council in Cardiff in 1998 strove to implement the principle by requesting different Councils to prepare strategies and programmes which integrated environmental concerns into their policy areas.

The Sixth Environmental Action Programme, *Environment 2010: Our Future, Our Choice,* represents a continuation of the principles of the Fifth Action Programme. In particular, it proposes five strategic actions to help the Union meet its environmental objectives. Two in particular have resonance for the theme of ecological modernization – the continuing focus on policy integration and the focus on 'finding new ways of working closer with the market via businesses and consumers' (Commission of the European Communities 2001: 15–16).

Conclusion

In an increasingly integrated world, the configuration of trade, investment and production chains is determined by market criteria rather than being constrained by borders which can often be sub-optimal from an economic perspective. Ecological modernization reflects this trend. However, governance structures often lag behind market reality. In environmental terms, this is certainly true both globally and at European level. However, partly because integration is more advanced and more planned at European level, EU environmental policy arrangements and institutions are more developed than supranational policy and institutions or the Multilateral Environment Agreements that have proliferated in recent years. Moreover, large differences in economic development between countries, means that environmental concerns do not have the same priority in the less developed as the developed world. As such, in the interim at least, regional arrangements present the greatest possibility of incorporating environmental concerns.

Despite the obvious differences, there are fundamental similarities at play in the Europeanization and globalization process. EM ideas are strongly represented in EU policy. They are present also, albeit less consistently and less strongly, at a global level. However, because of the similarity of forces at work in a European and international sense, and as multinational enterprises adapt EM ideas and practices, and assuming the environmental Kuznets curve effect kicks in, there is scope for greater spread of EM practices on a more global scale. The rapid acceptance of ISO 14001, a voluntary initiative which could supersede the EU's EMAS, is a prime example of how the corporate sector can respond quickly to EM-related ideas once there is recognition of their efficacy.

From the European perspective, the EU's experience of developing EM-related policies raises the possibility of the EU exercising a leadership role in the global environmental policy arena. Furthermore, the increasing penetration of EM ideas in the European corporate sector places the European business sector at a distinct competitive advantage if the anticipated greater demand for environmental quality manifests itself.

Notes

1 US-based NGO, the Worldwatch Institute, estimated that in 2000, there were 14 million environmentally-related jobs in existence with the potential for the creation of many more. The European Commission estimates that there are 3.5 million environmental jobs in Europe and that the world market for environmental services could reach €740 bn by 2010. Marx (2000) argues that environmental policy has a net positive effect on employment.
2 Preamble to the Treaty of Rome establishing the European Economic Community, the forerunner to the EU
3 After the conclusion of the Uruguay Round, the WTO incorporated the objective of sustainable development and the need 'to protect the environment' into the preamble of the WTO Treaty. The WTO's strengthened Dispute Settlement Procedure has also attracted a number of high profile cases regarding the interface between trade and the environment. However, the WTO remains primarily a trade organization.
4 NAFTA does have an environmental side-agreement, the North American Agreement on Environmental Cooperation which establishes an institutional framework which may, eventually, support transnational norms, policies and standards.

5 Other standards in the series cover environmental audit, environmental performance evaluation, life cycle assessment and eco-labelling and declarations.
6 Examples of how EMS, backed up by ISO 14001 registration, can help businesses, include:

- reduced costs from increased energy efficiency and lower water consumption;
- waste reduction from improved process yields of raw materials;
- the potential for new income streams resulting from the improved utilization of by-products and the conversion of waste into commercial products, such as energy;
- higher quality and more consistent products resulting from changes in the production process;
- lower packaging costs;
- reduced downtime;
- a safer working environment leading to lower accident rates and costs in the long term;
- improved public relations;
- reduced liability for environmental damage: given the growing tendency for companies to be held responsible for their contribution to environmental degradation, the financial and legal risks associated with poor environmental practices have increased over the years. An effective EMS reduces exposure to this risk. In some cases, insurance companies may even consider reduced environmental risk premiums for companies that adapt such systems.

7 US registrations, on the other hand, represent less than 5 per cent of total registrations. Initially, most US registrations were for US affiliates of companies registered elsewhere such as Akzo, BOC, Elf Atochem and Nobel Plastics. This is changing. The motor industry, which is under growing pressure to demonstrate its commitment to enhancing environmental performance, has played an important role in this. Following the lead of the Rover Group and the European operations of Toyota and Honda, General Motors and the Ford Motor Company have informed their suppliers that all their manufacturing operations must comply with ISO 14001 by the end of 2002 and mid-2003 respectively.

References

Banerjee, S. (2001) 'Managerial perceptions of corporate environmentalism: interpretations from industry and strategic implications for organisations', *Journal of Management Studies* 38: 489–514.

Bhagwati, J. (1997) 'Free trade and the environment', in V.N. Balasubramanyam (ed.) *Writings on International Economics*, Oxford: Oxford University Press.

Bøås, M. (2000) 'The trade-environment nexus and the potential of regional trade institutions', *New Political Economy* 5: 415–32.

Commission of the European Communities (2001) *Environment 2010: Our Future, Our Choice – The Sixth Environmental Action Programme*, Communication from the Commission to the Council, the European Parliament, the Economic and Social Committee and the Committee of the Regions, COM (2001) 31 final, Brussels.

Conca, K. (2000) 'The WTO and the undermining of global environmental governance', *Review of International Political Economy* 7: 484–94.

Liebig, K. (1999) 'The WTO and the trade-environment conflict: the new political economy of the world trading system', *Intereconomics* 34: 83–90.

Lundquist, L.J. (2000) 'The international spread of ecological modernisation ideas', paper presented at a workshop Diffusion of Environmental Policy Innovations, Berlin, 8–9 December 2000.

Marx, A. (2000) 'Ecological modernisation, environmental policy and employment: can environment protection and employment be reconciled?', *The European Journal of Social Sciences* 13: 311–16.

Mol, A. (2000) 'The environmental movement in an era of ecological modernisation', *Geoforum* 31: 45–56.

Mol, A. (2001) *Globalization and Environmental Reform: The Ecological Modernization of the Global Economy*, Cambridge, MA: MIT Press.

Mol, A. and Spaargaren, G. (2000) 'Ecological modernisation theory in debate: a review', *Environmental Politics* 9: 17–49.

Murphy, J. and Gouldson, A. (2000) 'Environmental policy and industrial innovation: integrating environment and economy through ecological modernisation', *Geoforum* 31: 33–44.

Najam, A. and Robins, N. (2001) 'Seizing the future: the South, sustainable development and international trade', *International Affairs* 77: 49–68.

Neumayer, E. (2001) 'Greening the WTO agreements: can the treaty establishing the European Community be of guidance?', *Journal of World Trade* 35: 145–66.

Porter, M. and Van der Linde, C. (1995) 'Green and competitive – ending the stalemate', *Harvard Business Review* 73: 120–34.

Renner, M. (2000) *Working for the Environment: A Growing Source of Jobs*, Washington, DC: Worldwatch Institute.

Rugman, A. and Verbeke, A. (2000) 'Environmental regulations and the global strategies of multinational enterprises' in J. Hart and A. Prakash (eds) *Coping with Globalization*, London: Routledge.

Runge, C. (2001) 'A Global Environment Organisation (GEO) and the world trading system', *Journal of World Trade Law* 35: 399–426.

Scott, A. (1999) 'Profiting from ISO 14000', *Chemical Week* 161: 83–5.

Toke, D. (2001) 'Ecological modernisation: a reformist review', *New Political Economy* 6: 279–91.

Trebilcock, M. and Howse, R. (1999) *The Regulation of International Trade*, 2nd edn, London: Routledge, Ch. 15.

Vaughan, S. and Nordström, H. (1999) *Trade and Environment*, WTO Special Studies 4, Geneva: WTO.

Weale, A. (1992) *The New Politics of Pollution*, Manchester: Manchester University Press.

Weinstein, M. and Charnowitz, S. (2001) 'The greening of the WTO', *Foreign Affairs* 80: 147–56.

World Commission on Environment and Development (1987) *Our Common Future*, Oxford: Oxford University Press.

Young, S. (ed.) (2000) *The Emergence of Ecological Modernisation: Integrating the Environment and the Economy*, London: Routledge.

10 The EU and sustainable development
The long road from Rio to Johannesburg

Jon Burchell and Simon Lightfoot

Introduction

The UN Conference on Environment and Development (better known as the Rio Earth Summit[1]) in Rio de Janeiro, 1992, was seen by many as the beginning of a new ecological era. At this conference, the EU was granted 'full participant status' giving it many of the same rights as the participating states (Bretherton and Vogler 1999: 91). At the same conference, the EU also committed itself to the concept of sustainable development. In 2002, the World Summit on Sustainable Development (WSSD), held in Johannesburg, set out to evaluate the obstacles to progress and the results achieved ten years on. The Johannesburg Summit must be seen as part of a post-millennium continuum that includes the trade talks in Doha and the development talks in Monterrey. The 2002 Summit marks the tenth anniversary of the EU's commitment to sustainable development and as such, provides the perfect opportunity for a critical reflection regarding the EU's engagement with the sustainability agenda. This chapter examines to what extent the barriers and constraints that have confronted EU attempts to implement sustainable development post-Rio provide important insights into the EU's behaviour at the World Summit. As such, it represents a timely critical assessment of the EU's relationship with the concept of sustainable development.

The fact that the EU is attempting to offer leadership at Johannesburg means that it is inevitable that the spotlight turns on its own internal track record on sustainable development (Wilkinson 2002: 22). This chapter serves as such as a spotlight as it examines the engagement of the EU with the Summit's priorities as outlined by Kofi Annan: water, health, biodiversity, energy and agriculture. It examines whether EU policies and actions in these five priority areas actual allow it to play the role of global green giant. It then goes on to contrast the priority areas for the EU with its own action. In doing so it examines the extent to which the EU's position for Johannesburg, and commitments made by the EU at Johannesburg, actually support the sustainability agenda.² In Goteburg, the EU committed itself to producing a Communication on how the Union is contributing and should further contribute to global sustainable development. Commissioner Wallström argues that the 'EU has to play the leading role in ensuring that Johannesburg delivers concrete progress towards sustainability goals' (Wallström 2002: 1). The Johannesburg Summit is therefore an important stage for the EU to prove that its commitment to sustainable development represents more than just Green rhetoric.

The WSSD agenda and the EU

Taking Kofi Annan's priority areas as a guide – water, health, biodiversity, energy and agriculture – the following discussion represents a form of initial mini-sustainability audit on the EU. It is clear that many of these priority issues have become more visible within the EU since the sixth EU environmental action programme was created.³ The sixth EAP, which focuses on climate change; protecting nature and diversity; environment and health; and resources and waste management, also forms an important input into the Rio +10 process. However, while the contents of the sixth Environmental Action Programme (EAP) suggests the possibility of significant improvements in the future, our current concern lies with presenting an accurate reflection of the current state of the union.

Water

Poor water is a major global environmental problem. The Water Framework Directive is designed to rationalize much of the EU's existing water policy. For the first time it provides an integrated framework for water policy based upon the idea that water is not static (Grant *et al.* 2000: 168). Crucially, this Directive allows Member States to use eco-taxes to meet its requirements. This raises many equity issues, as such taxation can often be seen as regressive (see Luckin and Lightfoot 1999). The EU's Summit goal was to meet the Millennium goal of halving the number of people without access to safe water by 2015 and sets a parallel target of halving the number of people without access to sanitation by the same date. Under the initiative, the Union will set up partnerships with developing countries, sharing EU expertise on sustainable management and distribution of water and providing financial support through the EU's development programme. The EU argues that dealing effectively with the water crisis in the developing world requires improvements in governance at international, national and regional level, in order to put in place the instruments necessary for legislation, regulation and implementation. They also believe it will involve large-scale investment through public–private partnerships and other more traditional forms of development assistance. This involvement of the private sector is reflective of both the EU's agenda and that of the Johannesburg Summit across many fields of sustainability policy. In this instance, it has lead to strong criticism from Oxfam, who argue that this is privatization of vulnerable water industries. Within the EU though, water quality has steadily improved and if the Water Framework Directive is fully implemented, water policy could be a sustainability success story, although the Spanish's National Hydrological Plan[4] shows how fragile the balance between environment and growth can be.

Health

The EU, via the sixth EAP, now for the first time makes an explicit link between health and the environment by calling for a holistic approach to environment and health. It argues for the full implementation of the precautionary principle due to the impact of a poor environment on vulnerable groups, such as children and the elderly. In this area the Commissioner gave a robust defence of the position not to set targets:

> How do we set limits when our health is at risk? In statistics the 'norm' is usually a male adult. But we also need to find out what limits apply to vulnerable groups, such as children and pregnant women, to avoid them being harmed.
> (*Environment for Europeans*, March 2001: 3)

'Our Future, Our Choice' stressed the need to decouple resource use from growth. As countries get richer, so their resource use increases, but their recycling does not. So while resources are being depleted, waste builds up, offering additional environmental and health problems. It is also clear that questions of health and the environment overlap with the whole issue of water quality. The explicit recognition of the health/environment link is a step forward for the EU but it is clear that unless more is done to prevent waste build up the rhetoric may not count for much (see Bomberg 1998: 161–8). On the issue of waste, poor practice within the EU prevents it from offering the global leadership its wishes.

Biodiversity

The sixth EAP acknowledges the threat of losing the unique resource of nature and biodiversity within Europe, with the biggest threats coming from unsustainable farming and fishing. The sixth EAP argues that Europe is seeing dramatic threats to the survival of many species and their habitats. The full establishment of the Natura 2000 network and a set of sectoral biodiversity action plans are the cornerstones of the approach to avert these threats. However, the janus face of the EU can be seen in its funding of the Alqueva dam (see Goncalves 2000) and the Via Baltica projects. Both provide evidence to show that the EU commitment to Natura 2000 diminishes when it conflicts with other policy goals.

The Via Baltica is a proposed four-lane motorway that forms part of the EU's plans for transport networks in accession countries (TINA) and is fuelled by dreams of an uninterrupted Cork-to-Helsinki highway. Unfortunately, the proposed route cuts across Biebrza marshes in Poland, one of Europe's most important wildlife sites. According to Zoltan Walinszky, the EU's role is very contradictory:

> On the one hand it insists accession countries draw up a list of Natura 2000 sites which would guarantee protection to the most important areas before entry into the EU. On the other it is promoting a transport network which takes no account of these areas.
>
> (in Coward 2002: 27)

One MEP, who is a member of the EU–Poland Joint Parliamentary Committee, said of this case that 'it's just a matter of weighing up the environmental concerns against the transport needs' (in Coward 2002: 27). This quote highlights many of the problems faced by the EU in attempting to promote sustainable development. In particular it reflects many of the problems with attempting to 'mainstream' sustainable development in the face of direct challenges and often outright hostility, from other policy sectors. Indeed, one Green MEP argues that 'the 'EU is structurally incapable of catering for environmental concerns' (Lucas 2001). She highlights that, for example, the promotion of Trans-European Networks are predicted to increase CO_2 emissions in the transport sector by up to 18 per cent (see Lucas 2001).

Agriculture

When examining the EU's position on agriculture, there emerges a strong dynamic between this sphere and the EU's attitudes towards sustainability through trade. The EU is a very powerful global trade actor and it has the power to really engage third countries with sustainable development issues. Indeed, it has included some environmental provisions in trade agreements with developing countries (Baker 2000: 319). Another recent development was the 'Everything but Arms' initiative which creates tariff- and quota-free market access for all products except arms from 49 Least Developed Countries (LDCs). The Commission argues that there is no conflict between international trade, especially trade liberalization, and environmental protection. It is therefore a major player for certain trade liberalization measures within world trade negotiations. It is in these negotiations that critics argue that the janus face of the EU's sustainability strategy comes to life. For example, Oxfam rank the EU first according to an index which measures protectionism, arguing that the EU places high tariffs on the two most important industries in developing countries: agriculture and textiles.

The main policy culprit according to Oxfam is, unsurprisingly, the CAP, which has a double whammy effect on developing countries. First, EU farmers are protected from cheaper imports by protectionism measures. Second, they receive subsidies, which despite recent reforms, leads to over-production and hence surpluses. These surpluses are then 'dumped' on the world market, undercutting farmers in the developing world. There is also the very real criticism that the EU's aid policy reflects a refusal to open up agricultural markets to neighbours. For example, the largest recipients of EU aid are Morocco, Egypt, Tunisia, Palestine, Jordan and Jamaica, yet the poorest countries include Ethiopia, Bangladesh and Vietnam. Indeed the top ten recipients of EU aid include only one sub-Saharan country. Critics argue that this state of affairs reflects the fact that member states, especially those with large agricultural sectors, would rather give aid than open up EU markets for trade, especially to states who could undercut them. 'The strategic interests of some southern European states has meant that politics rather than poverty has dictated the aid budget. An aid budget should be based on need' (*Independent*, 28 January 1999). Therefore, while developments like the 'Everything but Arms' initiative are welcomed, it still looks unlikely that LDCs will be granted full access to all EU markets, despite the recent mid-term review in June 2002. This was seen by Jonathan Porritt as a 'serious step in the right direction' (Porritt 2002: 8), while Zilbermann goes as far as to argue that 'one has to acknowledge that the prospects of a substantial reform of the CAP, expanding and promoting the role of rural development and environmental measures – sometimes viewed as the "Cinderella" of the CAP – are now stronger than ever' (Zilbermann 2002: 8). Indeed Fischler was the recent surprise choice as joint greenest Commissioner, as awarded by the Green Group of 8.

Energy

The energy sector is a major source of CO_2 emissions that contribute to global climate change. Climate change represents arguably the biggest global threat, and the energy commitment within the fifth EAP was designed to assist the EU in achieving its UN Climate Change Convention commitment of stabilizing CO_2 emissions by 2000 at 1990 levels and by reducing them to 8 per cent below the 1990 level by 2008–12. It uses a number of programmes to help it achieve this target. For example, SAVE I and II had the aim of stabilizing CO_2 emissions and achieving improvements in energy efficiency, while ALTENER encouraged the promotion of renewable energy sources. The latest report from the EEA in November 2000 appeared to show the EU was on track to meet the first of these targets, although it also highlighted that these results could be related to one-off emission reductions in Germany and the UK (*Environment for Europeans*, November 2000: 6). The problem is that energy policy has a direct impact upon environmental measures and in this crucial policy sector the EU only has weak powers. Although it has shared responsibility for energy policy, the instruments for energy policy are not integrated within the treaties (Barnes and Barnes 1999: 234). The proposed liberalization and deregulation of domestic energy markets compound this situation, pushed heavily by DG Competition. The critique from green NGOs and MEPs is that failure to use the full range of economic instruments, especially taxation, is likely to prevent the EU achieving its targets in this area (Lucas 2001).

In the broader Summit agenda, the EU has proposed an initiative that will provide technical assistance to developing countries' governments on energy issues. The initiative will support global targets to half the number of people without access to adequate, affordable and sustainable energy supply (see CEC 2001). However, there is the view that research rather than regulation is important, reflecting once again the problem-solving discourse where issues like global warming are treated as problems to be solved by new technology. This discourse is also more amenable to the business lobby.

The EU's WSSD agenda

Having examined the EU's track record in relation to the UN agenda, it is also interesting to compare this with the priorities identified within the Commission's WSSD agenda. A brief examination of this agenda highlights a significantly different focus for action and future development, which gives a strong indication of how the EU views future moves towards sustainability developing.

The Commissions agenda focuses upon increased global equity and effective partnerships for sustainable development; better integration and coherence at international level; adoption of environment and development targets; and more effective action at national level with international monitoring (see CEC 2001). Meeting these objectives, the Commission argues, will lead to the protection of natural resources as a basis for economic development, make globalization sustainable, and enhance good governance and participation (see CEC 2001).

Increased global equity and effective partnerships for sustainable development

The EU was actively supporting public–private partnerships to tackle many of the most pressing problems. The need for private money to bridge Rio's implementation gap is seen as one way of bringing business on board, in the same way NGOs were incorporated at Rio. The need for private money is also linked to the fact that the EU falls a long way short of its promised goal of reaching the United Nations' long-standing official development assistance target of 0.7 per cent of GDP before this summit. At present only four member states (Denmark, Sweden, the Netherlands and Luxembourg) meet this target. One Member State, Ireland, has a timetable to reach 0.33 per cent by 2006. In Monterrey, the EU pledged to boost aid by $5bn a year by 2006, after Germany dropped its opposition, but also said that they were constrained by stability and growth pact that sets limits on government spending and borrowing.

It is apparent that within the Commission there is support for increasing the use of market instruments and voluntary agreements to solve environment problems and these concerns are mirrored in the Johannesburg agenda. The use of voluntary agreements and self-regulation has a long tradition in two leader states, Denmark and the Netherlands. They offer a number of advantages to the policy maker. They tend to be preferred by the business lobby, as they do not increase regulation or cost in the same way as market-based instruments. The problem is that they only work if people are prepared to modify their behaviour. They also rely upon business to reach an agreement in the first place and then self-regulate (see Burchell and Lightfoot 2001).

The business community has, in the period since Rio, sought to represent itself as more focused upon issues of sustainability and more committed to developing a new role as a social actor. This is clearly evident in the increasing emphasis placed upon the concepts of Corporate Social Responsibility (CRS) and the emergence of Corporate Citizenship. However, the emphasis here is on development of policies that are not only voluntary, but which are also business led. It is argued that any attempt to regulate produces merely minimum standards that are hard to enforce whereas emphasizing the 'business case' for sustainability encourages companies to innovate.

However, critics argue that voluntary codes should not be seen as a replacement for effective legislation. Indeed there is still relatively little evidence of the impact of CSR beyond merely representing a public relations exercise. This is undoubtedly reflected in the difficulties experienced in encouraging the use of eco-labelling. Establishing acceptable standards through the process of eco-labelling has been met with a distinct lack of enthusiasm from the business community. Experience, it is argued, has so far suggested that 'firms seem reluctant to co-operate in establishing the criteria for, and then using, eco-labelling for their products unless there is a threat of binding regulation, except in a few technically homogeneous sectors' (Sbragia 2000: 312). Many critics argue that voluntary agreements are a 'cheat', as they allow business to escape stronger regulation. Commissioner Wallström has said she is in favour of making more use of these types of agreements, although she stressed that they are only an option if they present advantages compared to other instruments. She also stressed that if voluntary agreements do not work, the introduction of stricter EU legislation is unavoidable (Euro-op 2000). DG Environment is therefore pursuing a twin-track strategy of encouraging voluntary agreements with the veiled threat of legislation if this does not succeed. It is therefore no surprise that the EU wished to see Johannesburg push the idea of global voluntary agreements.

Better integration and coherence at international level

The Brundtland definition of sustainable development has implications for many policy sectors. Much like gender, environmental problems cut across a number of policy sectors; in this case trade, agriculture, industry, taxation, energy, transport, aid and scientific research. The EU wishes Johannesburg to develop an effective institutional framework for sustainable development at international, regional and national levels based upon the Cardiff Process. For example, it highlights the need to reinforce co-operation on sustainable development between UN bodies, the Bretton Woods institutions and the WTO (see CEC 2001: 13). This is a worthy aim, but it is clear that the EU cannot get its own house in order. The cross-cutting nature of the environment means that it cuts across policy sectors that are represented within the Commission by different DGs. This situation pits DG Environment against many other DGs and the strong vertical lines of division, the 'silo mentality', hamper intersectoral policy co-ordination within the Commission (Wilkinson 2002: 22). Each DG often finds it difficult to see beyond the limits of its competence, and research suggests that these competencies are jealously guarded (see Bulmer 1994: 361). These divisions, as shall be shown, have major implications for the EU's strategy for sustainable development. As Haigh foresaw in 1984, the simple sounding statement concerning the need for integration represented a considerable challenge for the DG Environment. The new departure entailed in this declaration means:

> that environmental policy will cease to be a fairly self-contained activity within the Commission and the Directorate-General for the Environment will have to involve itself much more in the work of others. This may well be seen as interference by those responsible for, say, agriculture, transport and energy policy, and anyone with experience of bureaucracies knows what that entails.
>
> (Haigh 1999: 110)

The problem too is that within many other DGs 'there is a widespread belief that the promotion of sustainable development is the business of those who deal with the environment' (Baker 2000: 314). This is despite the fact that sustainable development is seen to have three pillars: the environmental, the social and the economic (see Carter 2002: 195–203).

An excellent example of the problem of integration is the draft Groundwater Action Programme. The tortuous progress of this initiative, designed to combat water pollutants, especially agricultural, at source was attributed to the fact that DG Agriculture saw DG Environment as butting in to a key area of competence, namely the CAP. Although the draft has been included in the Water Framework Directive, it is clear that policy disputes between different DGs can be a crucial source of policy impasse (see Grant *et al.* 2000: 174–5).

NGOs see the incorporation of the environment into all other sectoral policies as crucial to its success. In this area, many believe there is still a long way to go towards changing the mentality of policy makers from thinking merely in sectoral compartments. This need to incorporate the environment fully was partially tackled at the Cardiff Summit in 1998. The outcome of the Summit was that different sectoral Councils agreed to take account of sustainable development issues in their actions, and report to future EU summits on their strategies for integration (Christie 1999: 28). At the Vienna summit in December 1998, the Transport, Energy and Agricultural Councils reported on their initial strategies. At the same summit, three more Councils – Industry, Internal Market and Development – were invited to submit similar reports to the next summit in Helsinki. The 'Cardiff Process' also required the Commission to strengthen its assessment of its own proposals as the 'green star' scheme had proved to be inadequate. It is clear from this discussion that for the first time the Member States are taking the issue of integration more seriously. This process has been followed through via the Lisbon and Gothenburg summits.[5] However, the 2002 Barcelona Summit, which was charged with undertaking the first comprehensive review of progress of all aspects of the EU's sustainable development strategy, was a big disappointment. It was clear that the environment pillar was not taken as seriously as the economic and social pillars, as the Summit focused almost exclusively on economic and employment issues (Wilkinson 2002: 22).

Towards the end of this fifth EAP in November 1999, the Commission launched a consultation, a Global Assessment of the fifth EAP that in turn was based upon a major report by the EEA (European Environment Agency) on the state of the environment. Both reports showed that issues such as poor implementation of legislation by Member States, the poor integration of the environment into other policy areas, and the failure of shared responsibility, continued to prevent the EU attaining the standards it set for itself. There was also the perennial problem of reconciling environmental imperatives with the socio-economic objectives of the EU. To try and counter these problems, in early 2001 the Commission launched its sixth EAP. To improve conditions in four priority areas, the sixth EAP argues it offers a strategic approach. It re-emphasizes the need to integrate environmental concerns into economic sectors and other policy areas to ensure the environmental objective of a sustainable society is achieved. Full integration of environmental concerns into the four policy priority areas is clearly crucial for the EU to meet its objectives, as is full implementation of existing legislation, such as the Water Framework Directive and the Noise Framework Directives. To ensure implementation, the EAP focuses upon legal action via the ECJ alongside a 'name and shame' policy. The EAP once again highlighted the business opportunities offered by clean technology and eco-labels. Commissioner Wallström sees this as cornerstone of her own agenda:

> I believe that 'greening' the market is a key to sustainable development. And I know that there are many pro-active companies out there who already benefit economically from the high environmental standards they apply, and which consumers are expecting more and more.
> (DG Environment website, accessed 8 May 2001)

This theme of working with business and consumers to achieve more environmentally friendly forms of production and consumption echoes the theme of shared responsibility found in the fifth EAP. Here, the Commission wants to have recourse to a raft of new instruments ranging from an Integrated Product Policy, which encourages a sustainable life for products from design to disposal, and environmental liability to fiscal measures and better information for citizens. This stress on working with the market appears to be part of a developing problem solving discourse, which clearly still exists within the EU.

Adoption of environment and development targets

The EU wishes to see environment and development targets from Johannesburg. Clearly the EU is proud that it ratified the Kyoto Protocol in May 2002 and in doing so demonstrated its global environmental leadership on this issue. According to the Swedish Government, which represented the Council Presidency during the first half of 2001, climate change is one of the biggest threats to sustainable development. The continuing need to reduce emissions was illustrated by an EEA Report in May 2001, which showed that a number of Member States had exceeded their emission targets agreed as part of the 'burden sharing' deal agreed in Luxembourg 1998. This deal was designed to allow the EU to meet the Kyoto Protocol target of an 8 per cent reduction in emissions over 1990 levels by 2008–12. Despite these problems, the Commission called for more far-reaching global emission cuts in the order of 40 per cent by 2020 and cites the scientific estimate that in the longer term a 70 per cent global greenhouse gas emission reduction as compared to 1990 levels will be needed. The programme pointed to the need for structural changes especially in the transport and energy sectors, called for stronger efforts in energy-efficiency and energy-saving, the establishment of an EU-wide emissions trading scheme, further research and technological development and awareness-raising with citizens so that they can contribute to reducing emissions. Commissioner Wallström stressed that 'the scientists have told us clearly that we must face up to climate change or else accept dramatic consequences. Making the Kyoto Protocol operational is not easy as everybody knows but it can really only be a first step' (DG Environment website accessed 8 May 2001). Many NGOs are concerned that the EEA figures suggest that a number of countries, including leader states, are on course to overshoot their targets.

There was also the problem outlined by the review of the fifth EAP that emission reductions in one sector could be offset by increases in another, as was seen in the transport and energy sectors. The sixth EAP tries to incorporate solutions to these problems, but in most areas is limited to setting general objectives rather than quantified targets. Commissioner Wallström argued that 'it is important that we discuss concrete actions that will start things moving rather than spend much time in debating what the specific target figures should be' (DG Environment website, accessed 8 May 2001).

The EU's position was welcomed by various green NGOs, with Dennis Pamlin, the Worldwide Fund for Nature (WWF) climate change campaign co-ordinator, stating that the 'EU continues to lead the world on climate change' (*Financial Times* 17 June 2001). On climate change it is clear that the EU is one of the greenest actors and could start to act as an environmental hegemony (see Bretherton 2002: 2). The problem is that the competition is not up to much. Although President Bush pledged not to block the Kyoto process, the fact that the world's largest polluter backed out of its commitments is a concern for global climate change. The EU's intense diplomatic effort to keep other industrialized countries on-side showed some success (see Leggett 1999: Ch. 11; Bretherton 2002: 12). However, Australia recently used world environment day to announce that it would not be signing the protocol. Therefore, while it is clear that on climate change the EU has moved further onto a sustainability agenda, there is a real problem that EU action alone will not be enough. As Hans Wolters, Director of Greenpeace International, argued 'we can't wait too long anymore to do something real about climate change ... or it will be too late' (European Policy Centre website accessed 8 May 2001). The fact that the EU is not pushing for a new Kyoto is one of the main critiques of its position for the WSSD.

More effective action at national level with international monitoring

The EU wishes to see more effective action at national level. Yet this is something that it finds difficult itself. Levels of implementation within the EU can be low and non-compliance is an important and often overlooked area of study, as implementation is at the 'sharp end' of the policy process

(Jordan 1999: 69). However, while monitoring the implementation of EU legislation still remains in the hands of Member States, the existing levels of implementation are unlikely to be radically improved. The sixth EAP highlights again the need for full implementation of existing legislation, such as the Water Framework Directive and the Noise Framework Directives. Commissioner Wallström noted that the environmental policy regulatory framework is broadly speaking in place, takes up this point that implementing existing legislation is a priority. 'If the member states were to fully apply our existing standards and rules, much would be gained already' (European Policy Centre website accessed 13 September 2000). One bright note is that every accession state (except Malta) has been able to provisionally close the environmental chapter of the *acquis*, with fewer transitional measures than anticipated (Bretherton 2002: 13). This has been highlighted by the Commission as perhaps the biggest contribution the EU can make to global sustainable development (CEC 2001: 13).

Talking past each other: from Bali via New York to Johannesburg

From the discussion so far, it is clear that the EU and its Member States have a number of problems with the Summit's proposed agenda. Indeed, it appears that all participants are finding it difficult to develop a clear picture of what Johannesburg should be seeking to achieve. The final PrepCom before Johannesburg was held in Bali. During this meeting it became clear that producing a plan of action for Johannesburg was not going to be easy. This section highlights some of the major areas of agreement and disagreement between the EU and other states. One of the EU's main proposals was that all countries should implement national sustainable development strategies by 2005. The Group of 77, which promotes the interests of developing countries in the UN, and China opposed this proposal and it appears likely that the US will become 'accidental allies' with the developing world. The EU was also the strongest supporter of time-bound targets. On these issues, the EU could be seen to be acting as a global leader. However, this proposal is likely to cost the EU very little. In contrast, the EU was the biggest opponent to a proposed world solidarity fund, arguing that the stated objective – poverty eradication – was too vague. However, the EU was supportive of linking human rights and health. It therefore appears that the EU was strong on rhetoric but unwilling to commit additional money, despite strong evidence highlighting the inescapable link between poverty, environmental degradation and poor health.

The main sticking points in Bali revolved around trade and finance issues. The EU's position was that market liberalization was the way out of poverty. This position is perhaps unsurprising, as the EU has long been on the establishment of a common market and to ensure economic growth.

Indeed it can be argued that, on the whole, the EU strategy has been 'economic development based on growth onto which environmental considerations can be grafted' (Baker 1997: 93). The preparation argued that 'Delegates should recognise the primary role of domestic resources, as well as the role that trade liberalisation and private financial flows, notably foreign direct investment (FDI) can play in generating more resources for sustainable development'. This position had become clear during the Doha Trade talks where the EU, under the guise of DG Trade, produced a 1,000-page document that set out liberalization demands. It is alleged that many of these demands were drafted by the European Services Network, made up of executives from 50 financial sector companies, which enjoyed privileged access to the Article 133 committee. Kevin Watkins of Oxfam called it a 'bananas for banking negotiating strategy', as the EU promises to open up its agricultural and textile markets to its competitors on the condition they liberalize access to banking and insurance markets, markets in which European companies have a competitive advantage.

During the Doha negotiations the EU argued that it won some important environmental concessions, including clarification of the relationship between Multilateral Environmental Agreements (MEAs) and WTO rules, negotiations on eco-labelling and the protection of the precautionary principle (see ENDS Report: 322). However, many environmental groups were not as positive as the EU arguing that many of the concessions that EU argued as successes were in fact vaguely worded or connected to significant riders.

The EU is suggesting supportive measures on a wide scale ranging from the integration of sustainability parameters into regional and bilateral agreements and preferential trade schemes, commitments from all countries to duty- and quota-free market access for all products originating in least developed countries, the promotion of markets for organic produce, environmentally friendly products and 'fair trade' measures to enhance the transparency of domestic trade procedures, the reform of environmentally harmful subsidies and the further development and support for sustainable impact assessments (SIAs).

This became clear in Bali when the EU struck a deal with G-77/China on trade issues and circulated a non-paper. The main problem was that in the end the language on subsidies was too much for some member states to go along with. One clear example focused upon CAP reform, where the mid-term review proposals are certainly likely to come under attack from a number of Member States resulting in them being watered-down. Indeed those states opposed to the reforms argue that Commissioner Fischler has exceeded the provisions outlined in Agenda 2000, which they argue only mandated a review of technical adjustments (Zilbermann 2002: 8).

This discussion of subsidies highlights a major problem faced by the EU in international negotiations: who negotiates what? The EU is an actor but so too are the Member States. It has been argued that, except in areas of exclusive competence such as trade, the EU's authority was unclear. This lack of a clear delineation was especially clear prior to the Summits in the PrepComs (see Baker 2000: 309–10). This situation requires strong leadership from the Council presidency. Much of the preparation for the EU's position was carried out by the Spanish Presidency of the European Council, which ran for the first six months of 2002. It was during the difficult negotiation throughout the Bali PrepCom that this leadership would be most appropriate, yet it was claimed that the EU was 'ineffectually led by Spain'. Although the Presidency had put environment as one of its goals, its record at the Barcelona Summit was seen to be disappointing. The controversial hydrological plans were also a sticking point during the Presidency. Despite the fact that the plans have failed a sustainability audit, they will still receive EU funding.

It was also interesting that the European Parliament, normally the greenest EU institution, did not pass a critical resolution, leading many to conclude that a deal was struck between the EPP and the ELDR to ensure the Presidency was not embarrassed. In many ways this corresponds to the fact that Spain has long been identified as a 'laggard' state in environmental terms. It will be interesting to see whether Denmark, a long-standing leader state (see Liefferink and Andersen 1998) that will represent the EU in Johannesburg, will produce stronger environmental leadership.

As mentioned earlier, mainstreaming sustainability produces significant difficulties. Sustainable development does not fall neatly into existing bureaucratic competencies. For example, the three pillars of sustainable development – trade, development and environment – reflect the remits of different DGs and Councils which caused problems as each meeting was negotiated by different ministers. For example, Doha focused upon negotiation by trade ministers, Monterrey by finance ministers, while Johannesburg currently appears to be a mixture of foreign, development and environment ministers. Once again, the cross-cutting nature of environmental issues causes problems, especially when the problem of competence is laid on top.

Critics of the EU's Johannesburg position argue that it reflects too much of DG Trade's neo-liberal ethos rather than the more trade with a social conscience views of DG Development or the ecological views of DG Environment. However, this reflects the overall pattern within sustainable development over recent years. The Rio Summit raised environmental expectations and the business lobby quickly realized that the process could be a threat. It therefore reacted to ensure that it was able to play a role in future summits. This meant that unlike many green groups, the business lobby was well prepared for the WSSD and able to hit the floor running. Johannesburg will see the business community emphasizing its commitment to socially responsible and sustainable activities and the development of voluntary codes of conduct and stakeholder engagement.

The high profile business lobbying has lead to accusations from

Christian Aid that the agenda has been 'hijacked' by the pro-trade lobby. It is claimed that the International Chambers of Commerce have been lobbying hard to ensure that less focus is placed upon the business-unfriendly aspects of sustainable development. For example, proposed binding regulations covering human rights and the environment have been replaced by voluntary codes. These findings are perhaps unsurprising, as the business lobby tends to be better funded, more organized and have more access than the green lobby (see Greenwood 1997: 183–4, Burchell and Lightfoot 2001). With this in mind it is crucial that DG Environment works closely with DG Development to ensure their concerns are heard. The main problem is that neither DG is seen as a strong DG. It is also argued that there is a lack of chemistry between Poul Nielson, Commissioner for Development and Humanitarian Aid, and Wallström, that could cause problems in both DGs influencing the EU's Johannesburg position (Ryborg 2002: 37). Added to this mix is Wallström's reluctance to network within the Commission. The need for a united position within the more ecologically minded parts of the Commission is crucial to counter the influence of the more neo-liberal DGs.

Conclusion

EU Commissioner Wallström argued that the World Summit offered a wake up call to the world and that the EU had a 'determination to exercise leadership' on global sustainable development issues at the Summit (Wallström 2002). Both the Swedish Presidency in 2001 and the subsequent Belgium Presidency identified the Sustainability Summit in Johannesburg in 2002 as a possible starting point to signal that the EU is ready to change its unsustainable consumption and production patterns. The fact that similar commitments were made back in 1992 highlight the difficulties faced in creating a sustainable Union: part of a long march towards sustainability. How far the EU needs to go was highlighted by Commissioner Wallström when she scored its implementation of sustainable development strategies as five out of ten (Wallström 2002: 7). This chapter has highlighted a number of the reasons for this low score, a decade on from the fifth EAP's calls to 'implement sustainable development'. She argues that there was a delivery gap in what the EU does, including the problem of integrating the environmental dimension into all the EU does, in line with Article 6 of the Treaty of Amsterdam. This Article, which states that 'environmental protection requirements must be integrated into the definition and implementation of Community policies and activities ... in particular with a view to promoting sustainable development' can be seen as firm commitment to sustainable development. As John Hontelez argues 'it's still words on paper, but the fact that sustainable development is part of the Treaty gives us a better political framework' (in Kazakina 2002: 12).

Critics argue that it is this political framework that is at fault. Baker (1997) distinguishes between two types of environmental policy:

1   Policies that have as their goal the management of environmental quality within the context of existing economic, political and social policy and that require marginal, incremental adjustments to the features of those policies.
2   Policies that have more radical goals, such as the reorganization of consumption patterns, the redefinition of what constitutes economic activity, the redistribution and radical altering of Western use of resources and the reform of the existing political and military structures.

She argues that as EU environmental policy making is characterized by incrementalism, as shown by the various deals struck to accommodate the leader/laggard division, which acts as a brake on the development of radically new policies. Therefore, she concludes that the EU has developed a weak understanding of sustainable development:

> Incrementalism makes the chances of successful translation of the commitment to sustainable development into actual policy dependent upon the extent to which the required policy changes can be fitted with existing policy commitments. Policy proposals that fit with the strategy of environmental quality management stand a greater chance of acceptance, while policies that fit more closely with the second, more radical, pattern have little, if any, chance of success. The concept of sustainable development has been interpreted by the Union (and its member states) to fit within the confines of managerial as opposed to radical policy solutions.
>
> (Baker 1997: 102)

Yet as the EEA argued:

> the long-term success of the more important initiatives such as the internal market and monetary union will be dependent upon the sustainability of the policies pursued in the fields of industry, energy, transport, agriculture and regional development ... This implies the integration of environmental considerations in the formulation and implementation of economic and sectoral policies, in the decisions of public authorities, in the conduct and development of production processes and individual behaviour and choice.
>
> (in Lenschow 1999: 93)

The Gothenburg decision on a strategy for sustainable development, was seen by the Swedish Prime Minister Persson as a 'huge one in European history', as it added an environment dimension to the EU's existing economic and social policy objectives. The Swedish Presidency and the European Commission wished to set firm environmental targets to mirror those for economic and social policies agreed at the Lisbon summit in 2000, but like the sixth EAP, the final strategy contained few concrete targets (see Lucas 2001).

Sustainable development should be central to the Lisbon process, yet the Commission itself noted that progress has been disappointing. These contradictions within the EU's sustainability strategy appear evident in its approach to Johannesburg. On the one hand it is pushing a trade liberalization agenda, while still unable to reform the CAP. It pushes the idea of national sustainable development strategies and strict environmental targets, but is reluctant to commit money. It can act as a global hegemon in climate change negotiations offering leadership against the US, although it is aided by the lack of serious competition. It is clear that the EU is some distance from the end of the long road towards sustainability.

Notes

1 For an illuminating description of Rio from an ecological viewpoint, see Leggett 1999.
2 Please note that this chapter was written before the Summit and therefore is unable to discuss Summit outcomes.
3 For more details on the development of the EU's EAPs, see Burchell and Lightfoot 2001: Ch. 4.
4 This plan involves the building of over 100 new dams on the River Ebro which would divert water from the North to the South of Spain.
5 For more information see (Fergusson *et al.* 2001).

References

Baker, S. (1997) 'The evolution of EU environmental policy: from growth to sustainable development?', in S. Baker *et al.* (eds) *The Politics of Sustainable Development: Theory, Policy and Practice Within the EU*, London: Routledge.
Baker, S. (2000) 'The EU: integration, competition and growth and sustainability', in W. Lafferty and J. Meadowcroft (eds) *Implementing Sustainable Development*, Oxford: Oxford University Press.
Barnes, P. and Barnes, I. (1999) *Environmental Policy in the EU*, Cheltenham: Edward Elgar.
Bomberg, E. (1998) *Green Parties and Politics in the EU*, London: Routledge.
Bretherton, C. (2002) 'International climate change management: the future role of the EU as a global actor', paper for workshop The Kyoto Protocol without America? Finding a way forward after Marrakech, European University Institute, Florence, 20–22 June.
Bretherton, C. and Vogler, J. (1999) *Europe as a Global Actor*, London: Routledge.
Bulmer, S. (1994) 'Institutions and policy change in the EC', *Public Administration* 72: 423–44.
Burchell, J. and Lightfoot, S. (2001) *The Greening of the EU: Examining the EU's Environmental Credentials*, London: Continuum/Sheffield Academic Press.

Carter, N. (2002) *The Politics of the Environment*, Cambridge: Cambridge University Press.
Christie, I. (1999) *Sustaining Europe: A Common Cause for the EU in the New Century*, London: Demos/Green Alliance.
Coward, R. (2002) 'EU-funded road set to ruin Poland's wildlife paradise', in the *Observer*, 19 May.
CEC (2001) 'Ten years after Rio: preparing for the World Summit on sustainable development in 2002', Communication from the Commission to the Council and European Parliament.
DG Environment website, http://www.europacu.int/comm/environment/index_en.htm (accessed 8 May 2001).
European Policy Centre www.theepc.be.
Fergusson, M., Coffey, C., Wilkinson, D., Baldock, D. with Farmer, A., Kraemer, R.A. and Mazurek, A.-G. (2001) *The Effectiveness of EU Council Integration Strategies and Options for Carrying Forward the 'Cardiff' Process*, Brussels: Institute for European Environmental Policy.
Grant, W., Matthews, D. and Newell, P. (2000) *The Effectiveness of EU Environmental Policy*, Basingstoke: Macmillan.
Greenwood, J. (1997) *Representing Interests in the EU*, Basingstoke: Macmillan.
Goncalves, E. (2000) 'Lies, dam lies' in *The Ecologist*, 22 May.
Haigh, N. (1999) 'EU Environment Policy at 25: retrospect and prospect', *Environment and Planning C: Government and Policy* 17: 109–12.
Jordan, A. (1999) 'The implementation of EU environmental policy', *Environment and Planning C: Government and Policy* 17: 69–90.
Kazakina, K. (2002) 'Patchy outlook ahead as summit of green goals looms in Johannesburg', in *European Voice* 1 August–4 September.
Leggett, J. (1999) *The Carbon Wars*, London: Penguin.
Lenschow, A. (1999) 'The greening of the EU: the CAP and the structural funds', *Environment and Planning C: Government and Policy* 17: 91–108.
Liefferink, D and Anderson, M.S. (1998) 'Strategies of the "green" member states in EU environmental policy-making', *Journal of European Public Policy* 5: 254–70.
Lucas, C. (2001) 'Free market Europe – a growing threat to the environment', *The Ecologist*, March.
Luckin, D. and Lightfoot, S. (1999) 'Environmental taxation in contemporary European politics', *Contemporary Politics* 5: 243–61.
Monbiot, G. (2001) *Captive State*, Basingstoke: Pan.
Porritt, J. (2002) 'Last gasp', in the *Guardian*, 17 July.
Ryborg, O. (2002) 'Wallström's green team' in *E!Sharp*, March.
Sbragia, A. (2000) 'Environmental policy' in H. Wallace and W. Wallace (eds) *Policy Making in the EU*, Oxford: Oxford University Press.
Wallström, M. (2002) 'A wake-up call for global sustainability', Speech at European Policy Centre Dialogue 'Sustainability and Globalisation: Towards Johannesburg', 26 February, Brussels.
Wilkinson, D. (2002) 'Jury out on sustainability impact assessment', in *European Voice* 1 August–4 September.
Zilbermann, M.K. (2002) 'Fischler's mid-term review: a further step towards sustainability', in *Corporate Seeds*, July, Issue 13, Brussels: Hill and Knowlton.

11 The WTO and sustainability after Doha
A time for re-assessment of the relationship between political science and law?

James Tunney

Introduction: sustainability after Doha – promised land or poisoned chalice?

The academic identification of the concept of sustainability may seem like explaining how to unravel a complex tartan. Just as 'sustainability' began to be effectively translated from political discourse into legal principle in the European Union (EU), the EU was nearing the end of the Uruguay Round of trade negotiations. On the one hand, the Community was grappling with ways to answer some of the searching questions that environmentalists were asking through re-alignments consistent with emergent notions such as sustainability. On the other hand, the Community was seeking to adhere to a new, unified regime in relation to trade. The World Trade Organization (WTO) was set to become the 'central, international, economic institution'. The enhanced Dispute Settling Mechanism (DSM) and the greater central focus provided by the new organizational structure in the Marrakesh Agreement was appreciated by certain legal observers. Involvement of people such as Peter Sutherland (the ex-EC Competition Commissioner) signalled perhaps that the supposedly neutral settlement of technical trade issues was undergoing a process of 'juridification'. The full import of Marrakesh in legal terms arguably represented an effort to implode the legal regulation on global matters into the central focus of trade. To many, this represented a culmination of a neo-liberal agenda happening in various ways towards the end of the twentieth century. While political science discourse recognized the novelty and revolutionary nature of the WTO, legal thinkers, as ever, often saunter slowly behind.

As a response perhaps to Seattle and growing opposition, the Doha Declaration sought to locate trade in its wider context. Thus sustainability figured in a way that it had not done before. Nevertheless, critics of the WTO see this as a cynical attempt to displace existing multilateral environmental regulation. In legal terms, GATT/WTO disputes demonstrated that the EU had sacrificed a degree of sovereignty, which it in turn had derived from the pooled sovereignty of nation states. The *Bananas* disputes were arguably perhaps crucially illustrative of this. Likewise the *Beef Hormones* disputes between US and Canada and the EU demonstrated how external trade obligations could counteract the freedom of regional legal communities. The 'precautionary principle' seemed to some to have been effectively buried here for example. Similarly the argument of interference with national choice may be seen in relation to the *Tuna/Dolphin* case between the US and Mexico and the *Shrimp/Turtles* case. The question arises as a matter of law as to the locus of rule making in areas such as the environment and in particular in relation to sustainability. Is the cession of discourse to the WTO the start of a radical transportation of legal authority or a mere reflection of a new status quo?

Occasion for articulating ground rules

The approach of a jurist to the discussion of issues such as sustainable development may differ significantly from that of a political scientist or an economist. Arguably, the role of law is being eclipsed, partly due to the fault of legal writers. Thus it is submitted that there are a few observations worth emphasizing, so that a sound inter-disciplinary dialogue may take place and the proper role of law is understood in the dynamic environment of world trade regulation, post-Doha. It is argued here that examining concepts such as sustainability provides the occasion, at least, if not the cause to suggest that there is a need to:

1 facilitate a triangular dialogue between politics, political science and law;
2 recognize and embrace paradigm shifts in law and the emergence of new frontiers of debate (such as culture);
3 understand the legal processes and limitation of emerging regional legal models (such as the EU);
4 understand the process of conceptual integration of new ideas through new legal structures;
5 locate the WTO in the hierarchy of legal developments, and identify particular effects thereof;
6 conceive strategies of 'comprehensive engagement' in relation to sustainability, which include legal strategies;
7 conceive of 'sustainable legal systems' as part of those strategies.

While recognizing the high level work done on the frontier of law and politics by academics such as Howse (2002) it is still worth articulating a basic framework of dialogue. These propositions will be advanced against the backdrop of the continuing evolution of discourse in relation to sustainability in the world trade context.

The need to facilitate a triangular dialogue between politics, political science and law: from the politics of sustainability to sustainability and the law.

Politics and policy of sustainability

The Public Symposium at the end of April 2002 at the WTO building in Geneva revealed (at least) a fairly open field of issues facing the WTO. Thus the debate covered capacity building, democracy, government, politics, institutions, corruption, functionality, rule making, law and governance to reform. It crossed themes of accountability, representation, communication, information, technology, measurement, mechanisms, knowledge, research, transparency, enforcement, justice, equality, credit and debt. It alighted on issues of environment, famine, food, public health, welfare, trade policy and all the tools thereof, protectionism, investment, industry, finance, monetary policy, economics, poverty, resources, comparative advantage, assets, liberalization, ownership, bargaining and labour. It circled issues of movement of people, goods, services, capital, migration and transport. Sustainability appeared among this forest of issues under a wide, world tradescape.

The concept of sustainability has been re-articulated in recent decades as an antidote to environmental degradation. Indigenous peoples would claim that they have pursued the principle for a long time, although some of their record is contestable in this domain. A comprehensive sense of sustainability should lie at the heart of the environmental struggle. While narrower definitions are necessary for functionality in particular contexts, it is difficult to see how anything other than a comprehensive sense of sustainability is desirable. Analysts therefore should treat the entire web of contexts, and not seek to draw artificial boundaries. Accordingly the environmental movement, indigenous struggles, international development, bio-diversity, economic fairness and other agendas overlap. It is unsurprising therefore that such pervasive concepts trigger multiple political debates.

Sustainability is not an easy option for some politicians and neither are pro-environmental policies. It could be countered that expecting too much from politics *per se* is naïve. The fact of environmental devastation is increasingly clear to many people, even those who were sceptical hitherto. Arguments based on the negative consequences of population growth, climate change, diminishing water resources, fish, species of plants, animals and habitats, deforestation, deteriorating air quality, and the growth of environmental refugees are well known. The cost of environmental damage is also evident. Preventable environmental disadvantage, causing massive economic disadvantage underlines the inescapable relationship. But it is nevertheless often argued that the short-term interests of corporate forces can successfully ignore costs, not directly impinging on them. The experience with the US reaction to the Kyoto Protocol has created a great deal of cynicism about the presumption of nobility among state actors. Prospects for the World Summit on Sustainable Development in Johannesburg were accordingly questioned (Porritt 2002). Many agreements or declarations are merely 'political' in nature. It is easy to commit oneself and one's nation to noble causes but not adhere to them in the absence of sophisticated enforcement mechanisms. Porritt's argument is a standard one from environmentalists. He states:

> But all the principal global institutions are 'genetically predisposed' (as it were) to give precedence to the economic over the ecological. The IMF, the World Bank, the WTO, most UN agencies and all regional and international banks take their marching orders from white men in dark suits whose mission (for the most part, it should be said, a wholly honourable if misguided mission) is to expand the global economy on behalf of OECD governments and address poverty elsewhere through more of the same kind of earth-bashing growth that has got us into such a mess. Agencies such as the UN Environmental Programme are impotent in the face of hegemonic control; global treaties designed to slow the pace of ecological destruction invariably come off worst in any clash with the titans of international trade and economic liberalisation.
> (Porritt 2002: 9)

Porritt then goes on to mention certain strategies which could be utilized to address the problems. For example he suggests the need for the internalization of environmental costs, improved efficient use of resources, enhancement of 'natural capital', control of population growth and restraint of the power of multi-nationals. However it is noteworthy that his primary argument is a trade argument. Thus he starts his wish-list:

> Start by doing right by conventional market economics: get rid of all perverse subsidies that pay people to destroy the environment. Franz Fischler's new proposals for common agricultural policy (CAP) reform are a serious step in the right direction. But George Bush's US farm bill (pumping $180bn of new subsidies into US agriculture over the next 10 years) is an even more serious step in the wrong direction- and yet another kind of redneck unilateralism that is persuading more and more people of the status of the US as the number one rogue state.
> (Porritt 2002: 9)

The reliance on the economic argument is not the only paradox. Such arguments are predicated presumably on enforceable rules-based systems. A lawyer would think of law, yet many environmentalists seem to remain in the arena of political debate content with promoting Cassandra-like arguments.

Politics to political science

Political science is surely the place to look for analysis and explanation. But the dynamism of world trade discourse emphasizes the need to clarify modalities of disciplinary, inter-disciplinary and trans-disciplinary engagement. Sometimes this must be simply done. Otherwise, there will be a number of concepts appearing just like misleadingly similar words in language contexts, where one thinks one knows the meaning of a word, but does not. Linguistic 'false friends' will have counterparts in the conceptual terrain of world trade. Therefore, the gulf between disciplinary worldviews needs to be bridged. From an outsider's perspective it seems that there are some criticisms that could be levelled against the approach of political science to the issues outlined above, at a time when it should be uniquely placed to set the agenda. One is that politicians do not always find it relevant, and neither do neighbouring disciplines such as law. Politicians sometimes point to the failure of political theorists in their ability to operate in real-world political environments. It also seems more concerned with the construction of Platonically ideal concepts, driven by academic concept bagging without care for accessibility or transmutability. This may create more of a pseudo-science feel at times which allows writers to mask the norms they advance while being very quick to criticize the normative approach of others. Yet political science is still uniquely placed to inform and clarify. If it does so, then it would seem to have to fit into the triangle between politics and law, in a far more sophisticated way. The criticisms of the legal academy are just as pronounced and part of the benefit of such inter-relationships is to allow for conceptual reform within it. It is also noteworthy that jurists tend to analyse the world in terms of different and very diverse jurisprudential starting points, and that sometimes other disciplines looking at law look in upon a very narrow range of contexts.

Political science to law

The charge of environmentalists (such as that made out by Porritt above) is slightly simplistic. In the US, the success (internally) of the environmental movement has been in its creative use of legal possibilities through the courts. This has helped prevent dams being built, habitats destroyed and other actual and potential environmental damage. While it is indisputable that the US has been extremely cavalier in its approach to multilateral agreements in relation to the environment, it is nonsense to argue that it is a 'rogue state' as a result. The US, more so than many other states, is a society based on the rule of law, however much it is unilateralist and however much one may disagree with some of its internal policies. This simple rule of law basis was most amply demonstrated in the case of the US versus Nixon (1974). In this case the Supreme Court established that the President was not above the constitution and answered the challenge posed by the Special Prosecutor Archibald Cox to consider whether people were governed by the rule of law or the rule of man. This illustrates the importance of the question of the comprehension of the phenomenon of law outside its core conceptual territory. While legal essentialism must be avoided, that should not blind others to the requirement to adequately locate, identify and integrate legal phenomena on the overall terrain.

In relation to multinationals or large US companies, for example, they are subject to the law. The laws of antitrust are perhaps the best example. The Sherman Act of 1890 was intended to regulate the conduct of large companies as the *US v Microsoft* case demonstrates (Brinkley and Lohr 2001). Ultimately they can be closed down. This important body of law is seldom mentioned in environmental arguments often calculated to demonstrate the impotence of governments in the face of corporations. Competition law could be linked to culture to a greater extent (Tunney 2002). Many environmentalists oppose the integration of the 'Singapore issues', such as competition law, without advancing much credible argument to support their propositions. Meanwhile other engagements have been successful, such as where the consumer movement has successfully conditioned the behaviour of large companies through litigation and class actions, although the link within supposedly distinct bodies of law needs to also be made (Tunney 2002). Romantic revolution often appeals over dull, grinding reform. When even such commentators as Henry Kissinger identify the need for reform in world trade contexts, the extent of the opportunity becomes clear.

Creating enhanced dialogue

A prism needs to be held up sometimes to remind certain disciplines to separate out the distinct elements, in order to enhance the soundness of their analyses and to avoid the tendency of all disciplines (including law) to create their own conceptual prisons. International lawyers in the academic world have often remained inertly in quite well defined camps, such as 'international economic law'. Such inertia, when combined with the dearth of inspiration from 'jurisprudence', underlines the need for outside forces to compel the legal world to reshape itself anew. At the moment, it seems that those jurists who do embrace other disciplines sometimes serve to obscure rather than enlighten. Even on a simpler level, the common modes of reference in legal discourse and political science make dialogue more difficult than it should be. While the recent work of people such as Habermas (1997) is undoubtedly a welcome addition, particularly in the identification of 'world' dimensions, the question of its ease of operational integration into the law machine is a far more difficult one. Other ideas such as 'cosmopolitanism' for example, which draw on politics and law, are often articulated in political science contexts on premises which are difficult to translate into legal discourse. In a process of dialogue there is a need to identify respective terms of art and appropriate methodologies in order to avoid charges of methodological freestyle. Different audiences need to be appreciated. Insights, observations, principles and practices need then to be translatable into political, legal and public domains. An important part of the practice of law is the ability to predict what will happen given particular factors. Politics, political science and law should inform each other, but the differences must be respected first. The threads of the concept of sustainability cross a vibrant theoretical tartan.

The need to recognize paradigm shifts in law and the emergence of new frontiers of debate (such as 'culture'): the opportunity presented by the re-mastering of jurisdiction.

The example of the evolution of the concept of 'jurisdiction'

There are many ways to look at emergent, world economic structures. Certain lawyers are in the thick of this discourse and are contributing to its evolution and an appropriate sense of the nature of law. Although it is still remarkable how many texts in relation to international and world trade regulation, emerge from economic and political science contexts. Certain lawyers argue for example that 'economic globalization' is:

> governed by the totality of strategically determined, situationally specific, and often episodic conjunctions of a multiplicity of sites throughout the world. These sites for example, include, EU law, US law, Chinese law, multinational corporation and trade association codes of conduct, international customs conventions, and WTO law. Each of these sites has institutional, normative and processual characteristics. Although the sites are not isolated from each other, each has its own history, internal dynamics and distinctive features. Taken together, they represent a new form of global legal pluralism.
> (Snyder 2002: 1)

Global legal pluralism and ideas of 'inter-legality' nevertheless presume some sense of what was there before. One of the examples of political science discourse venturing into legal territory is in relation to what might be termed 'Post-Westphalian State discourse'. It is worth re-iterating such starting points (and that is all they are) in order to emphasize the dynamic, contemporary context of legal evolution and to underscore the opportunity presented, particularly by the re-engineering of the concept of jurisdiction. The Peace of Westphalia, after the 30 Years War (1618–1648), is seen to represent the beginning of the concept of the State as we know it, and the development of fundamentally related ones of jurisdiction and sovereignty (Shearer 1994: 11). A pragmatic approach in the vein of William James, would seek to identify the consequences of the evolution rather than seek to fit it into neat compartments. While the post-Westphalian state construct is over-simplified and contested and may be characterized by some as merely one type of sovereignty, the process of evolution would ultimately ripen into the principles such as that articulated in Article 1 of the *Montevideo Convention of 1933 on the Rights and Duties of States*. The concepts had a degree of dynamism (Shearer 1994: 90), thus '"Sovereignty" has a much more restricted meaning today than in the eighteenth and nineteenth centuries when, with the emergence of powerful highly nationalised states, few limits on state autonomy were acknowledged'.

In one way, the emergent secular concept of jurisdiction was a feeble being, a pale imitation of its previous self, in that it represented a contraction from earlier divinely authorized regal or imperial justifications for exercise of jurisdiction. During the Middle Ages the Church courts exercised civil jurisdiction. The Reformation began to erode the civil jurisdiction of the Church. Law merchant and commercial law would be subsequently emphasized to a greater extent and the blossoming of international lawyers from the theology faculties would be largely ignored.

The more recent phase of the concept might be characterized by the reconstruction of the concept for an inter-dependent and increasingly regionalized world, characterized by the development of measures to combat the limitations of a purely national concept of jurisdiction. Examples of this phase could include the Tokyo Convention on Offences and other Acts Committed on Board Aircraft of 1963; the EC Convention on Jurisdiction and the Enforcement in Civil and Commercial Judgments of 1968; the Hague Convention for the Suppression of Unlawful Seizure of Aircraft 1970. Movement revealed fault-lines in the foundation of the State–Territorial–Sovereignty–Jurisdiction relationship. The State of Israel, for example, was often involved in disputes where it rejected existing conceptions of jurisdiction such as in relation to Eichmann and the raid on Entebbe. The development of transport and communications, *inter alia*, diluted the effectiveness of territorial-based conceptions and required remedial treatment. This was done with the aid of the 'subjective' and 'objective' territorial principles. Thus counterfeit and drugs for example, were grafted on as exceptions. Personal and universal jurisdiction were also essentially exceptional, of which Piracy and War Crimes are the most celebrated examples. International law might even be seen as a product of the need to mitigate the limitations of the concepts of territorial jurisdiction in particular. Other domains of development included the evolution of conceptions based on the common concerns of mankind.

Anachronism to conceptual anarchy?

Jurisdiction is perhaps the major consequence of Statehood and the practical manifestation of the politico-legal concept of sovereignty. In many ways it is the *grundnorm* although based on relatively static, inert fictions, located in a particular time and place. Shadows of the feudal system fall over the castellated conceptual terrain, ruled by the king, knight and horse. Just as part of the development of the feudal system has been explained by the number of people necessary to help an armoured knight mount, so the concept of jurisdiction might be explained by the context of a fairly local, relatively immobile populace. It is thus unsurprising that the limitations of the concept are revealed when the law tries to deal with things and people that move, or boundaries that in reality are permeable, or contexts where the notional international legal analysis is not coterminous with the realities of political, military or commercial might. Such concepts were never calculated to deal with things, people or vessels that moved quickly or indeed moved at all, although it might work well for men and domesticated animals. Traditional, orthodox conceptions of jurisdiction, a fellow of cannons, carriages, muskets and wigs, is anachronistic in an age of space travel, mass communications, mass travel, nuclear weapons, cloning and proliferating war. The digital age altered the reality that permeates much legal thinking. The logic of the satellite, conceived by Arthur C. Clarke, had implications for the way the world works and not least for the concept of jurisdiction. Telecommunications, the internet and the emergence of convergence and digitization are facilitating the growth of the electronic circulatory network of the globe, further accelerating the intercourse that leaves traditional concepts of jurisdiction some way behind (Tunney 1998).

Reconstruction through human rights and commercial law

The illusory aspect of the nature of frontiers based on national jurisdictions also reveals the subordination of inadequate and unsustainable legal principle to other realities, such as when mass movements of people occur, as with the fall of the Berlin Wall or the events in Rwanda. With decentralized and diffuse wars and growing international crime, the inevitable establishment of international criminal courts accelerates. With the evolution of global environmental problems, the old concept of jurisdiction ostensibly becomes irrelevant. With the development of indigenous rights, new regional communities and world trade institutions, borders are being rubbed from the globe. With the reassessment of legal doctrines such as the *terra nullius* doctrine in the light of more enlightened analyses, pillars of the construct of jurisdiction are felled (Tunney 2000). With the clash of competing exercises of extra-territorial jurisdiction, such as in relation to the Boeing–McDonnell Douglas merger, calls for an international antitrust enforcement agency by writers such as Eleanor Fox will become amplified. All these factors point to solutions which are global and which will hasten the departure of a virginal concept of jurisdiction. The contemporary events in Iraq might testify to this. It is surprising that the US and the UK have not argued that they are building a genuine international law regime from scratch as none (properly so called) has arguably ever existed. Law and legal systems will have to test out ways to translate universal principles of law and workable legal systems. Law provides one of the only mechanisms to allow for the coexistence of competing cultural constructs in a shrinking, competing world. For example, it seems that legal concepts of culture (as opposed to 'merely' anthropological, economic, sociological ones) inevitably come centre-stage (Tunney 2001).

Other academics such as Teubner will focus legitimately on the significance of the *Lex Mercatoria*. Recent legal texts by writers such as Berger have used this significant legal tradition in contemporary contexts (Berger 1999). Apart from this arguable continuity, specific contexts such as communications technology have provided a significant part of the shift in legal landscape. The Council of Europe Convention on Cybercrime 2001 is an important example of international co-operation in the legal domain aspiring to a higher level, albeit built on existing national systems. The WIPO Conventions of 1996, calculated to bring copyright laws into the digital age, are also interesting in this perspective. In the competition domain, it is worth remembering the exercise by the EU of extraterritorial jurisdiction in order to exert control of huge mergers in the US, which had assumed that such were purely issues of domestic regulation. Then the work of separate regional human rights courts and *ad hoc* tribunals must be considered (Higgins 2003). But many legal academics still seem to suggest that nothing has really changed. While it is true that law is more malleable, adaptable and versatile than many others think, it is impossible to assume the persistence of predominantly local, legal constructs. If the concept of sustainability is not conceived with a sense of such kaleidoscopic paradigmatic shifts within law itself, then it is doomed to dysfunctionality in real world scenarios. One crucial change has been in the emergence of regional legal communities such as the EU, which should be re-iterated here in view of its role in the development of, and supposed commitment to, sustainability.

The need to understand the legal processes and limitations of emerging regional legal models (such as EU): restating the legal obvious.

Revisiting origins

Sustainability in the EU emerges in a unique way from its structural womb. Again, the evolution and development of the EU is at the heart of political discourse in Europe. However, there are different emphases from a legal and a political perspective. It is widely accepted that the drenching of the fields of Europe with blood and eventual war-weariness and fight-fatigue that followed the wars, created the conditions for the re-definition and re-alignment of legal conceptions, which hitherto had been relatively persistent. They become all the more persistent because they are ignored and assumed. When they become understood, it is largely as the misunderstood progeny of political thinking. Instead, it is forgotten that politics creates law, but that once formed it also reflexively creates politics and again creates law as the wheel of human affairs turns. Those who study politics should not underestimate this nexus. Law has its own nature, its own logic and its own force despite its diversity. It is not a closed system, but it has a unique set of characteristics. Of course, all 'legal realists' would be more than aware of the political context and origin of law. Additionally, they would ensure that law is informed by other disciplines, but presumably expect reciprocity of intellectual comprehensiveness. Likewise, there is no suggestion that law should provide a predominant analysis. This approach may be negatively labelled as premised on a type of romantic progressivism, but is arguably predicated on the inherent nature of legal rules.

The legal nature of the EU, and the European Community (EC) at the heart of it, is understood by many lawyers and political scientists. The nature of the legal enterprise is confirmed by some core principles articulated by the European Court of Justice (ECJ). It has authority to interpret the founding Treaties. Two core EC cases *Costa* (Case 6/64) and *Van Gend En Loos* (Case 26/62), allowed the ECJ to judicially identify and articulate the simple proposition that the Treaties had set up a new type of legal Community, as testified by its novel legal set-up. That Community establishes a new international legal order with legal capacity and personality, and entitlement to representation on the international plane. Member states had limited their sovereign rights. Implicitly it was consistent with the exercise of sovereignty that elements of it may be given away. Such sovereignty had been 'pooled', or perhaps transfused into the new legal community. Member states were confined by their membership not to act inconsistently with it. Thus the Member State's rights may be limited. The Member State cannot plead its own laws to escape consequences deriving from legislation within the EC's competence or otherwise act inconsistently with the legally binding obligations they have adhered to directly or indirectly. Individuals may in certain circumstances obtain rights, enforceable in the national courts of the Member States.

Rules that are real

Thus, through the alchemy of law and the magic of judges, rules became law and not 'mere' politics. Classic definitions or understanding of law imply that it is composed of rules of the authority of a community (usually the state),' which are backed up by force. Machinery of force, with a general degree of legitimacy, distinguishes legal rules from non-binding, non-legal rules. Under such a definition, there never has been a fully matured body of 'international law' properly so-called, pending the establishment of a mechanism of coercion based on some legitimate authority. Unlike national judges with multifarious interests to consider, or international judges with limited enforcement powers, the ECJ both had a mechanism of enforcement and a clear context of integration.

The radicalism manifest in the above decisions and the boldness of cases such as *Defrenne* (Case 43/75) and *Barber* (Case C-262/88) indicate the power of judicial development, which is often insufficiently studied outside the mechanistic approach of law. The nature of judicial independence gives a freedom to think long term in a radical way. This inherent rule-articulation potential should be borne in mind in relation to the WTO. There is much debate about the nature of WTO rules. Jackson uses the term 'rule orientation' as opposed to the terms 'rule of law' or 'rule-based system'. He says that the term 'rule orientation' implies a less rigid adherence to rules and allows for more fluidity in approach, thereby facilitating a 'system of bargaining and negotiating which permeate the WTO system' (Jackson 2000). A desire to avoid legalization of rules has been clear at certain stages of the evolution of the international economic order, notwithstanding the 'poets of Bretton Woods' tag that lawyers earned early on. Such an approach is arguably based on the intention to exclude lawyers and associated dangers with the undeniable risk-adverse nature that their presence may bring. Sometimes it may be a pragmatic response to avoid frightening away states, who may want room to manoeuvre in future circumstances. More specifically, it may be based on the more pragmatic basis of seeking to make negotiations work. Alternatively, it could be argued that it is better to allow for the evolution towards legally binding rules, having camouflaged intentions for diplomatic reasons until law clearly emerges from its political chrysalis.

From imitation to limitation

The subsequent regional developments in Asia such as the Association of Southeast Asian Nations (ASEAN) and in the Asia-Pacific region the Asia Pacific Economic Cooperation (APEC), in South America El Mercado Común del Sur, (MERCOSUR), in Africa the Southern African Development Community (SADC) and Economic Community of West African States (ECOWAS), as well as the North American Free Trade Agreement (NAFTA) and the Free Trade Area of the Americas (FTAA) for example, could be seen as a replication of the EU model or inspired by the EU model. Obviously, there is a phenomenon of regionalism which is independent of this proto-type, and which is, for example, a function of national strategy and opportunity. Certain regionalisms, such as East Asian regionalism, may have explicitly rejected the deeper integration *á la* EU, and therefore are not replications, but may be modifications. Certain experiments such as the South Pacific Forum (SPF) are quite *sui generis*. Within regions there is 'sub-regionalism', such as the Indonesia, Malaysia and Thailand Growth Triangle (IMT-GT) that may be quite bespoke. So in some senses it is not hugely useful to think in terms of the extension or replication of the deeply-integrated, mature state entity which is the EU, although elements of it are reproduced, happen to be reproduced or are mirrored. But regionalism (in the sense of regional legal communities) is here to stay, as long as other such constructs can persist. Recent financial crises do not seem to have frightened states away from regionalism as a model of development. There is also need to consider the attempt to spread competing models from the US and from China.

The limitations of the EC/EU must be remembered. There are many, depending on political perspectives. As a question of functionality of legal systems, it should be pointed out that there are competing interests within the EU, which will legally contest meanings and interpretations, impinging on their interests. Homogeneity of purpose cannot be assumed. Second, the efforts to replicate the legal model may not succeed due to the lack of similarity of starting points of other regions. Third, the model is largely based on the legal theory of transfer of sovereignty. This assumes that it is consistent with the possession of sovereignty, that one can relinquish it. It must be remembered that this theory should also apply in relation to the EC itself and its membership of international organizations. The EC is unusual in that it has itself joined the WTO. This clearly leads to a new hierarchy of legal relations, whose exact inter-linkages need articulation. Some of the associated answers are more legal in their complexion than others and should be treated as such. The need to understand new legal models such as the EU is part of the comprehension of the new international legal order and the need to re-align outdated ideas of international law that may be preserved in formaldehyde in other disciplines. There is a large literature on this matter. Sustainability as a concept must grow in such soil. Only then can one grapple with finer points such as the vexed question of implementation and enforcement of WTO law in the EU (Eeckhout 2002) and how the EU complies with WTO decisions (Branton 2002) and finer contexts which may impact on issues of sustainability.

The need to understand the process of conceptual integration of new ideas through new legal structures: the example of the relationship between tourism, culture and heritage in relation to sustainability in the EU.

Sustainability in the EU

In relation to the specific context of sustainability, there is a fairly clear trajectory of development. Sustainability entered the Treaties with Article 2 of the Treaty on European Union at Maastricht. The Commission Communication (COM (2001) 264 final) entitled '*A Sustainable Europe for a Better World: A European Union Strategy for Sustainable Development*', is typical. It recognized sustainability as a global objective, and the implementation of its specific Rio obligations, in preparation for Johannesburg. Sustainability is recognizably related to economic growth, social cohesion and environmental protection. The communication focuses on a diverse range of issues which is seen to be related to sustainability, such as global warming, antibiotic resistant strains of some disease, poverty, loss of biodiversity, ageing population, and transport congestion. It is difficult to see conceptual coherence in the principle as used. Sustainability is recommended to be a pervasive policy, although there is little indication of how this can realistically and effectively be achieved. In the context of the environment, the Commission Communication *On the Sixth Environment Action Programme of the European Community, Environment 2010: Our Future, Our Choice*, states that:

> A prudent use of the world's natural resources and protection of the global eco-system are a condition for sustainable development, together with economic prosperity and a balanced social development. Sustainable development is concerned with our long-term welfare here in Europe and at the global level and with the heritage we leave to our children and grandchildren.

The priority issues of climate change, bio-diversity, environment and health, and sustainable management of natural resources and waste are focused on. There are many examples of specific development of policy in relation to sustainable development, such as in relation to urban spaces, leisure and tourism. It is worth mentioning this context, merely as an example of policy formation and to stress how removed it seems from a legal world.

Specific policy contexts of sustainability

Leisure and tourism is increasingly being mentioned in Commission policies. Concepts such as that of 'sustainability' have been used in such contexts to meld some other ones together. One context where the link between tourism and culture became clear was in the context of sustainability as applied to cities. The *European Sustainable Cities Report* was prepared by the European Commission Expert group on the Urban Environment with the assistance of Euronet in its role as the Scientific and Technical Secretariat. In the abstract of that report it is noted that:

> Tourism and leisure activities can have significant impacts on the quality of a city's cultural heritage. Planning for tourism, leisure and cultural heritage should be integrated in national guidelines and regional policies and regional policies addressing economic, social, environmental and cultural aspects. In addition tourism, leisure and cultural heritage issues should form an integral part of the spatial planning process...
>
> Leisure and tourism activities can have a significant impact on the quality of a city's cultural heritage. A historic city or a city with special architecture is attractive for tourists, which has positive economic and social effects on the one hand, but on the other can be a threat, specifically in social and environmental aspects, for the sustainable development of a city.

In addition to the internal issue of sustainability, it is also relevant in external contexts. The Commission Communication to the Council and the European Parliament entitled, *A European Community Strategy to Support the Development of Sustainable Tourism*, focuses on the issue of sustainability and tourism externally, and thus links tourism and culture. In the introduction, the Commission states:

> So, in the light of the challenges posed by the development of tourism, for the economy and in terms of its impact on the environment and civil society, and of the lessons learnt from past co-operation policy in this field, this communication seeks to map out a strategic framework for the EU and Member States support for developing sustainable tourism. The aim of this strategy, taking account of Community measures (*acquis communautaire*) in the field of tourism, is to ensure that co-operation schemes dovetail better with the EC's development objectives and to enhance the effectiveness of projects in the light of experience.

Thus at the level of the regional legal community, the new legal bases give rise to new policies which will eventually be implemented in legal contexts, and thus possibly create emergent standards in relation to culture and heritage. These may have an upwardly constitutive effect on the law at a higher level, but not necessarily so. Other specific commitments such as the Urban Waste Water Directive 1991 create specific legally binding obligations.

From policy context to legal context

Back in the legal domain, a few concerns arise. The first is that of what a lawyer might term 'justiciability'. Legal concepts must work in circumstance of dispute. Legal principle is often hammered out in the courts in contested situations. The dialectical method is inherent to most legal systems, even ones that would claim to be more inquisitorial. It is difficult to see how the vague and abstract language of policy associated with sustainability will invariably give rise to operational legal principles which function in contested situations. Associated with this difficulty is the issue of transferability. While the Organisation for Economic Co-operation and Development (OECD) concept of sustainability (also used in the EU) talks of it in a global context, the specific EU elucidation in relation to a conglomeration of developed, mature states is all too clear. It is difficult to see how a general jurisprudence can emerge from that specificity. At the same time, the persistence of the Common Agricultural Policy (CAP), the apparent lack of interest in indigenous rights and the uncompromising protection of IP rights, leave the EU achievement open to question in relation to the sincerity of its commitment to sustainability. In combination with the suspicions of developing countries of the EU promotion of environmental issues, US unilateralism and uncertainty about the status of the Multilateral Environmental Agreements (MEAs), the opportunity to ignore sustainability as a justification will surely present itself to any WTO Panel when faced with a clearer trade based counter-obligation. Theorists must look to the institutional consumers and operational implementability of their theories. It is accordingly useful to be reminded of the role of the WTO.

The need to locate the WTO in the hierarchy of legal developments and identify particular effects thereof: the process of 'juridification' and the need for re-conceptualization of culture, heritage and the environment.

Origins and nature of the WTO

As sustainability enters other rule-based systems, at the behest of players such as the EU, it is worth noting the origin and nature of entities such as the WTO, in order to locate it in the hierarchy of legal developments and disciplinary self re-assessments. In 1947, the General Agreement on Tariffs and Trade (GATT) came into existence. It sought to create a degree of harmonization in the rules of international trade. Bitter experience of the early part of the century had underlined the potential destructive nature of the use of state policies for protectionist purposes. The exact intentions and conceptions behind GATT were unclear. Nevertheless an organizational and conceptual framework began to emerge in a type of organic way. Since the 1947 Agreement, there have been several rounds of talks that lay the foundations of inter-state trade. The stalled Uruguay Round gathered momentum with the arrival of key personnel, agreement on some critical agricultural issues, and out of this *inter alia,* emerged the Charter forming the basis of the WTO. This is now the 'central economic institution' in the world. It is seen by some to be the basis of a new 'global constitutionalism'. Significant differences between it and its previous incarnations involved the creation of a sophisticated institutional structure, combined with a new Dispute Settling Mechanism (DSM). For a lawyer (and bearing in mind that some of the crucial creators of the new institutional and DSM structures were lawyers) the enhancement of the DSM was a great leap on the road to a new legal system. The commitment to enforceability is a *sine qua non* of legally binding rules. While the proponents of the newly evolved WTO sought to portray their achievement as a non-law one, in reality it was. Others have long since described the process of 'juridification' of trade matters. Not understanding the significance of legal mechanisms, made it difficult for some to recognize the creative achievement the new structures represented as an emerging legal phenomenon.

The Ministerial Conference at the top of the structure, has representatives from all the member states involved and by its nature can only really meet infrequently. But on a more regular basis, there is a General Council and there are a number of specific Councils that meet more consistently to review and recommend within particular domains, such as the Council on Trade in Goods and the Council for the Trade Related Aspect of Intellectual Property. While GATT had focused on goods, these new agreements introduced *inter alia* services and IP. From a developing country perspective, the new regime is different in that it deals with issues hitherto seen as domestic, regulatory ones, within the domain of national sovereignty. Less freedom is seen as an impediment to development policies. The lack of a pre-existing, level playing field seems to distort the integrity of the principle of reciprocity. Apart from the environment there are clear fault lines associated with culture and heritage that colour comprehension of concepts such as sustainability. As well as being part of the panorama of understanding it is submitted that these theoretical and political, philosophical clashes will increasingly become legal ones.

The tension between trade and cultural heritage and environmental issues in world trade

Sustainability floats on broader currents. On the thirtieth anniversary of the World Heritage Convention, it is noteworthy that the philosophical basis of the concept of world heritage is still difficult to articulate. While this makes sure that the horses of state are not frightened away, and allows room for creative ambiguity necessary for growth, it does not help in the real world context of dispute. The Australian courts have remarked on this difficulty. While heritage and emerging world trade rules as of yet have not clashed, they may do so in the future. There are international conventions dealing with cultural property, but we can expect some major conflicts in the future particularly considering the likelihood of privatization of heritage management.

Apart from notional conflicts, particular disputes in the GATT/WTO context have underlined the significant actual consequences of the agreements. Recent disputes over steel and foreign sales corporation taxes have hit the headlines. This adds to the increasingly known cases such as the *Bananas* case, the *Shrimp/Turtles* case, the *Beef Hormones* case and the *Dolphin/Tuna* case. These decisions illustrate how signatory states have yielded a degree of sovereignty in the interests of free trade. Such decisions are seen to be unduly narrow to many analysts (Scott 2002). There is also an emerging series of cases, which commentators suggest are significant in relation to the regulation of the creative industries and culture, such as the Canadian Periodicals case. It has been argued that:

> free trade is generally meant to promote non-discrimination, not homogenization. In replacing national societies of culture with a global society of efficiency, one risks losing something intangible that is more valuable than economics and that goes to the very heart of human well-being. The tension between trade and culture can be regarded as a modern manifestation of the age-old debate between society (Gesellschaft) and community (Gemeinschaft).
>
> (Carmody 1999: 236)

Commentators such as Footer and Graber (2000) have looked quite specifically at the possible cultural policy responses to trade liberalization. This complements trends of recognition of issues in relation to cultural policy in the EU (Cunningham 2001).

The ideological basis of the WTO arguably rests on a new legalism, which provides a framework for a free trade agenda. While a free trade agenda may be value neutral to many, to others it is not. Many would see a clash between culture and economics, free trade and community, tradition and progression. There is a contest of values implicit in some of the developments and discourse. Before the trouble at Seattle and various summits, and before September 11 and the discourse on 'cultural clashes', some economists within the western world were approaching their discipline and its links with culture in a critical way. They had explored the relationship between economics and culture and inevitably had to deal with ideas of 'the cultural industries' and the 'creative economy'. Such economists identify a tension between the supposed individuality of creative production and the supposed collective nature of cultural production. This involves a dialogue with anthropology and other disciplines, and notions of 'cultural materialism'. The more enlightened of those economists would not make boldly exclusive claims for their endeavour, but rather recognize that their discourse is an inseparable dimension to cultural production, of which creativity is a central driving force. Limitations of particular disciplinary approaches are very clear and often recognized. The symbolic values of cultural production cannot be easily accommodated or represented in transactional terms and the accusations of 'commodification' have come quick.

To deal with the tensions, economists such as Throsby call for a greater 'human-centred' notion of economics (Throsby 2001). But there are some essentially legal questions emerging from the evolution of the WTO, and the prospective interpretations of GATT, GATS and TRIPS. Questions arise about the implications of these binding Conventions on the access to, ownership and management of culture and heritage in the widest sense. However it seems clear that while specification of purpose and rule is well advanced in relation to trade rules, the same cannot be said of macro-concepts such as culture and indeed sustainability.

Sustainability in particular

Elements of the difficulty of conceptualization of culture and heritage and the environment manifest in the context of the concept of sustainability. The sustainability notion is based on standard definitions, such as that used by the OECD, following the Brundtland Commission. The concept of sustainability was crucial in the Rio Conference that approved Agenda 21. The UN Commission on Sustainable Development also plays an important role. The EU has adopted the standard international conception which states that it is development which 'meets the needs of the present without compromising the ability of future generations to meet their own needs'.

Such vagueness required more specific elucidation, and advocates would identify the broad concept with a collection of subsidiary concepts. The distillation of workable, operational methods to implement the macro-concept would seem to be difficult. The possibility of enforceability may be compromised by the inherent vagueness of the concept. Sustainable development is mentioned in the preamble to, and in the WTO Agreement.

Article XX of the GATT allows protective action to be taken to protect human, animal plant life or health and to conserve natural resources. This was relied on without success in the *Tuna/Dolphin* case. Furthermore it had no extraterritorial dimension. Many developing countries are suspicious of the agenda of the environmental movement, no matter how much they are told that it is for their own good. Thus many such advocates believe that the WTO context is not the appropriate place to deal with such issues. Accordingly the following argument has been put forward:

> Given the unequal bargaining strengths of the North and South in the WTO, the complex issues in relation to PPMs, cost internalization, the trade-related environmental measures should not be negotiated within the WTO. If they are discussed at all, the venue should be the

United Nations (for example, in the framework of the Commission on Sustainable Development) in which the broader perspective of environment and development and of the UNCED can be brought to bear.

(Khor 2000: 44)

Other bases of discontent are reflected in statements by critical western analysts such as this one by Lomberg. He has said in relation to sustainable development:

Sustainable development is a hollow concept if limited to the rich world while forgetting the poor, or focused on the future while forgetting the present. The summit in Johannesburg must rediscover the obligation to fulfil the needs of all those in the current generation as well as everyone in future generations that was laid down in the 1987 Brundtland report.

(Lomberg 2002: 21)

Doha to Johannesburg

For many, the Doha Ministerial Conference that concluded on the fourteenth of November 2001, was a politic response to the trouble in Seattle. Many development advocates stressed the persistence of existing inadequacies such as asymmetrical starting positions, and inadequately representative procedural mechanisms. It is well recognized that developing countries cannot partake to the same extent as developed countries, due to a lack of resources. The efforts to secure enhanced Special and Differential Treatment (S&DT) were a key strategy, as well as the effort to reduce agricultural subsidies and domestic support by developed countries. Protectionism has often been seen as the preserve of developed countries only. The developing countries were suspicious of environmental arguments (bearing in mind the major sources of pollution) and realized that they could suffer if onerous standards were introduced at the cusp of a developmental transition. Likewise, labour commitments are seen to be unhelpful to developing countries.

Doha was seen by some to provide some benefits. Jeremy Hobbs in his speech on behalf of Oxfam International to the WTO Symposium on April 29, 2002, cited the Doha Declaration on TRIPS and Public Health as a positive example. This was seen to be one of the few real successes secured by developing countries, although it was seen as purely political. He was very critical of the WTO, again because of tariffs and subsidies, and lack of market access for developing countries. He was critical of the sincerity of commitment to phasing out the Multi-Fibre Agreement by 2005. Another key related issue is that of food security. This will increasingly become entwined with the issue of IP protection. As well as the issues of public health and food security, the protection of Traditional Knowledge and Traditional Environmental Knowledge should be borne in mind. There has been no serious attempt to deal with these in a trade context, although trade and IP are now inextricably linked. Some commentators see the linkage of trade and IP as representing a successful campaign by the US to avoid a perhaps more inclusive agenda being promoted by the World Intellectual Property Organisation (WIPO).

But nevertheless, the determinative issues in relation to the context in which issues such as sustainability are decided are legal ones. For example, in regard to the relationship between MEAs and the WTO, in relation to the Summit, it was suggested that it was desirable to:

> affirm that MEAs and the WTO are equal bodies of law, and that trade measures pursuant to MEAs are consistent with WTO rules. Governments should identify mechanisms to ensure that trade liberalisation is accompanied by parallel efforts to strengthen environmental governance, at both the national and international levels.
> (WWF 2001: 20)

The EC had sought at Doha to clarify the relationship between MEAs and the WTO regime. That they are seen as separate bodies of law has caused some concern to WTO members (WTO 1996). The Doha Agenda was calculated to push sustainable development to the top, so that it becomes an overarching goal.

Many would dispute that Doha represents a 'development agenda'. Sustainability has become a relatively uncontested term in an intra-EU context. This has led to a failure to develop a more robust and indeed sustainable concept of sustainability. If it is not allied to recognition of transitional contexts, S&DTs, indigenous rights, development assistance, technology transfer and capacity building for the LDDS, then it will not receive support. The achievements at the Doha conference may have been slim. Some saw the compromising attitude of the US to anti-dumping and the Declaration on the TRIPs agreement and Public Health as important (Schott 2002: 191–219). It is interesting that the Declarations at Doha raised debate about whether they were legally binding or merely political (Charnovitz 2002: 207). This is hugely significant in relation to the question of the nature of the WTO and whether the Ministerial Conference can be seen as a legislative body which can set the agenda for world trade law. Politically however, it may be remembered in time for the emergent sense of bargaining power from the developing and LDCs (Larson 2002: 6–8). The EU's major focus was seen by some to be its environmental agenda. Thus the preamble affirms the objective of sustainable development and the right of each country to take whatever measures are necessary to protect human, animal or plant life or health, subject to adherence to WTO obligations. The issue of the relationship between existing WTO rules and specific trade obligations set out in (MEAs) was expressly recognized as necessitating further study.

The issues remain within the framework of Doha and existing rules. Developing countries have continued to call for genuine liberalization on textiles, the phasing out of export subsidies and credit, the prohibition of the dumping of subsidized food, the associated re-orientation of agricultural promotion to environmental concerns, the introduction of a genuine 'development box' in the Agreement on Agriculture and the implementation of the Marrakesh Decision regarding food aid (Save the Children 2002). The use of anti-dumping rules as protectionist measures by developed countries has been raised. A re-assessment of GATS has been called for. Flexibility and variable geometry to facilitate growth is sought. Food security in the context of IP rights in relation to genetic resources will remain controversial. The question of the relationship between TRIPS and the International Treaty on Plant Genetic Resources for Food and Agriculture (PGRGA) and the Convention on Biological Diversity (CBD) is an important one. National and regional regulation of trade in fish is assuming a higher profile. In relation to the LDCs, many advocates would seek what would effectively amount to a general exemption from the onus of adherence to standard rules, while securing the benefit of the key ones. Debt cancellation is increasingly being linked to the trade agenda. Sustainability is inextricably linked to all of these issues. EU enlargement and the persistence of the politics of subsidies remains a great threat. The pro-subsidies forces were at work behind the scenes at Doha. Diverse, dynamic and disputed contexts drive any genuine debate about sustainability in relation to world trade.

The need to conceive strategies of comprehensive engagement that include legal strategies: all for one and one for all.

More effective engagement

The proponents of sustainability and those committed to environmental concerns need a more comprehensive engagement than a merely economic or political one. A danger of the growth of environmental militancy may be to cause the further retreat from existing commitments. Strategic engagement in the evolution of World Trade law through the WTO in particular could be a useful approach for those who want to advance the cause of sustainability. The danger of a merely pious and sanctimonious approach is clear. While it may satisfy the conscience of western liberal intellectuals, it will not achieve actual results. The MEAs will continue to be crucial, but the exact mode of treatment within existing world trade rules needs elaboration and advocacy. At the moment it is seen to be a rarefied domain of legal investigation. If sustainability is to become a reality, it must be done within existing and emergent systems.

The complexity of evolution of global institutions that have the capacity to make binding legal determinations, requires a sophisticated level of engagement on a more comprehensive basis than hitherto. While the results of such engagement may not be miraculous, the failure to do so could be disastrous and the political commitment fictitious. As a matter of *realpolitik*, there will have to be some recognition of the deep divisions between the developed and developing countries; otherwise the well intentioned will rightly be accused of an effective type of veiled protectionism. It is still noteworthy that the United States has not gone cold on the WTO, to date at least. The success of a rules-based system does not solely depend on the fact of breach of the rules, but rather on response thereto.

Other struggles are fundamentally linked with environmental ones and sustainability and lessons may be learnt from there. The indigenous movement is part of it. Achievements have been limited. One noteworthy characteristic has been the frustration with legal systems leading to calls for non-legal solutions. The Zapatista movement was rejectionist of trade liberalization, which is unsurprising from an indigenous perspective. The environmental movement needs to see the value of law and the connections between diverse domains of law. It should address the role of sustainable law systems as part of an holistic attempt to develop a philosophically sustainable concept of sustainability itself. Injustice breeds contempt for particular systems of law encountered.

Cause for optimism?

There has been a growing appreciation of the need to ensure linkage between environmental and development policies for example. Thus the UK Minister argued that:

> The most important prize to be had out of the Earth Summit on sustainable development in Johannesburg would be the creation of a new partnership between the environment and development policies.
> (Short 2002: 6)

She seems positive about the Doha agenda as part of an emerging consensus. She states:

> In recent years, we have been building a new international consensus focused on the need to reduce global poverty. At Doha, last November, an agenda was set aiming to make trade rules fairer to poor countries. At Monterrey, we reached international agreement to financing development, including a commitment to reverse the decline in aid. Now at Johannesburg, there is a chance to bring sustainability into the consensus.

Short sees the environment as one pillar of sustainability, with other social and economic ones. She emphasizes the need to respect the needs of the local community. She recognizes the fears of the developing countries that environmental concerns can be used as a mechanism of protection. Those fears were articulated in Seattle in 1999. She puts it thus:

> As we saw at the 1999 World Trade Organisation Ministerial Conference. Developing countries are fearful that the OECD countries, having plundered and polluted the planet as we developed, are now planning to pull the ladder up behind them by imposing rules and environmental standards that create enormous barriers to their economic growth.
>
> (Short 2002: 6–7)

Nevertheless she still feels that Doha, provided an opportunity to address these concerns through the re-articulation of world trade rules. Like Porritt, she identifies the CAP as a major obstacle.

The need to conceive of 'sustainable legal systems' as part of those strategies: the World Bank wakes up.

Re-imagining legal futures

Sustainability might usefully be integrated into evolving notions of the rule of law, apart from as a specific justiciable legal consideration. One of the greatest failings of the conceptualization of systems of global governance has been the failure to understand the role of institutions, legal systems and law. It seems strange to lawyers that the discourse on 'governance' often seems to ignore law and legal systems which is the *sina qua non* of governance. The Washington Consensus foundered on the issue of institutions. The World Bank has recognized its own failure to respect the role of institutions. In its recent report on sustainable development, it has continued its zealous conversion (World Bank 2002: 25). In its conclusion it states (in customary sustainability-speak vagueness):

> The key is to act now to initiate virtuous rather than vicious circles – to create constituencies for sustainability, not for environmental degradation and social polarization. Much will be possible if we plant now the seeds of adaptive, durable institutions that respond to the interests of all citizens.

The Report does stress the role of property rights, security of tenure, monitoring and enforcement, institutions, police, judges and the rule of law at various stages. This is nothing new, in that Adam Smith emphasized their significance a long time ago. On page 1, the Report states that:

> Institutions such as property rights and the rule of law are essential for the creation of human-made assets and the efficient operation of markets as a coordinating institution.

Additional institutions are needed to coordinate and ensure an adequate supply of the assets that are not spontaneously provided by markets: environmental assets (clean water, clean air, fisheries, and forests) and social assets (mutual trust, ability to network, and security of persons and property).

Competent institutions for coordination pick up signals about problems, balance interests fairly and efficiently in formulating policies, and execute policies in an accountable fashion. Such institutions enable societies to negotiate paths to 'win-win' opportunities – paths that can be elusive when the costs to some groups go uncompensated.

Nevertheless, it emphasizes that the lack of a holistic approach seeking to integrate law and the legal systems will effectively mean that any pretence to the achievement of sustainability should be forgotten.

Conclusion: Doha is also a matter of strategy and choice

Recent academic work in the political domain such as that of Callinicos (2003) and so-called interdisciplinary legal studies (Posner 2001) shows how difficult the bridge between law and political science will be to cross, in relation to issues such as sustainability in world trade contexts. Some legal textbooks, particularly from the US, demonstrate a more welcome holistic approach (Jackson: 2002), although they do challenge other disciplines to develop their rules. Nevertheless, it has been submitted here that there is a need to facilitate an increased triangular dialogue between politics, political science and law. Part of that dialogue (which has commenced) will be to recognize and embrace the paradigm shift in law and recognize new frontiers such as the legal articulation of culture. This, it is suggested, will require a broader effort to understand the legal processes of emerging regional models such as EU and its clones. Understanding the structural set-up should make it easier to understand the process of conceptual integration of new ideas through such new legal structures. The WTO should be located in this hierarchy of legal developments, and particular effects should be thus contextualized. In relation to contexts such as sustainable development, this should allow the conception of strategies of comprehensive engagement, which include legal strategies.

If those strategies are to be successful, then there must be some conception of commitment to what might be termed 'sustainable legal systems' as part of a wider strategy. Otherwise noble commitments will remain mere aspirations, and the advocates of environmentalism will remain stuck in the rut of *schadenfraude* or crowing their pyrrhic victory amid environmental devastation. The charges against those regressive elements in the evolution of world trade from a developing country perspective may be better tested. For example the doublespeak of the European Commission in relation to eradication of poverty and its conduct in relation to agricultural subsidies might be better attacked in the interests of equity. The US has shown that it is politically free to oppose softening of patent rights to promote public health objectives. The complexity of emergent world regulatory orders must not be allowed to camouflage hypocritical policies. Furthermore, recent fishery debates indicate that the public directly affected by the consequences of dealing with sustainability needs convincing of its value. Pure economic arguments and trade rules that do not promote sustainability but benefit from their simplicity of application will persist in the absence of development of more complex structured and enforceable rules that can for example deal with issues such as internalization of external costs. At the same time, it is increasingly being accepted by theorists such as Braithwaite and Drahos, that the 'ratcheting up' of global standards is possible instead of the drive to the bottom. However that seems to presuppose proactive, effective responses, predicated on robust analyses that recognize the reflexive disciplinary relationships that exist. Sustainability could be usefully developed and refined as a concept itself by sending it into the forge of legal debate to be fashioned into something applicable to its own world.

References

Barber versus GRE, (Case 262/88) [1990] ECR I-1889, [1990] 2 CMLR 513.
Berger, K.P. (1999) *The Creeping Codification of the Lex Mercatoria*, The Hague: Kluwer Law International.
Branton, J. (2002) 'The E.C. washes its dirty bed linen – is the saga over yet?', *International Trade Law and Regulation* 8: 2, 64–7.
Brinkley, J. *et al.* (2001) *US v Microsoft: The Inside Story of the Landmark Case*, London: McGraw-Hill.
Callinicos, A. (2003) *An Anti-Capitalist Manifesto*, Polity Press.
Carmody, C. (1999) 'When "cultural identity was not at issue": thinking about Canada – certain measures concerning periodicals', *Law and Policy in International Business* 30: 2, 231–320.
Charnovitz, S. (2002) 'The legal status of the Doha Declarations', *Journal of International Economic Law* 5: 1, 207–11.
Com (2001) 31 final, *On the Sixth Environment Action Programme of the European Community: Environment 2010: Our Future, Our Choice*, Brussels.
Com (2001) 264 final, *A Sustainable Europe for a Better World: A European Union Strategy for Sustainable Development*, Brussels.
Costa versus ENEL, Case 6/64 [1964] ECR 585, [1964] CMLR 425.
Cunningham, C. (2001) 'In defence of member state culture: the unrealised potential of Article 151(4) of the EC treaty and the consequences for EC cultural policy', Cornell *International Law Journal* 34: 1, 119–63.
Defrenne versus SABENA, Case 43/75 [1976] ECR 455, [1976] 2 CMLR 98.
Eeckhout, P. (2002) 'Judicial enforcement of WTO law in the European Union – some further reflections', *Journal of International Economic Law* 5: 1, 91–110.

Footer, M. and Graber, C.B. (2000) 'Trade liberalization and cultural policy', *Journal of International Economic Law* 3: 1, 115–44.
Habermas, J. (1997) *Between Facts and Norms*, Cambridge: Polity Press.
Higgins, R. (2003) 'The ICJ, the ECJ and the integrity of international law', *International Comparative Law Quarterly* 52: 1–20.
Howse, R. (2002) 'From politics to technocracy and back again; the fate of the multilateral trading regime', *American Journal of International Law* 96: 94–117.
Jackson, J.H. (2000) *The Jurisprudence of GATT and the WTO; Insights on Treaty Law and Economic Relations*, Cambridge: Cambridge University Press.
Jackson, J.H. et al. (2002) *Legal Problems of International Economic Relations: Cases, Material and Text*, 4th edn, St. Paul: West Group.
Khor, M. (2000) 'How the South is getting a raw deal', in S. Anderson (ed.) *Views from the South: The Effects of Globalization and the WTO on Third World Countries*, Chicago, IL: International Forum on Globalization and Food First.
Larson, A. (2002) 'A new negotiating dynamic at Doha', *Economic Perspectives*, Electronic Journal, Washington, DC: US Department of State.
Lomberg, B. (2002) 'Only the well fed worry about tomorrow', *The Guardian*, August 22.
Porritt, J. (2002) 'Last Gasp', the *Guardian*, July 17.
Posner, R. (2001) *Frontiers of Legal Theory*, London: Harvard University Press.
Save the Children (2002) *A Genuine Development Agenda for the Doha Round of WTO Negotiations*, London: Save the Children.
Schott, J. (2002) 'Comment on the Doha Ministerial', *Journal of International Economic Law* 5: 1, 191–5.
Scott, K. (2002) 'On kith and kine (and crustaceans): trade and the environment in the EU and the WTO', in J. Weiler (ed.) *The EU, the WTO and the NAFTA*, Oxford: Oxford University Press.
Shearer, I. (1994) *Starkes International Law*, 11th edn, London: Butterworths.
Short, C. (2002) 'Prize Fight', the *Guardian*, August 21.
Snyder, F. (ed.) (2002) *Regional and Global Regulation of International Trade*, Oxford: Hart.
Throsby, D. (2001) *Economics and Culture*, Cambridge: Cambridge University Press.
Tunney, J. (1998) 'The digital re-mastering of the concept of jurisdiction law or opportunity for paradigm in law?', Dublin: BILETA Conference Proceedings.
—— (2000) 'Native title and the search for justice: Mabo (1992)', in E. O'Dell (ed.) *Leading Cases of the Twentieth Century*, Dublin: Round Hall Press.
—— (2001) 'Is the emerging legal concept of culture the cuckoo's egg in the E.U. competition law nest?', *European Competition Law Review* 22: 5, May.
—— (2002) 'The neglected tension between disclosure of information in consumer and competition law contexts', *Journal of Consumer Policy* 25: 329–343.
US versus Nixon (1974) 418 U.S. 683.
Van Gend en Loos versus Nederlandse Administratie der Belastingen, Case 26/62 [1963] ECR 1, [1963] CMLR 105.
World Bank (2002) *World Development Report 2003: Sustainable Development in a Dynamic World*, Washington, DC: World Bank.
WTO (1996) *Report of the WTO Committee on Trade and the Environment*, 14 November 1996, Geneva: WTO.
World Wide Fund for Nature and Center for International Environmental Law (2001) discussion paper, Gland, Switzerland: WWF & CIEL.

Index

Tables are indicated by *italics*.

Aarhus convention 5, 94–104
action: collective 53–6
action programmes: environmental 162
activists 43–4; anti-capitalist 8–9; anti-globalization 8–9; *see also* demonstrations; militancy; protests
agriculture 171–2; *see also* Common Agricultural Policy (CAP)
aid policy: EU 172
air quality 158
animal welfare issues 55, 57
anti-capitalist activists 8–9, 43–4
anti-globalism 31–45, 153
anti-globalization activists 8–9, 43–4
audits: environmental 163
Austria *137*, 138, *140*, *142–3*, 144–6

Baker, Susan 3–4, 183
Bali PrepCom 179–80
Barcelona Summit (2002) 176
BAT (best available technology) 138
Bauman, Zygmunt 39
Beauvoir, Simone de 19–20
Biehl, Janet 20
biodiversity 170–1
biological determinism 20, 25
Blunkett, David: UK secretary of state (2003–) 125
Bové, José 42
boycotts 43–4
Britain *see* United Kingdom (UK)
British EMOs 52
Brundtland Report 6, 36, 156
business community: EU 174
business lobby: EU 181–2

capitalism xviii, 32, 33–4, 36, 41
capital budgeting xviii–xx
carbon emissions 144, 172–3; tax 162
Cardiff Summit (1998) 176
Castells, Manuel 39
chemicals 144
citizenship 73–91; environmental 4–5, 116–28

civilization: Western 37
civil society 77–8
climate change 172–3, 177–8; *see also* global warming
Collard, Andrée 27
Common Agricultural Policy (CAP) 11, 172, 180, 189
communitarianism 40
competitive trade xxi
compliance costs 153–5
compound interest xviii–xix
computer technology 38–9
Confédération Paysanne (French farmers' federation) 42
consultation model 88–9
consultative elitism 5, 86–90
corporate globalization xx
Corporate Social Responsibility (CSR) 174
Crick, Professor Bernard 121
Crickian consultation model 88–9
'critical natural capital' 2–3
cultural ecofeminism 16–22
cultural production 203–4
cyberpunk 38

defining technologies 37–9
degradation: environmental 24
dehierarchization 75
deliberative democracy 88–9
Delors, Jacques: president of EC (1985–1995) xxi–xxii
demonstrations 43–4, 53, 56; *see also* activists; militancy; protests
denationalization: of the nation-state 75–6
Denmark 174
developing countries 158–9, 169–70, 171–2, 173, 208
dialogue: interdisciplinary 191–2
difference: politics of 26–7
Directives: EU 145–6
Discounted Cash Flow (DCF) xix
Dispute Settling Mechanism (DSM) 186, 202
Dobson, Andrew 4, 31–2, 79–80
Doha Declaration 186

Index

Doha Ministerial Conference (2001) 180, 205–7
domestic policy change *134*
dualistic thinking 17
duties: citizenship *see* obligations

Earth First! 65
ecofeminism 4, 15–29
ecological citizenship 79–82, 116–28
ecological footprint 4, 122–3
ecological modernization (EM) 10, 152, 155–9, 160
ecologism 31–45
eco-taxes 169
education: citizenship 116, 121, 125–8; environmental 99
emissions 144, 172–3, 177–8
energy 172–3; nuclear 57, 144
Environment 2010: Our Future, Our Choice see Sixth Environmental Action Programme
environmental impact 122–3
environmental justice movement 119–20
Environmental Kuznets Curve (EKC) 158–9
Environmental Management and Audit Scheme (EMAS) 163–4
environmental movement: definition of 49; and ecofeminism 27–8
Environmental Movement Organizations (EMOs) 6–7, 48–53; European Parliament 60–4; institutionalization 57–60, 66–7; national differences 51–60
environmental radicalism 65–6
environmental rights 118–20
environmental standards: European Union (EU) 134
equality 26–7; *see also* inequality
essentialism 19–22
ethics 108
Europe xii, 5–7
European Commission (EC) 48
European Community (EC) 94, 96
European Court of Justice (ECJ) 196
European Environmental Bureau (EEB) 48–9, 50
European environmental movement 47–67
European integration: of EMOs 57–60
Europeanization 6–7, 152–64; of EMOs 47–67; extent of *143*; of national policy 130–49
European Parliament (EP): EMOs (Environmental Movement Organisations) 60–4
European Sustainable Cities Report 199–200
European Union (EU) 6–7, 47, 130, 186; aid policy 172; environmental policy 132–49, 160–4, 183; environmental standards 134; legal model 195–6; sustainability audit 169–73
'Everything but Arms' initiative 171
exclusion: environmental and social 117, 119–20

Falk, Richard 34, 41

feminism 3–4; *see also* ecofeminism; radical feminism
Fifth Environmental Action Programme (EAP:1992-2002) 162, 164, 172
Finland 136–44
footprint: ecological 4, 122–3
fragmented citizenship 77–86
France 42, 136–8, *140*–5
Freeden, Michael 32
free trade xxi, 40–2, 171–2, 203
Friends of the Earth (FoE) 50
Fukuyama, Francis xvi
fundamentalism 37
'fuzzy politics' 82–6

Geddes, Professor Sir Patrick xiii–xvi
General Agreement on Tariffs and Trade (GATT) 201–2
Geneva Public Symposium (2002) 188
Germany 133, *137,* 138–46, 148, 160, 161, 174
Giddens, Anthony 33, 121
global capitalism 32, 35
global climate change *see* global warming
global communication 38–9
global injustice 39
global institutions 207–8
globalization xii, 7–9, 32, 33, 36, 37, 39, 73, 152–64; capital budgeting xviii–xx; corporate xx; economic 75, 192; space–time schism xv–xviii
global legal pluralism 192
global trade 40–2
'global village' 37
global warming 57, 123–4; *see also* climate change
Gothenburg European Council strategy 183–4
Greece 136–8, *140*–4, 146–8
greenhouse gases 158
Green ideology 31–45
Green Party of England and Wales 8
Greenpeace 50
Green political parties 7, 8
growth: economic 1–5
Growth, Competitiveness, Employment: White Paper (1993) 162
growth–environmental incompatibility 1–3, 155

Hardt, Michael 35
health 170; adequate environment for 95–7
Hobbs, Jeremy 205
Hooker Chemical 119
household waste 115

ideologies 31–2, 105
impact: environmental 122–3
implementation levels: EU 178–9
improvement: environmental 96–7
inclusion: environmental and social 116–17
incompossibility 86; of rights 76–7
inequality 41, 42; *see also* equality

information: access to 97, 99
information technology 38–9
injustice: global 39; social 41
institutionalization: of EMOs 57–60, 66–7
institutions 209–10; global 207–8; of the state 33–5
Integrated Product Policy 177
integration: policy 175–7; economic 159
interdisciplinary dialogue 191–2
interest: compound xviii–xix
international environmental obligations 122–4
International Organisation for Standardisation (ISO) 163–4
international trade 171–2
Ireland 136–8, *140*–4, 146–8, 174
ISO 14001 163–4

job losses 154–5
Johannesburg Summit 10–11, 168–84
jurisdiction: evolution of concept 192–5
justice: access to 97, 99; citizenship 116–17, 123–4

Klein, Naomi 8–9
Kyoto Protocol 177–8

landfill sites 115
law: role of 187; rule of 190–1
Leadbetter, Charles xvi, xvii
Least Developed Countries (LDCs) 171–2
legal contexts 200–1
legal debate 11–12
legal models: regional 195–6
legal systems 144, 209–10
legislation 174–5
Le Monde diplomatique 35
liberal feminists 27
litigation: importance of 190–1
lobbying 51, 53, 64
Locke, John xvi
Love Canal: USA 119
Lucas, Caroline: British Green MEP 54
Luxembourg 174

Maastricht Treaty 162
market instruments 174
market liberalization 179–80
Marshall, T.H. 117
Marshallian citizens 77–9
McDonalds: restaurants 42
'McWorld' 37
media: role of 43–4
Mellors, M. 23
Members of the European Parliament (MEPs) 54
militancy 207; *see also* activists; demonstrations; protests
modernity 33–7

nation-states: sovereignty 75–6
Natura 2000 170–1
'natural order' 15–16

natural world: and women 17
nature conservation 57, 146
neoliberalism 34–5, 41
Netherlands, the 133, 136–46, 148, 160, 161, 174
networks: of environmental groups 49–53
'network society' 38, 39
neutrality: of the state 105
Newell, Peter 42–3
new environmental policy instruments (NEPIs) 138
New Labour 121, 125, 128
Non-Governmental Organizations (NGOs) 42–3, 100; environmental 139
nostalgia xvii
nuclear power 57, 144
nuclear tests 55

obligations: of citizenship 117–18, 120–4; to international environmental issues 122–4
Our Common Future see *Brundtland Report*
Our Future, Our Choice see Sixth Environmental Action Programme
Oxfam 171–2

participation 102–4; in environmental decision making 97–101
patriarchy 18, 23
Patterson, Matthew 34
Persson, Göran: Prime Minister of Sweden 183–4
Pitkin, Hanna 83
place xiii–xiv; centrality of xii
plan of life doctrine 85–6
Plumwood, Val 17, 21
Poland 42
policies: environmental 62; EU 132–49, 160–4, 183; integration 164
policy change: EU and national *134*
policy content 135–8, 136–8, 142–3, 145
policy instruments 135, 136; *see also* new environmental policy instruments (NEPIs)
policy integration 161–2
policy structure 135, 138–41, 142–3
policy style 135–6, 141–3
political action styles 64–6
political pluralization 4–5, 73–7, 82
politics of difference 26–7
'polluter pays' principle (PPP) 161, 162
pollution 56–7, 144, 153; air 146; Britain 59–60; water 158
pollution havens 153–5, 158
Porritt, Jonathan 189
post-cosmopolitan citizenship 79–82
poverty: world 41
power: nuclear 57, 144; political 87; of state governments 75–6; *see also* energy
preservation: of the environment 96–7
'prevention' principle 161
private–public partnerships 173–4
'propaganda war' 43–4
protection: of the environment 96–7; role of democracy 101–2

protectionism 171–2, 205, 208
protests 55–7; *see also* activists; demonstrations; militancy
public participation 97–101, 102–4, 106–7
Public Symposium (Geneva: 2002) 188

'race to the bottom' hypothesis 153–5, 161
radical feminism 16–22
radicalism: environmental 65–6
Randall, Vicky 20–1
'Reclaim the Streets' movement 39–40
regionalism: developments 197–8
regional legal models 195–6
relocation of firms 153–5
renewal: Aarhus Convention 97
representation 82–6, 87–8
rights: of citizenship 117–18; environmental 118–20
Rio Earth Summit (UN Conference on Environment and Development: 1992) 168
road fuel: protests 55
rubbish tax 115
rule of law 190–1
'rule orientation' 197
rulers: as citizens 87–90

Sachs, Wolfgang 36–7
Samoobrona: Polish political party 42
Sbragia, Alberta 143
Second Treatise of Government: John Locke xvi
second-wave feminism 19–20
Short, Clare 208–9
Single European Act (SEA:1987) 161
Sixth Environmental Action Programme: *Environment 2010: Our Future, Our Choice* 160, 164, 169, 170, 176, 199
social cohesion xxi–xxii
social exclusion 119–20
social inclusion 116–17; and sustainability 124
social injustice 41
socialist ecofeminism 22–4
sovereignty 193, 196, 198; of the nation-state 75
space: 'of flows and places' 39–40
Spain *137*–44, 146–8
Spanish Presidency of European Council 181
spiritual dimension: sustainability 3
standards 163–4; *see also* environmental standards
state: institutions of 33–5
Strong version: sustainable development 2–3
subsidies 172, 180–1, 189, 205
substantive representation 83–6, 87–8
substitution: Aarhus Convention 97
sustainability xii, 1–5; Aarhus conception 95–7; concept of 186, 204; in the EU 199–200; and law 190–1; and political science 190; politics of 188–90; and social inclusion 124; and world trade 187–9
sustainable behaviour 115–16

sustainable development 1–5
Sutherland, Peter 186
Sweden 136, *137*, 138, 139, *140*, 141, *142*, *143*, 144, 145, 146, 148, 174

tariffs 171–2, 205
Tarrow, Sidney 47
taxation 169
tax policy: environmental 162–3
TEA project 56
technologies: defining 37–9
Third World: ecofeminism and 24–5
tourism 199–200
trade 40–2; free and competitive xxi
trade liberalization 171–2, 203
trade patterns 153–5
Transformation of Environmental Activism (TEA) project 52
transnational corporations 41–3; *see also* international corporations
transnational networking 51–3
transport networks: EU 170–1
Treaty of Rome 160

UN Conference on Environment and Development (Rio Earth Summit: 1992) 168
United Kingdom (UK) 115, 125, 136–48
United Nations Economic Commission for Europe (UNECE) 94
USA 119–20, 190–1
usury xviii–xx

values 105, 108
Verhofstadt, Guy 8
Via Baltica project 170–1
voluntary agreements 174–5

Walinszky, Zoltan 171
Wallström, Margot: Commissioner for the Environment 182
waste: household 115
water: access to 169–70; EU policy 169–70; pollution 158; supply, Europe 144, 145
Weak version: sustainable development 2–3
Weale, Albert 134
well-being: adequate environment for 95–7
Western civilization 37
White Paper: *Growth, Competitiveness, Employment* (1993) 162
Women's Environmental Network (WEN) 24
women's movement 26; *see also* ecofeminism; feminism
World Bank 209–10
World Heritage Convention 202
world market 41
World Summit on Sustainable Development (WSSD) 10–11, 168
world trade law 207
World Trade Organization (WTO) 186, 188, 201–6; rules 197
World Wide Fund for Nature (WWF) 50